A Life Apart

The fate of an outsider

Patrick Grigsby

Pen Press

First published in Great Britain by Pen Press

All paper used in the printing of this book has been made from wood grown in managed, sustainable forests.

ISBN13: 978-1-907172-46-5

Printed and bound in the UK
Pen Press is an imprint of Indepenpress Publishing Limited
25 Eastern Place
Brighton
BN2 1GJ

A catalogue record of this book is available from the British Library

Cover design by Jacqueline Abromeit

To my wife and soul mate
Beryl
our three wonderful daughters
and our eight brilliant grandchildren

Acknowledgements

Dr.W.D Cussins for his unstinting help with preparation of the many ancient photographs, Andrew Fawcett for stepping in at the last minute to organise my website, Sheila Parker for reading and correcting my early work, Brenda Cave for her inspiration, John Craddock for his technical advice. Finally and by no means least Joseph O'Neill for his invaluable guidance on publishing and for putting me in touch with Penpress.

Author's Note

To add to its authenticity, throughout Patrick's narrative all the people who feature are known by their proper names.

Chapter 1

It was one of our traditional family reunions with much emotional hugging and kissing to greet each other. Everyone had so much to say at the table; laughter, animated cross-talk and more laughter. Much warmth radiated from the human closeness, like a breath from the furthermost corners of the Mediterranean, where I had grown up. It's a deep rooted habit now carried on through three generations that all 16 of us foregather, usually for lunch. Dinner ceased to be an option once grandchildren were around. Apart from our three daughters and their husbands, the tally of grandchildren had risen to eight – four boys and four girls. This particular party was at Edwin's Gastro restaurant in Bramley village outside Guildford two days after Christmas 2006. The occasion also served to celebrate my 75th birthday which took place on that very day.

You will deduce from what I have said, that I was born on the 27th December 1931. I am unable to dream up some clever clue that might lead you to the place of my birth. It was in fact Port Said in Egypt. It would be harder still to point you towards the origins of my mother, Theodosia. As for my father William Henry Grigsby, my own name Patrick, points unambiguously to his Irish origins!

Setting out to map this long journey through time and space and to include the people and places I have frequented along the way, I am conscious of pitfalls, as with memory the further back one goes it becomes increasingly unreliable. Worse still, it can merge with one's fantasies. One can end up with convincingly real perceptions that in truth are figments of one's imagination. I will not let myself fall into this trap. So, to begin with I will tell you about something tangible that I have possessed, which goes back to my early childhood in that most celebrated of towns in Egypt, Alexandria.

* * *

This possession of mine is nothing much and of no intrinsic value. It is a greetings card. In fact a Christmas card. It is not particularly attractive, nothing like the splendid ones of today. The illustration on it depicts a wise looking owl reading from a large book to three baby robins. They appear to be listening intently, perched below him on the branches of a holly tree, which has an abundance of red berries. With the years that have passed, the card has visibly aged, the narrow once gold edging is now frayed and the colours have also faded. Inside the card the bold handwriting in ink reads:

To my son Patrick, For 1934
From his loving Dad

The handwriting is unmistakably my father's as it matches the writing on some documents in my possession which belonged to him.

It is likely that the Christmas card was posted in Beyrouth when his ship called there. It appears that he had not expected to be back home in Alexandria for the Christmas of 1934. Being apart from their loved ones was the price ship's captains paid for pursuing their chosen occupations. I have often been told my father loved the sea. My mother kept the card safe, along with a few other mementoes. Sadly, my father was never to return home. Now, this faded scrap of cardboard, more than 70 years old, remains the only keepsake from him.

Captain W.H. Grigsby, known to family and friends as Harry. The father that I lost in early childhood.

Patrick and Dosia, his mother from whom he was destined to live a life apart

That furthest corner of the Mediterranean Sea is renowned for sudden treacherous storms. In those days, Beyrouth was an open roadstead with visiting ships anchored off shore. Anchored out at sea, they could only be reached by rowing boats or tugs. As master responsible for his ship and crew, he was duty bound to return to the vessel in spite of advice to remain on shore until the tempest abated. Going out to sea in a tug, he was swept overboard by a freak wave. His body was recovered some days later. So it was that at not even four years old I was separated from him. I was destined to continue '*a life apart*' though at the time I could have known little about it.

My mother Theodosia became a widow just seven years after marrying my father in Beyrouth on the 17th June 1927. She would have had many friends in Egypt, and particularly in Alexandria – the preferred place to live for those who could afford it. In any case, there was a good train service between the capital Cairo and Alexandria. The modest beginnings of the Egyptian State Railway.

My mother's family connections, and even their roots through my grandfather, go a long way back to Egypt. Comparatively recently, during the First World War, with her men folk away fighting the Germans and their allies, my grandmother, with my mother and her two younger daughters Olga and Rosie had fled to Egypt. Turkey was allied with Germany. By all accounts, the three young women had a grand time socialising at parties, dances and soirees with the local '*beau monde*'. There were also some British officers lucky enough to be stationed in Egypt who acted as their escorts.

I have some photographs taken on board the SS Carniola before it left Alexandria on the 5th July 1919 for Mersina, as it was then called. What is so interesting about the group of people in the photograph is that they are all descendants of an Englishman who spent his entire adult life in the Middle East in the service of the Ottoman Empire. General Henry Selby Rickards, my great grandfather, was also known in Egypt as Abdullah Pasha, el Ingilizi – when converting to Islam, General Henry Selby Rickards adopted the name Abdullah, meaning 'Servant of God' in Arabic. As for his title of Pasha, this is the highest civil and military designation bestowed by the Ottomans.

A heavy, leather bound booklike album lay flat on a marble topped dresser in my grandparents' sitting room. I recall as a child seeing my mother open this to show its contents to special guests. This was a rare occurrence indeed as it was only visitors from England who were so favoured. She would release the small clasp to open it. Inside there were two coloured portraits in gold coloured metal frames. I recall hearing snatches of what my mother had to say. She rarely deviated from her introduction of the bearded man in uniform seated by a table on which rested his gold handled ceremonial sword. She referred to him as "General Rickards, my grandfather." pointing to the second portrait she would go on to say – "and that is Catherine his second wife. She had been sent out from England as a governess. You know, his first wife was an Egyptian princess. He had converted to Islam and gone on the *hajj* to Mecca so that they could get married. When his Egyptian wife died, he married Catherine and lived in London where my father was born."

In the snap taken on the SS Carniola, my grandfather Rickards is wearing a '*sola topi*' and William his son, safely back from France, is in a grey fedora. With them are my grandmother and mother with her younger sisters Olga and Rosie. The evacuation of the four of them to Egypt had brought them together with their Egyptian relatives. All descendants of the General and his first wife. He was known to them as Abdullah Pasha. It was said at the time that she was an Egyptian princess. The man in the photograph wearing a '*tarboosh*' is believed to

SS Carniola before departure from Alex for Mersina July 1919.
From left back row – William, Br.Officer, Olga, Uncle Amin, Seza Nabarawi, Cousin Bertie, Dosia, Henry Rickards & Rosie

be either a half cousin, Bertie or my mother's half uncle Amin Abdullah. He and my grandfather were half brothers. Ceza Nabarawi, one of Egypt's three famous feminists is seen in the photograph wearing a black headdress. The two of them resident in Egypt must have boarded the SS Carniola to see my grandfather and his family off on their voyage back to what hopefully had survived of the extensive Rickards properties in Turkey.

Returning to the untimely death of my father, bereavements in that part of the world are very different occasions from the restrained British tradition. Mourning there is neither private nor quiet. People, relatives, friends all feel they must share in the grief being experienced by the next of kin and her close family. Some Muslim bereavements are attended by professional mourners who are paid to wail and let out hooting cries. Their '*ululations*' can be heard many doors away. My mother would not have been short of people calling to pay their respects and condole with her. They will have also consoled her, enquiring as to her plans:

"Dosia, with Harry gone, God rest his soul, how are you going to manage?"

"I can't stay here in Alex. I have no means of supporting myself and Harry did not have any security with the people he was employed by other than his salary. I now have Patrick to think of as well. No, I have no choice; I will have to go back to Mersin. Mother is expecting us and I will just have to wait and see how things work out."

"Well, I will say goodbye. Have a safe journey '*inshallah*', God willing. My heartfelt '*salaamat*' and respects to *sit* Mariam and the rest of your people in Mersin. God be with you and your boy Dosia."

In those days, girls from better off families did not receive an education or training intended to fit them for a career. Middle class young ladies were not meant to work. It was not the done thing. Even so, my grandfather made the financial effort to give all his children, his three daughters included, a good education away in Europe. My mother was sent to Marlborough College, a girl's boarding school in Buxton. Her two sisters attended a girls boarding *Lycee* in Montpellier, both ending up fluent in French. Olga later trained at the London Hospital and once qualified as a nurse, she went on to live and work for a period in England.

The little recollection I have of our journey out of Egypt, through Syria and into Turkey is hazy. I recall just two things. Al Kantara, a crossing point on the Suez Canal; a bustling place, with mostly fishermen carrying baskets of fish that they had caught. It was night time but warm. Also Aleppo, the second largest town in Syria after the capital Damascus. My recollection though is strangely of mother cautioning me to be aware of the '*Aleppo Fly* ':

"The dreaded '*Aleppo Fly*'. I have never heard of them any where else, they are found only here in Aleppo. If you allow them to settle on you and they have a chance to sting you, it seems you would get a fever. The infected surface from the sting takes a long time to heal. You are left with a deep unsightly scar. Patrick, look that poor chap over there. Can you see the several scars on the side of his face?" Thus alerted, I saw several other people with the pockmarks, all victims of that dreaded fly that my mother had told me about.

I have no memory of our arrival in Mersin (as it came to be called with the formation of the new Turkish Republic). It was a coastal town that my mother had brought me to in 1935. Historically it had benefited greatly from the construction of the Suez Canal and the American civil war. The much needed timber for the canal came from the vast forests in the Taurus Mountains. Cotton grown in the arid plains of Cukurova was processed and baled in Adana, and shipped to Europe in place of cotton imports that had dried up from America.

This boom in the 1860s attracted wealthy families from Syria, and Egypt. A massacre of Christians by the Druze had brought an influx from Lebanon also. These émigrés brought finance and know-how as entrepreneurs, merchants, exporters and shipping agents.

Settlers, most of them Christians, belonged to prominent families from whence they came – Barbour, Chelfoun, Nakkash, Chachaty, Dumani, Diab, Nader and Debbane. It was the Nader family who in 1854 had commissioned the building of the small picturesque orthodox church. There were also well known Muslim families like Gandour, Miskavi, Safa, Hamis the Chiftci. The last mentioned were the first millionaires in Mersin. There were many others who were less well known. It is said that as recently as the 1840s the place then known as Mersina was little more than a fishing village, with one small wooden jetty.

It was the descendents of these families who continued to provide the trade and commerce in Mersin. There was nothing much by way of industrialisation in the town, just a soap factory owned by the Gandours, and brick works going out on the road to Tarsus where deposits of clay had been discovered. I remember hearing that all the olive groves that surrounded the town were owned and commercialised by the Nader family, believed to be amongst the very earliest to have settled in Mersin.

Not surprisingly, it was these people who owned the best properties and the grandest houses. The exterior of the buildings had much in common. They were built from locally quarried limestone that was cut and dressed into large blocks. They had shallow pitch, red-tiled roofs. All had balconies and some large terraces as well. All windows were fitted with vertical thick steel bars for security. Wooden shutters with adjustable slats provided some coolness and shade during the long hot summer days. The ground floors of these buildings were used for

Syrian Orthodox Church

Mass in Syrian Orthodox Church – modestly decorated tree, the only public evidence of Christmas tide in Mersin

various commercial purposes, mostly shops and storage depots. The lived-in house portion was always on the first floor.

My grandfather's two houses were built on a prime corner site along the main coastal road or '*corniche*' with large rambling gardens. The grounds of the house that my mother and I were destined to live in were encircled by a high stone wall. A stone archway connected the wall to the house. A heavy wooden double door with massive forged steel hinges was built into the archway. My mother's bedroom, which I shared with her, was on the first floor.

Its two windows overlooked the entrance where there was a small courtyard with flower beds. I can remember a profusion of violets because of their distinctive purple colour. An outside stone staircase led up to the entrance of the house itself. The steps were so shallow I was soon able to run up them. I had also come to notice the sweet smelling white jasmine and lemon verbena, both climbers that twined round the stair rails. I grew accustomed to their distinctive yet very different scents. A lemon verbena now grows against our south facing garden wall in Sutton Coldfield, a living reminder of the past. It still needs to be protected every winter from the English frosts.

Just beyond the courtyard growing almost against the stone wall was an enormous eucalyptus tree, much bigger than any I have seen in England. I picked up its then strange sounding name quickly as they are very common in the hot regions of Turkey. Pigeons had built their nests amongst its branches. I used to lie in bed listening to their cooing – a wistful memory that has remained with me. Now, years on, I am transported back whenever I hear those doleful calls.

The two Rickards houses had been built by my grandmother Mariam's father Hanna Kerroum, a master builder, soon after she and my grandfather were married. Both were roomy houses. The one that my

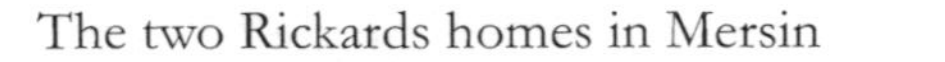

The two Rickards homes in Mersin

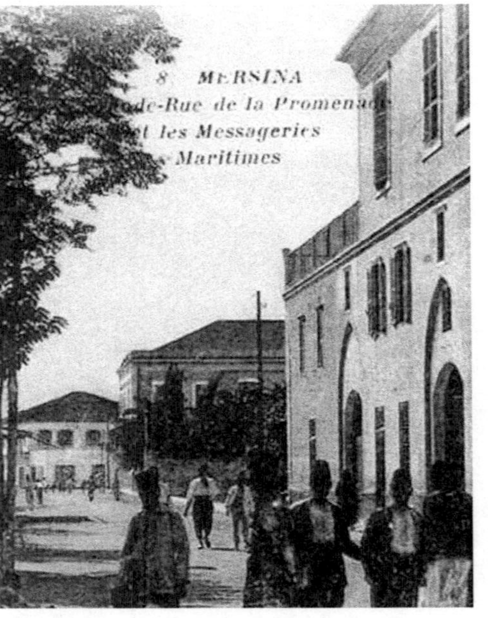

Mersina as it was in 1914-18, World War era. *'Kishla caddesi'* main sea front road devoid of traffic, men still wearing the *'fez'*. The house at the very end where my grandparents lived was where my mother brought me from Egypt

grandfather rented had a covered balcony and distinctive arches on two sides which made it look most attractive.

In the house where my grandparents lived, the front door opened into a big rectangular hall with a white marble floor. In summer when the carpets were taken up it was the coolest place. In all, there were seven rooms positioned on three sides of this hall. Five of these were bedrooms with wooden floors. They all had large sash windows opening on to the hall. My mother and her sisters sometimes invited friends to parties in the hall. My aunts were in their mid thirties and as yet unmarried. They had many young admiring suitors. There was a great deal of talking, people spoke in loud voices, gesticulating. Jokes were bandied around giving rise to much laughter and sometimes hand clapping. Those evenings were memorable. My bed was under one of these sash windows. By standing on the sill I could peer over the top of the window and watch, understanding little of what was being said. Hardly surprising as everyone there would have been speaking a hotchpotch of several languages.

The *'outsider'* families who had come and settled in Mersin all spoke more than one language. Members of the Rickards family, apart from English spoke French, Arabic and Turkish. Other languages spoken as mother tongues also included Italian, Greek and Armenian. By far the biggest group of settlers in the town came from Syria and spoke Arabic. There were several Italian families – Levante, Bertamini, Damiani. Mantovani. Of the Greek families, it was the Tahinci and Mavrumati households who were the most prominent. My family knew the Keshishian and Jambazians who were well established Armenians in the town.

The following statistics point to the unique composition of its population. The figures are taken from a book in Turkish, titled *"From Yesterday up to Today – Mersin – 1836-1987" by Lawyer, H Sinasi Develi.*

Mersina Population breakdown – 1890

Muslim:	5240	58.20 %
Greek Orthodox:	2700	30.00 %
Armenian:	800	8.90 %
Catholic:	260	2.90 %
TOTAL:	9000	(100 %)

The population of Mersina in 1890 included a disproportionately large number of Christians – 41.80%. By contrast, the figure for the whole of Turkey at the time would almost certainly have been a fraction of this, given that today Christians are lumped into the 5% non-Muslim minority. Another interesting statistic – the same census ascribed a population of 20,185 to the 87 outlying villages administered by Mersina. In 1890 all villagers, unlike the poorer mass of town people, were indigenous Turks and all of them were Muslim. The figures serve to demonstrate that the town of Mersina was a unique enclave, to which émigrés, largely Christian had been drawn. They came largely from the neighbouring countries to Turkey's south.

The large Christian population was served by the two Greek Orthodox, a Catholic and a Maronite church. Four Christian places of worship compared with one solitary Mosque in the town itself. At the time of the First World War Turkey, a Muslim country, was still the epicentre of the Ottoman Empire. Though culturally different, the wealthy and better educated Christian *'outsiders'* of Mersin rubbed shoulders and lived in harmony with the town's indigenous Muslims. A way of life that my family had willingly practised. My mother in particular, the eldest child of a mixed marriage followed this way of life; something that I picked up from her and went on to practise myself. After the formation in 1923 of the Turkish Republic, any of these émigrés who had not already acquired Turkish citizenship, were obliged to do so.

Coincidentally, it was also in 1890 that my grandfather arrived in Mersina. Apart from his houses and other properties in Mersin, he owned a substantial stone built summer house. This was in Gozne, one of the many villages tied to Mersin. Its local inhabitants were '*koylu',* villagers or peasants who in those days rarely ventured out of their '*koy*', village. They were all Muslims, as in the rest of Anatolia. They were loyal to their origins, leading stable, hard working lives in these remote villages. On the rare occasions that villagers from Gozne ventured down to Mersin, they would do so on horse back. They would spend the night with their horse in one of the town's four '*hans'* – a combination of inn and stable, common in Turkey.

Candir Kale, one of these villages in the Taurus Mountains, is situated near to Gozne. Its only link with the outside world is a rough mountain track, a bridle path. As is general in Turkey, bread is the staple diet. However, unlike anywhere else in the region, the women scribe a cross in the dough before baking. Strange, since all the inhabitants of *Candir Kale* are Muslims. An archaeologist from the UK who witnessed this said it most certainly must be a custom left from the Crusaders! This bears testimony to the unchanging and parochial nature of these isolated Anatolian villages.

The figures thrown up by the 1890 census make Mersin demographically unique. Add to this the benefits of a semi tropical climate and a desirable coastal position and you have a veritable oasis. It was not surprising that most of the short stay European visitors, notably those in their respective country's consular services, always yearned to return. Sentiments they expressed often in the letters they wrote to friends who remained in Mersin.

Though the climate in winter was temperate, my mother told me one day – "It will start getting colder now, I have been down town and seen *usta* Nedeem. He is going to make me a *soba*, a simple wood burning stove."

My mother would only ever get things made or supplied by tradesmen whose name was preceded by *usta,* what we call a master craftsman. However, in Turkey the term *usta* had come to mean a great deal more. One might say that a dentist or a surgeon is very *usta* meaning he is most accomplished in his chosen profession. My mother must have known every *usta* in the town. I had become almost proficient in Turkish thanks to attending Murshida Abla's little kindergarten where only Turkish was spoken. At that time and in that part of the country many Arabic words and expressions were in common use.

Not long after my mother had told me about the stove she had ordered, it turned up. A big black thing. There were also several large diameter metal tubes and a round tray, all in a matching black. Nedeem *usta* had come up the outside stairs and was met at the door by the servant girl. My mother appeared. He nodded his head saying '*selam aleykum*' to which my mother replied instinctively '*aleykum el selam*', as she shook hands with the *usta.*

Behind him at a respectful distance, carrying the parts for my mother's stove came three ragamuffins – they were his trade apprentices, *chirak* as they are known. Every tradesman, from tinker to tailor in the town had one or two *chirak,* learning the ins and outs of his trade.

"Where do you want it, madam?" *usta* Nedeem enquired.

My mother pointed out our bedroom. He signalled his troupe to bring the parts in. I must have gone off somewhere. When I returned the stove was installed. It sat on its tray in the middle of our bedroom. The assembled tubes were fitted, coming out of the back of the stove. They went almost up to the ceiling and out through the wall to the outside. An all-black monstrosity made all the more conspicuous by the manner in which it stretched up and along almost touching the light coloured ceiling. Not a pretty sight. More of an eye sore. I saw my mother and *usta* Nedeem in deep conversation eyeing his creation. I heard the *usta* telling my mother, "Madam, I always include a good size tray when one of my stoves is going into a bedroom. It is better like this, the floor you see. One has to protect it. It's wood!!" My mother nodded in an absent minded manner then spoke, "Tell me… this tray, it is included in the price you gave me, isn't it?" *Usta* Nedeem replied without hesitation, "Yes, of course, *Madam*." His reply brought the smile back to my mother's face. With that, the *usta* said goodbye, departing with his young helpers but not before my mother gave each of his *chirak* a generous handful of sweets. Their gratitude was only exceeded by their self-consciousness as they left.

It was not very long after its installation that my mother decided one night before we retired to light the stove. It was to be a trial run so to speak. The nights were getting noticeably cooler than they had been for months. "It will soon warm the room." She said to me with an approving look of anticipation. Sure enough, it did. As was customary, a good quantity of dry sand had been loaded into a basin constructed in the top of the stove for this very purpose. Before long this was baking hot. The pipes conveying the smoke and fumes to the outside were groaning and crackling with the heat. Next thing, I noticed the sides of the stove itself were starting to glow, a dark orangey red. At the sight of this, my mother must have lost her confidence. "Quick, Patrick go and call your uncle." My mother told me as the red glow had turned incandescent. I ran barefoot to call my uncle, I could feel the wooden floor under my feet near the stove had become quite hot. The whole thing sounded ready to erupt. It was quite alarming.

I fetched my uncle who hurried back in his pyjamas. He was not at all pleased to have been woken up. I could sense this from his silence on the way back to my mother. "Good heavens Dosia, you are going to burn the whole place down!"

My uncle used his handkerchief to protect his hand as he busied himself. He pushed in some metal parts and also closed the door on the front of the stove. Gradually the roaring abated. The excitement had kept me awake. I could tell from her regular heavy breathing that my mother had dropped off to sleep. I listened to the different crackling sounds as everything gradually returned to normal. The stove eventually lost its glow and merged into the darkness of the room.

None of the Rickards' houses or their many other properties, I was to find out many years later, had ever been insured. The displeasure my uncle showed at the time was hardly surprising. As far as I can find out, in those days no one in Mersin insured their homes or anything else. Nobody was prepared to believe nor trust that by paying some insurance company premiums year after year, that when disaster struck, their losses would be made good. Spending hard earned money on insurance against fire or theft made no sense. Instead, far better to put in place measures that would give protection from the risks. There were no private cars at the time, it was with the advent of private car ownership that insurance began to catch on and gain some credence. This is but one of many examples of how different the world that I grew up in was compared with the England that I would in time get to know.

My mother had married late in life; she would have been in her early 40s when my father died. Left a widow with me to bring up she was fortunate to be able to return to her family home in Mersin. Aware of my grand parents' devotion to peace and quiet, she must have felt duty bound to take me with her wherever she went. My grandfather suffered a condition that might be brought on if he was upset. In any case, he had little patience. Once I was five, my mother had enrolled me at Murshida Abla's kindergarten. She took me there the first day, thereafter I was left to find my own way.

My mother's freedom was short lived as I got tetanus following a fall in the kindergarten playground. I was laid up in bed and I seem to recall my whole body was stiff. I remember little else about that incident.

A year or two later, I was struck down with amoebic dysentery, a common complaint in that part of the world. With no antibiotics available at the time, I was put on what was then alarmingly called '*a starvation diet'*. I was allowed nothing to eat or drink but boiled water. My mother explained what the doctor had said, which I seem to recall went something like this: "Doctor Kamel has told me that you will have to be kept on a diet of boiled water only. You must have nothing nutritious to eat or drink, whatsoever. The purpose is to starve the amoebas inside you." Hearing how the enemy within was to be dealt with, I might have had the wit to enquire, "But what about me!" It never occurred to me at the time to do so. Had I enquired, I now suspect the answer could have been predictably evasive: "We will have to wait and see."

On the other hand, as my family's attitude to children 'who were to be seen and not heard' discouraged any questions, my mother might have dismissed my query still more brusquely: "You ask too many questions. Just do as you are told." After all, she with her brother and sisters had been brought up in the Victorian manner that my grandfather favoured.

Without the medicines of today, it is not surprising how fatalistic people were in those times. I was lucky to recover, a great many did not. Both my mother and I lived with the dread of a recurrence which was also usual as the amoeba could survive and remain dormant for years.

Great care had to be taken, particularly with fruit and vegetables. I remember my mother, for a time, rinsing them in a weak solution of potassium permanganate.

I used to be told how lucky I was as conditions had become so much better. My mother as a young girl, long before she was sent to school in England in around 1910, had a tooth extracted by the butcher in lower Gozne. I can well remember her very words of explanation: "Mother could not face having to take me down to the sweltering summer heat in Mersin on horse back; a journey of many hours. She put my mind at ease telling me that the butcher was experienced as he dealt with all the villagers and had a good set of instruments."

Times must have indeed got better. Even so, I dreaded being taken by my own mother to Doctor Bahir's dental practice in Mersin. He was reputed to be the best in town. His surgery was on the second floor above shops in a building that was once a substantial stone built house, not far from the then British Consulate. We used to go up a steep wooden stairway in near darkness to reach his large waiting room. It smelled of strong disinfectant.

On the wall facing us as we sat on uncomfortable wooden chairs were several coloured caricatures in cheap wooden frames. I used to gaze in wonderment and dread at these bizarre images – one in particular I can still bring to mind. The scene depicted was titled – "*A tricky extraction*", even then I had thought it a grotesque choice for a patients' waiting room. Think what I may, I recall gawping at the lurid scene. The dentist with his knee on the patient's chest as he struggled to draw the tooth. I stared at this image of the wretched patient, his eyes popping out and blood spurting from his gaping mouth. The fiendish looking dentist sweating as he struggles with his victim. On a hot day I recall Doctor Bahir himself did also sweat. It was a consequence of his exertion as his foot worked a pedal that operated the dental drill through a complex arrangement of pulleys.

My mother made me aware of the many hazards that surrounded us in Gozne that primitive yet much loved village in the Taurus Mountains where we went to escape the coastal heat each and every summer. "Patrick, there are a lot of scorpions here. They find their way into the house and could be lurking almost any where. Don't ever go into cupboards feeling around without having a really careful look first. Use a torch as the inner most parts of the cupboards are always dark."

A villager who had turned up at the house on one occasion gave a remarkable demonstration of what he claimed was *"a scorpion committing suicide."* The scorpion was placed in the middle of a ring of red hot embers. Having tried unsuccessfully to escape sure enough it curled its long tail over and injected itself with its own venom. It did not take long to expire.

A big black snake had its nest in the rock face that ran along the back of the house. Though it was about four feet long and over two inches in diameter, it was not venomous. They were common to that part of the Taurus Mountains. The Gozne villagers called them '*kara boga'*. Though harmless my mother was taking no chances, she told me, "Don't go round the back of the house in the dark, you may tread on it." I particularly recall that she was also most upset as she was convinced that it was stealing and devouring some of the eggs laid by the two chickens she had bought to provide us with fresh eggs for breakfast.

Several of us children liked to dive into the sweet smelling hay that was stored for the winter in a hayloft until we heard that it was supposed to be infested with some small snakes. They were said to be venomous. We did not have to be told twice. We had all grown up with a keen sense of what was safe and what wasn't. The freedom from constant parental control had taught us to use our own judgement. We also had some rudimentary knowledge of first aid. We knew for example if we were stung by a wasp or some unidentified insect to immediately urinate on the stung spot. If we could not access the place, a friend would be called on to oblige. I was to hear much later that it was the ammonia in urine that did indeed offer relief.

During the summer months in Gozne I spent most of my waking hours with the children of family friends from Mersin. The rest of the year in Mersin things were different, particularly early on before I started going to the Gazi Pasha primary school. We children had less freedom in the town where we were deprived of the opportunities to run wild exploring the wilderness of the Taurus Mountains.

It was back in Mersin one particular day about mid morning when my mother was making for the shops, and as usual I was by her side when we came upon the scene. There was an almost festive atmosphere about the place. A large crowd of men, women and children had come from far and wide to witness the spectacle. After all, public hangings were not that common but when they were staged, it was a veritable bonanza time for the peddlers with their carts loaded with snacks and drinks for sale. I recall my mother remarked, "Poor things, who knows when they will have such a wonderful opportunity again." Since becoming a widow, my mother empathised with all those who like her and all other widows, had a struggle to get by.

From the distance where we had stopped, all I could make out was an inanimate shape clad in a white gown suspended motionless from a tripod of telegraph poles that had been lashed together. I was intrigued by a large notice hanging from the victim's neck. It was covered with black writing. That sight, even at the time, did not particularly upset or frighten me. I have come to the conclusion that this was because we had not been near enough to the lifeless human on the end of the rope to be able to pick out the grisly details. My mother had not wanted us to be part of the jostling crowd. The great unwashed, the riff raff, mostly youths who barged their way right up to the brutal scene to gawp. As we moved on, my mother said to me, "Patrick, be warned, this is the consequence of doing wrong!"

Her words of warning remained locked in my mind. It was of course the body displayed so publicly that had moved her. Perhaps with me growing up without a father, she felt compelled to say what she did in the belief that it was for my good. My devoted mother was forever striving to do her best for me. However well intended, my early up-bringing left a disturbing mark on me.

That day, had we ventured close under that lifeless body clad in its white gown, as I was to find out on a later occasion, I would have seen the ghoulish reality of the corpse. The neck twisted by the sudden pull on the rope causing the head to tilt unnaturally. Facial features distorted, puce, bloated tongue hanging out of the open mouth. In keeping with custom, the notice affixed to the corpses spelled out in a few words the crime that had caused him to be there. In later years, encouraged by each other, I had in company with my friends seen the entire ghoulish spectacle in the market square just by Doctor Bahir the dentist's surgery. There were other scenes that did distress me even more such as the sight of animals being butchered.

I recall much talk about the modern '*salhane*', slaughterhouse in Adana. My mother and uncle were invited by the architect, Semih *Bey* to join a party from Mersin who went over when it was opened. It must have been quite a show piece and unique in the entire region. But then

Adana was the biggest and most important town in South Eastern Turkey to warrant such a magnificent '*salhane*'. Otherwise, animals were killed by the '*helal*' butchers themselves at their shops, often in full view of passers-by. Slaughter was performed as humanely as possible, and in accordance with *sharia law*, always with the same prayer being uttered as the razor sharp knife was deftly drawn across the animal's throat: *"Bi issim, Allah il raham, Allah il rahim."*, in the name of God the merciful, God the compassionate.

I saw sheep being killed by Adil the village butcher in this manner when we were up in Gozne for the summer. It must have been curiosity that drew us children to watch. We were transfixed. A sort of numbness overcame me as I looked on helplessly. In a split second I had caught sight of the sheep's wide open eyes. They had a pleading look that remained to haunt me. I did wonder what had drawn me to the scene. The same morbid excitement that draws the crowds to bull fights. In our case the terrifying act was mercifully over very quickly. Adil, was a powerful, thick set chap. He had trussed the animal first then despatched it with great skill saying to us children, "Through the grace of God, my sheep do not suffer!"

Adil then set about skinning the dead animal. He cut slits in the hide half way up all four of its legs. Getting down on his knees he put his mouth to each in turn and blew hard. In effect he inflated the upper part of the leg and as he continued, I could see the hide swelling. He stopped from time to time to rest and get his breath back. It was hard work. Whilst thus recovering from blowing, he put his hand over the slit and beat the swelling to disperse the air. Adil repeated this procedure on each of the four legs. In time, the whole body had visibly swelled and looked bloated. The hide was thus separated from the carcass. Adil cut the hide from the front of its neck down and removed it in one piece intact. Finally, the belly was cut open so that the entrails

The customary daily scene outside my grandparents' summer house in Gozne at sunset.
From the left – Henry Rickards & Mariam, Rosie nursing Billy, her husband Riri Levante seated on chair, standing Itel Lochner and his brother Ronnie next to him. I am in the centre near my cousin Billy.

The Roman remains are said to be of a castle that served as a lookout post when Cilecia was part of the Roman empire. The village beneath the castle nestles in a sheltered valley with a panoramic view of Mersin and the blue Mediterranean.

poured out into a shallow basin. The performance over, we children dispersed.

Up in Gozne there were other distractions. But first of all, to set the scene, let me tell you a bit about the place. Even in 1935 when I was first brought to Gozne, it was primitive. It did have a charm of its own, largely created by its cosmopolitan visitors, Christian families from Mersin including my own. These people first started going up there after the mid 1800s to escape the unbearable summer heat of the coastal plain. Originally the village would have been a cluster of flat roofed dwellings typical of what one still sees in the remote parts of Anatolia.

My grandfather's house like the ones in Mersin, was stone built with a red-tiled pitched roof. The ground floor comprised of two rooms and a large hall at each end of which there were double doors to the outside. When these were opened, there would be a pleasant flow of cool air. This part of the house, referred to as the '*downstairs*', was where the family spent the day. At times there were as many as eight of us in the house. All meals were taken at a large table around which we sat on wooden benches. The kitchen, which also at times served as a bathroom, must have been an after thought as it was built on to the house and had a sloping corrugated iron roof.

Access to the timber built first floor was by a wooden staircase from the hall. There were three bedrooms and a large open space which served as a sitting room. A door from this opened out onto a large covered balcony where the family spent the evenings.

Some distance from the house stood the '*privy*'. An upright wooden construction with a corrugated iron top akin to a sentry box. By the standards of the time, our house permitted us to live in relative comfort even though water on tap, gas, electricity, waste disposal did not exist. In short '*mod cons*', that piece of Estate Agents' jargon, were nowhere to be found in Gozne.

On the other hand, there was the fresh, cool mountain air at night. Stars sparkled in the clear night sky. When there was a full moon it was claimed that one could sit out side and read the paper. The bright lights of Mersin could be seen in the distance from the many balconies where people sat chatting after their dinners. Those distant lights were often likened to a diamond necklace. There was absolutely no traffic nor any man made noise to disturb those lost in reverie. Well maybe just the lilt of a refrain drifting across from a party, couples dancing to a record on a wind up gramophone. The French singing idol from Corsica, Tino Rossi was all the rage.

Deprived though we were of civilisation's basic conveniences which we all now take for granted, my mother made sure every night that I was well washed before going to bed. I had been told at some time that 'cleanliness was next to Godliness.' So it was that my mother, with the limited resources available to us in Gozne supervised and assisted me. With a carefully rationed supply of tepid water that she dispensed, I washed using a large enamelled basin. This rested on a box in our bedroom. I had to be careful that water did not wet the floor as I carefully dried myself at each stage. These nightly *'ablutions'* or as dictionaries define – '*the ceremonial washing of parts of the body*' – were in my case a lengthy performance. I started with my face and neck, moving down in stages, the water in the basin getting murkier as I progressed. This created a nightly dilemma, whether to wash my private parts and bottom before or after my feet.

With the benefit of hindsight, taking a bath would have been so much quicker. Arguably, I might even have stepped out of it the cleaner.

The fact is there wasn't a single bath in Gozne, not many in Mersin either. Most people there went to their local *'hamam'*. Had some forward thinker with Western pretensions invested in a bath he would have had to have it delivered by camel to his abode in Gozne. After all that, he would not have been able to get it plumbed into a water supply nor for that matter was there any electricity or gas for the heating of the water.

All water had to be carried from the fountain. My family were lucky as the big '*Mufti*' fountain was reasonably close, some 200 metres away. There was a large cauldron in our hall, my grandmother used to pay one of the villagers to fill it. This took several trips to and from the fountain. Little wonder my mother was sparing with the water for me to have my wash each night.

Later in the night, when all the lights were extinguished and absolute silence fell, nocturnal wildlife would be on the prowl. The surrounding mountains were home to foxes, hyenas, wolves and wild boar. They foraged for scraps of food. Winters in Gozne were severe with up to three metres of snow. These wild animals were then joined by wolves and brown bears. The *'koylu'* were the sole inhabitants of the village as all the townsfolk would have returned to their more comfortable homes in Mersin for the mild winters by the coast.

These reminiscences are of my earliest experiences living with my mother, bachelor uncle and grandparents in the Rickards' house in Mersin. Memories of an unusual infancy, though I was spared the conscious awareness of the loss of my father. I was beginning to sense the hardships that my mother was going through as a consequence of my father's untimely demise. My very existence at times must have been a bone of contention. After all, infants do make their presence felt. Little wonder that my mother must have at times felt she had been taken in by her family on sufferance. Insecurity plagued her. On occasions I overheard her in the company of her closest friends lamenting *"What is to become of us."*

A strange question that I recall both puzzled and frightened me.

Chapter 2

I could not have predicted how much my life in Mersin would change starting that morning in September 1938, though I now wonder whether as a seven year old I would have really been given to such speculation. The fact of the matter is that until then, I had been by my mother's side going wherever she went. I recall she visited a great deal. There was little else to occupy her in Mersin. She seemed to know no end of people in the town, mostly ladies, many of whom she used to refer to as "an old and very dear friend". Listening to their conversations, I had picked up Arabic and French words and phrases, even some that I dared not repeat. Brought up this way, and constantly hearing adult talk, I must have been privy to topics way ahead of my years. By then, I was able to speak Turkish fluently. At home as a family we spoke English though my mother and grandmother lapsed into Arabic when together in the kitchen.

That September morning started with my mother helping me into my new school uniform. The garb for the local Government primary schools throughout Turkey was 'uniform' in every sense of the word – egalitarian. All these primary schools were co-educational. Boys wore shorts and a belted tunic made entirely from a thick dark grey cotton material. Girls, a knee length dress in a black shiny cotton material, embellished with a detachable white fabric collar. Material for these uniforms was manufactured and retailed by the Sumerbank, a state enterprise founded by The Gazi[1] Mustafa Kemal himself, with

[1] The word, used as a title for one who fights on behalf of Islam. A prestigious title given to high-ranking generals for outstanding exploits.

branches in most towns. Sumerbank prices were deemed to be within the reach of the poorest. "Ataturk" – father of the Turks! made sure that 'all his children' would be schooled without putting their families to financial hardship.

Throughout Turkey, attendance at these schools was free. The nearest one to our house was the Gazi Pasha. The well-to-do Christian families of Mersin who were minded to, sent their children abroad. The Syrians to Beirut, the Italians to Rhodes and the rest, opted for the Greek, Italian and French schools in Istanbul. The younger Christian children, like myself were enrolled at the Gazi Pasha. Proof to my family that their choice had been a good one. My mother clipped the stiff cardboard badge with the initials "*GP*" onto my tunic. This would identify me to the world at large as a Gazi Pasha pupil.

It did not take long for us to walk to the school. Inside the high stone wall that went all the way round the school buildings and the grounds, there were boys and girls all in exactly the same uniforms that I have described with their black and orange "*GP*" badges. My mother spotted a girl and waved to her, she came over and greeted my mother, *"Good morning Madam Dosia."*

My mother smiled, returning her greeting she said to the girl, "Victoria, this is my son Patrick. Could you keep an eye on him until he gets settled in?"

"Of course! This is my second year. I can remember how I felt when I started. Don't worry; I will look after him for you."

"Thank you Victoria, he is an orphan, poor chap!"

I did not forget the choice of my mother's words. She had used the word *'yetim'* many times before. It means 'orphan' in Arabic and also in Turkish. I recall how embarrassed it made me feel every time I heard her describe me that way. I could not have explained then why I wished she did not persist in calling me *'yetim'*. What is more, by adding *'poor chap'*, the way she often did, still further compounding my discomfort. I would realise later on why I felt this aversion to being labelled *'yetim'*, for no one likes to be an object of pity.

As I mentioned earlier, due to its location the Gazi Pasha attracted children from some of the better-off families. A very small minority. There were no fewer than 80 children in my class. We sat three to a desk. As luck would have it, in my class there were Yalcin, the son of the Regional Governor, Atila the elder son of the town's Mayor, and a handful of children whose fathers were in business or one of the professions. The rest, an overwhelming majority, came from poor homes, like Cevdet with whom I was particularly friendly. I used to come across him after school selling *'simits'*, ring shaped hard bread rolls, which he had in a tray balanced on his head. Metin's father I remember was unique – he had a most unusual job, he was the lighthouse keeper. Metin invited me to his home and to my surprise it was the lighthouse itself! His family were poor, but not as poor as some of the others I visited.

The least fortunate children attended the other primary schools, situated in the poor quarters at the back of the town. At the time in Mersin, the absence of mechanisation meant that whatever work there was could only be done manually. The parents of these children were able to eke out a living doing such manual work that came their way. Poverty was a way of life for the vast majority. It was easy to pick out the deprived. In place of shoes many of them made do with rubber galoshes, often a size or two too big for them. Few wore socks, the winters were mild.

All the boys had their heads shaved, a precaution my mother told me that helped guard against the spread of disease and lice. Girls must have been deemed to be immune as they all had long hair, which was often platted. Proud as she had been of my auburn thatch, my mother had wheedled a certificate out of Doctor Kamel which she presented to the school authorities. This exempted me on medical or some related grounds from having my head shorn. A dispensation that pleased me as well because I had become conscious of my ears, which stuck out.

Barely a decade and a half had gone by since Ataturk had founded the Turkish Republic from the ashes of the Ottoman Empire. Gone were the fez, the '*yashmak*', and the Arabic alphabet. In their place, a new Westernised vision for Turkey was emerging amongst her population of about 18 million; an enormous undertaking which inevitably required drastic and sometimes unpopular measures to ensure success. Even at that early age, I must have become aware of saying anything, however innocent, that might offend the sensibilities of the locals. More particularly, it was a time when any form of dissent was given short shrift. The creed to Turkish-ness quoted below and recited every morning in all schools, laudable though it was at the time, bred strong feelings of chauvinistic nationalism:

> *I am a Turk, I am honest, I am hard working*
> *Foremost, I protect my juniors, I respect my elders, I love my country and nation*
> *My country, to rise up, to go forward*
> Oh Great Ataturk
>
> *I vow to follow unceasingly the way that you have shown to our destination*
> *May my existence be a gift to Turkish existence*
> *Lucky is he who says – "I am a Turk"*

Every morning before lessons, on a signal from our teacher all 80 children in my class, including myself, stood stiffly to attention, eyes facing the front and heads held high to recite this creed. As this was going on in all five classes simultaneously, though not necessarily in unison, you can imagine the cacophony that could be heard several blocks away. Each child called out the words at the top of their voices and with great fervour. I felt compelled to join in. I did ponder on the start of the first line – "I am a Turk!" Each time I said this it played on my mind, I felt uneasy. The same thought went through my mind every time – "Just a minute, why am I saying this! I'm not a Turk!" It was the loud forcefulness with which the entire class, including the teacher facing us, recited this creed that compelled me to do likewise. It created in me a guilty feeling of 'disloyalty' and ambivalence.

I never mentioned the matter to a soul, not even to anyone in my family. On the one hand was the absurdity of reciting the creed and my reluctance to do so, but on the other hand, what might befall me if I did not? Might I be taken to task for refusing to participate in this daily pledge? Paying homage and expressing allegiance. The quandary played on my mind, yet I chose to keep it to myself for reasons that I still find problematic. All this might now sound absurd. Even at the time might it have been an over reaction! The over sensitised thoughts of a mere child confused by the daily ritual made by all those around him, yet meaning nothing to him personally.

Grandfather Rickards had been reunited with his considerable collection of properties when the family returned to Turkey on the SS Carniola after WW l. A significant good will gesture by the Turkish authorities when one remembers Gallipoli. The Rickards family had always been well integrated into life in Mersin. They had many good friends amongst the indigenous population. My mother used to talk to me and tell me things about past experiences. Tannus Farris, her aunt's husband, is said to have had a hand in safeguarding the Rickards family interests during the war when they were evacuated to Egypt. However, the dramatic changes started in 1923 were still going on and it was inevitable that attitudes were changing. A mere child at the time, I would have understood little of the matters that were discussed amongst the grown ups. It is surprising though, how a child gets to sense things. The need to be discrete. So it was that I learned early in life when to keep quiet.

Back at school, there was a further weekly ceremony. Every Friday before breaking up for the weekend and again first thing on Monday mornings, we mustered by class in the school yard near the flag mast. After a brief address by the headmaster Ali Fuat Firat on Friday the '*al bayrak'* – the crimson flag, oft used slang for the Turkish flag – was lowered to be raised again on Monday., on both occasions accompanied by the singing of the National Anthem.

So much for my personal experiences. There were however much more serious undercurrents. Long past historical events that reflected badly on the country during the fall of the Ottoman Empire and after. Events that I heard my family speak about from time to time and understood only vaguely but which even so left an impression on me. Most incriminating, the massacres of the Armenians across the South East of Turkey. My mother herself had witnessed some incidents whilst she was at school in Tarsus. Too distressing, she never dwelt on what she had seen take place. Later the routing of the Greeks, entire communities who had been living in Turkey for years were victimised, forced to abandon their homes and businesses in a desperate bid to save at least their lives. Many did not make it and perished. In both these instances the victims were Orthodox Christians.

It has to be said that there continued to be minor incidents from time to time. A word that never failed to offend the Christian community, including members of my family was *'gavur'* – literally *'infidel'*. A word that I did occasionally hear as a child growing up in Turkey. In my Redhouse Turkish/Ottoman – English Dictionary *'gavur'* is shown to have several definitions in English, *viz.* *'non-Muslim'* and *'Christian'* neither of which in themselves are in any way insulting. The same word is shown to also mean *'infidel'* and *'unbeliever'* both of which are insulting to a practicing Christian. It depends therefore on the context in which and the tone in which the word *'gavur'* is used.

Prejudice often stems from misinformation or even ignorance. However unpleasant, sometimes the incident can provide some amusement as I recall on one occasion. I was on the balcony of our summer house in Gozne. There were some children whom I had never seen before playing on the dusty road. When they spotted me, they shouted out the evocative word *'gavur'*! One of the bigger boys then drew a cross in the dust and urinated on it much to the delight of the others who staggered about laughing and then proceeded also to relieve their bladders, shouting out, "This is what we think of the *'istavros'* – the Cross, that you *'gavurs'* worship."

Not wishing to give them the satisfaction of an audience, I left the balcony and went into the house. When I came out again, they had gone their separate ways. The behaviour of those children can be explained, though certainly not condoned, by an all too common misconception. In Mosques, there are no images of man nor beast. The devotional paintings and carvings of Christ and other holy figures in Churches are incorrectly assumed by some Muslims to be idols, false Gods, worshipped by Christians. Including the Cross. Whereas in fact they are no more than *'emblems of Christianity'*. I now know that this perception of Christianity is one of the major misunderstandings that the less well informed Muslims have.

I mentioned earlier the sensibilities of people following the creation of the new Turkish Republic and how easily they could sometimes be offended. This brings to my mind the incident of Dora and her dog. An example of righteous indignation that was met by bravado. A potentially tricky political situation that with the passage of time makes for an amusing anecdote.

Dora was young, as yet unmarried at the time. One of the Nakkash females, like all her sisters she was multi-lingual – she spoke her mother tongue Arabic, French learned at boarding school, English and of course Turkish. She was a good looking woman. Her quick wit and outgoing personality gave her added appeal. In company she was a most entertaining comedienne and an accomplished mimic. It was her wit that landed her in trouble as she stood talking to a couple of friends. They had stopped to admire her pet dog – few people in Mersin had pets. They were speaking in French, loudly as usual. A young Turkish Army officer happened to be going by, stopping he addressed Dora courteously in Turkish, "*Madam* I heard you speaking in a foreign language."

"You are correct, we were speaking in French. Is there some thing wrong?" The young officer evidently did think there was something wrong. What is more, he had set his mind on putting the matter right. "*Madam*, as a citizen of our country, you should speak our language, Turkish." On an impulse and without a thought as to its consequences, Dora smiled charmingly and looking down at her pooch told it in Turkish, "Bobby! You too, speak in Turkish."

The officer was outraged. The Turkish Republic, the Turkish Army he belonged to, his Officer's Uniform with the Star and Crescent had been insulted. The matter was duly put in the hands of a civil policeman. In next to no time Dora Nakkash found herself in the local police station under arrest on a charge of '*hakaret*', insulting talk. "Insulting the Turkish Republic by telling a dog to speak Turkish!"

For the times, nothing too much out of the ordinary. It is what followed that makes the story so memorable. It serves to illustrate how strong the ties of friendship can be in Turkey and in particular the roll of *'hatir'* best explained in English as *'the consideration that one person might expect from another'*. As luck would have it, even then, all was not lost. The duty police officer happened to know Dora's uncle Iskender Nakkash. A lot of local Mersin people knew him, but of course, not the young army officer who had been posted to Mersin for his military service. His home was hundreds of miles away in Anatolia. He was not a *Mersinli.*

"So you are from the Nakkash family. You say Iskender *Bey* is your uncle. *Madam* Dora it's a pity you upset the officer. The best thing will be to get your uncle to come down here. There will be some formalities and Iskender *Bey* will have to sign some papers."

In due course her uncle, known to his family and closest friends as Vizi, turned up in one of the town's horse drawn carriages. My mother had once told me that 'Vizi' was an abbreviation from Visigoth, but she never explained why he came to be called Vizi. He was a small man, always dressed impeccably in a three-piece suit. He nearly always wore a bow tie. His sartorial elegance was completed by the spats he wore to protect his well polished shoes. For all his wizened, rather chimp-like appearance, *Iskender el Kibir* – or as we would say Alexander the Great, was indeed a character.

The police officer who told Dora he knew her uncle Iskender *Bey* would have received him with a warm handshake. If nothing else, his age would have earned him this due respect which is part of the culture in that part of the world. He would have been found a seat and the usual hospitality, a cup of Turkish coffee. The formalities concluded, possibly a fine paid, *Iskender el Kibir* would have departed with his niece Dora and her pet dog Bobby.

"Hatir" knows no bounds whether religious, ethnic or national. It is simply an act of friendship, often turning a blind eye to either what has happened or to authority. To my earlier definition – '*the consideration that one person expects from another*', many others can be added; not to refuse something for the sake of the person, to acknowledge somebody's stature and position, to pay respect to feelings, rank or position. A Turkish proverb pays tribute to "*Hatir*" thus – *"One can even eat raw chicken out of friendship!"* I have to say, the very thought of eating raw chicken turns my stomach. It stretches my notion of friendship to breaking point. Surely then the proverb most be a most apt tribute to friendship or *"Hatir"*.

Mixing at the Gazi Pasha primary school with much older children, it wasn't long before I became more venturesome. Each day, lessons finished at 3.30 in the afternoon. Depending on the weather and the time of the year, I had quickly got into the habit of calling round to see my cousin Jorj who was at another school a couple of hundred metres away. Accompanying my mother on her frequent visits there, I was familiar with the quarter of the town where he lived.

My cousin Jorj was a bit older than me. A rather serious boy with a dry sense of humour. He was popular and seemed to know everyone in that part of the town. It was through him that I first met Hammoudi. He had a sister called Ayadda who was older than him, they were orphans and black. They had come to Turkey from outside the country but no one seemed to know much about their origins, believed to be African. They lived with and were cared for by one of the Christian families. Ayadda did much of the family's housework in return for her brother's and her own keep. She was what was known in Turkish a '*besleme*', loosely speaking it can be taken to mean '*adopted*' though not quite as an adoptive child would be in the West. In practice, a girl servant raised in the household. Much depended on the kindness and generosity of the family. In those times, there were many '*besleme*'.

We played about in the surrounding streets and open places very much I suppose like children of our age did anywhere else. There was one thing though that might well have set us apart; it was kite flying. We all made our own kites using strips of bamboo, tissue paper and string glued together with a thin paste of flour mixed with water. My grandmother used to save the tissue paper from her shopping. She bought me a roll of string. The height to which we could fly the kites we made was limited by their fragility. Some of the older boys made much bigger and stronger kites. The height they reached appeared almost without limit using strong twine. The pull on the twine was enormous, few of us who were still at primary school would have had the strength to hang on to some of those enormous kites.

One day some boys from another quarter grabbed Hammoudi's kite and ran off with it before we could stop them. He was very upset and cried. I gave him all the tissue paper my grandmother could get hold off. I never knew whether it was his distress at the loss of his kite that drew me to him. I had seen others bullied without feeling upset. He and his sister were the first and only Negroes I had come across in Mersin.

I would often go with Jorj back to his home. His mother Saada used to give me a hug and kisses and get me to sit down and join them for their evening meal saying, "Your mother is next door, I've called across to the neighbour to tell her you are here. She will wait for you. You can go round when we have finished eating." I enjoyed eating with them as they sometimes had unusual dishes. One of my favourite was something called *'sourky'* which was made from a special goats cheese with some added herbs. Rolled into a ball, it used to be left to dry hard in the region's baking sun which turned it almost black. It was sliced fine, mixed with fresh tomatoes and smothered with olive oil to be eaten with large quantities of the local bread. During the meal, Saada used to always serve her husband Yussef a small glass of *raki* which diluted with water turned white. It gave off a pleasant odour of aniseed. In Turkey it was jokingly called '*arslan sutu*', the milk of lions. It was potent.

It would have started to turn dark by the time I walked back through the two side streets to the main road, I would find my mother sitting with several others outside Aunt Fouteen's house. People sitting outside their homes were separated from the main road by a strip of common land. Their sole means of entertainment was conversation. Occasionally one of the visitors would have a fund of anecdotes, yet unheard to pass on to those present. Some recent or even distant experiences, the more unusual the better, gained on a journey or at some destination. The constant sound of cracking would accompany these tales as all present would nibble roasted watermelon, sunflower or melon seeds. Small cups of Turkish coffee or tea in small tulip shaped glasses would be served by the youngest of the daughters of the house.

It was these visits "to Aunt's" that left an indelible impression on me from my earliest days in Mersin. These frequent calls familiarised and drew me ever closer to the other half of our relatives, the Syrian side of the family. My mother was particularly attached to her aunt and used to spend a lot of time with her. She used to unburden herself on occasions, sometimes in tears. I can well remember hearing my grandmother shout, "Take your boy and go. He has been making a noise and upsetting father." My mother put her coat on and set off with me. As usual, we headed for her aunt's house.

'Aunt Fouteen', for that is what I knew her as. Indeed I had got in the habit myself of always addressing her as *'Aunt Fouteen'* though she was really my great aunt. She was a very kind, compassionate and generous woman. As such persons often also are, she was humble. Even at the time I sensed that she and her husband, Tannus Farris must have had a struggle to raise their five children on his modest income as a tailor yet they were so hospitable to the Rickards family. My mother always conversed in Arabic with her relatives. She addressed her uncle Tannus in the Arabic form – 'joz halti' this translates into English as '*my aunt's husband'*.

Very few, if any of the material trappings of today existed in the Mersin of the 1930s. There were no private cars to speak off, no television, few households had a telephone. People in town dressed conventionally. The fascination with designer labels was a long way off – garments were judged on their intrinsic worth and not some logo. There were meat safes but few refrigerators. No electric irons, but many heated with incandescent charcoal. Charcoal was also used for cooking. Cookers, whether gas or electric were unheard of.

There being little by way of material things, paraphernalia to show off, social standing was judged by real substance – property, education and life style. By these three criteria, the Rickards family was accepted amongst the top ones in Mersin's hierarchy. The head of the household, my grandfather was a child of the world's greatest empire, educated and brought up to be the archetypal *'English gentleman'*. His British credentials, prestigious as they were, gave good standing to his entire family in Mersin. I was yet to find out that the rest of his family in England, disapproved strongly of his marriage. His sisters would not even receive his children into their home in England.

Ironically, Henry Rickards an *'outsider'* in Mersin though of course not in England, by marrying Mariam Karroum had spawned a whole new generation who would be *'outsiders'* both in Turkey and also in England. In the mid 1930s and earlier, there were a whole lot of what could be termed *'outsiders'* in Mersin. Most of those families collectively known as Syrian émigrés were *'outsiders'*, even the ones who had become Turkish subjects. Syrian Orthodox, Maronite and some Catholics spoke Arabic in their homes. The wealthier ones sent their children to Jesuit boarding schools where they were taught in French and this became their adopted language. These were the people in whose midst my family lived and amongst whom I grew up.

My grandfather by that time would have been in his mid 60s and as I have already said, I had little contact with him. Looking back, I believe he must have felt detached from most of the people around him even though he spoke the languages in common use. Being the only Englishman living in that South Eastern region of Turkey, and given his credentials, my grandfather was well known. He was referred to in Mersin affectionately as *'topal Ingiliz'* – 'the lame Englishman'. In the days before the founding of the new Turkish republic, few indigenous people had surnames. They were known either by their occupation or some distinguishing feature, often coupled to their first name. Interestingly, as an infant I can recall on occasions being spoken off as – *the grandson of the 'topal Ingiliz'*. My grandfather's limp was due to paralysis down one side of his body from early childhood.

From as far back as the 1890s when he arrived in Mersin, he got to know missionaries from the USA and the British Consuls who happened to be the two sets of English speaking visitors to the region. It was through the American evangelist Dr David Metheny and his family that Henry Rickards met and subsequently married Mariam Kerroum, my grandmother in 1892. Descendents of Dr Metheny's family who might still be alive in the USA may not even be aware that the mortal remains of their forebears rest in a quiet corner shaded by pines and eucalyptus trees in the Mersin cemetery. The grave is surrounded by a rectangle of what has become over the years rusty ironwork. The polished centre of the rugged granite head stone is inscribed –

> Here lies what was mortal of
> DAVID METHENY, M.D.
> Minister of the Gospel
> OCT 16 1836 – JUNE 4 1897

It was the British Consul, Colonel Massey assigned to Mersin in 1896 with his wife and baby daughter Cynthia who was to become my grandfather's closest English friend. The Masseys left Mersin in September 1903 on completion of his seven year posting. During this time the two families became close to each other, a friendship that was kept alive for more than another 50 years. My mother's youngest sister Rosie was christened Rosamund in memory of my grandparents' dear friend Mrs Rosamund Massey.

I was to revive this family connection, staying with Mrs Cynthia Osmond at The Glade, Tyrrells Wood, Leatherhead when I was at school in England after the WWII.

Chapter 3

Artie Shaw's *Begin the Beguine* will always transport me back to Gozne in the summer season of 1938. Inextricably, associated in my mind with Artie Shaw's ageless hit was a striking woman in her mid 30s, Olga Alexandra Rickards, my aunt. She might well have seen me before as a baby. As far as I was aware, I was meeting her for the first time that summer when she came out from England. I can hear Artie Shaw's clarinet solo even now. It was first released in the July of that year making him "The King of Swing" almost overnight. Captivated by it, Olga must have bought the record before leaving England. She played that 78 disc over and over again on the family's wind up gramophone much to the delight of our neighbours in lower Gozne.

I can now understand why she seemed to me to be so different from any body else that I knew in Mersin. The years she had spent with the Scotts on their Pelsham Estate at Peasmarsh after finishing her nurses training at The London Hospital had given her a very English upper crust cachet. Yet, in appearance she was undoubtedly a native of the South Eastern region of the Mediterranean. It must have been these two contrasts that people, particularly the English, found so fascinating.

As time went by, I was to hear more about Olga. She had turned out to be unique in the Rickards family of Mersin, in that she had lived and worked in England for several years. No one else amongst her siblings had lived, leave alone worked there. Her lucky break came when Betty Scott, paralysed from a riding accident chose her to be a nurse-companion. It is said that several nurses had been short listed for Betty to make her final choice.

In those days, training at the handful of famous Teaching Hospitals in London was the prerogative of 'well educated gals with good family backgrounds' and predominantly coming from London and the home counties. Olga at the time must have been very much the '*outsider*' given also that she had been educated in France at a lycee in Montpellier. Her acceptance into the London Hospital had been largely thanks to a family friend, Dr Ernest Herga who had strong connections with it. That said, once she had completed her training as a nurse, it was Olga's very own allure, her charm of manner and speech that were to win Betty's heart.

Olga soon merged into the upper crust Scotts family. Though not titled, the men folk were all ex-Etonians, landed gentry and wealthy. "*Pops*" the head of the family, a successful stockbroker, had the means and the determination for his daughter Betty to enjoy the life style that would have been hers but for the tragic accident. "*Ricky*", as my aunt came to be called by the Scotts became the prime mover in "*Pops*" scheme of things. Chosen by Betty herself, the two of them had hit it off from the word go. They become inseparable – the patient and her "*Lady of the lamp*". Together, they participated in the fullest imaginable social schedule that money could provide. Visits to the West End theatres, restaurants, opera and ballet. Also country pursuits. The Scotts had their own cricket week at Pelsham, on their own ground which included its cricket pavilion where Betty and Ricky would have had pride of place doubtless in the company of their sons Peter and Robert with their guests.

The gathering clouds of World War II intervened. It must have been a distressing parting for all concerned when Olga left England. Not least of all for Betty who had not only become accustomed to her nursing skills but also the strong bond that had developed between them. The worsening political situation had left her with no choice.

She arrived in Mersin by sea. Generous to a fault, she had brought an unimaginable array of garments, house hold effects, ornaments and other treasures from London's stores. Many, things not seen or even dreamed of. I recall seeing her standing in her bedroom amidst the several partially unpacked cases from which she was handing gifts out to the family. "Dosia look at this. As soon as I saw it I knew it would be just right for you, isn't it lovely! Go on try it on. I am sure it will be the right size!" She dismissed any blandishments with a wave – "Oh, just a little gift from England dahling!"

Qualities that might have remained dormant as part of her nature, the life-style of the Scotts had brought to the surface making Olga a larger than life character. Loud and flamboyant. Her lavishness never deserted her even when not flush with funds. I recall when she had lost large sums at the gambling tables she used to dismiss the matter, declaring "Oh what the hell! –Easy come, easy go!"

"*Ricky*" had also brought away with her a lasting legacy of the years she spent at Pelsham. Peter Scott, the younger of Betty's two brothers, a senior ranking officer for his age was tragically killed in a tank battle in the North African desert early in the War. She continued to carry a torch for him. As to the extent of this failed love affair, no one in our family chose to disclose or discuss the details. Almost certainly it must have been the morning following her arrival that I witnessed my aunt overwhelming the entire family with the many lavish gifts she had brought with her to Mersin.

I remember something else, an envelope that she had brought from England. From this she took some papers that she was showing to my uncle saying to him "William, dahling! Look what I have brought you. A printed copy of the Rickards coat of Arms, a Saracen's head on a Tower. Peter Scott arranged for me to visit the School of Heraldry in

London. A charming young man attended to me, he was most knowledgeable and helpful."

At the sight of the document she handed him and hearing what she had to say, I could see that my uncle was quite overcome with emotion. "*Ricky*" continued enthusiastically suggesting to my uncle, "You could get one of the goldsmiths downtown to make you a signet ring engraved with our family crest. The Saracen's head, how very appropriate don't you think?"

My other aunt Rosie, the younger of the two, had the fine cut features of my grandfather and like him was fair skinned. She was reputed to be one of the prettiest females in the town, but she did not have her sister Olga's fascinating allure. In character she was also very different. Quick witted with a fiery disposition to match but steadfast. Unlike her siblings, she got married young. It was, I remember, my mother who told me, "Rosie had several suitors after her. She and Mary Nader were the two prettiest girls amongst the Christians of Mersin. She was spoiled for choice. She turned down proposals of marriage from some very wealthy admirers. In the end she married one of the Levante brothers. It was a real love match. Rosie and Enrico, though everyone knew him as Riri. He had served his military service in Italy and come back to Mersin to work in his father, Emilio Levante's Shipping Agency."

Rosie and Riri, after they were married, lived in the Rickard's house. Two years or so after my mother had brought me to Mersin I recall the hustle and bustle of my aunt giving birth. They had the biggest of the rooms presumably in anticipation of the new arrival, a boy christened Emilio Maria Levante. He was only ever called "Billy" a nickname that stuck with him throughout his life. To celebrate the occasion, I was given some 'Pierot Gourmand' sweets – a long remembered treat!

Soon after the happy event, Rosie and Riri moved into a rented house with their baby. The war had started and things were not going at all well for the Allies in the winter of 1939. A sad time also for the family as my grandfather passed away. A cold turned to pneumonia and with no antibiotics, he died a week later at the age of 69. The only Anglican church in Turkey was in Istanbul. Arrangements had to be hastily made to have a service in the house. It was taken in English by Mr Woolworth the headmaster of the Tarsus American College. Like the Methenys, whom my grandfather had got to know almost half a century earlier, the Woolworths were American missionaries.

I hardly knew my grandfather Rickards yet many of the circumstances surrounding his demise have remained vivid. It was early evening, the winter darkness had come early and suddenly. I was with my uncle and grandmother in our dining room, my mother had taken him a cup of hot milk to his bed side. Shortly afterwards she came rushing back in a distraught state, "Father has gone." She sobbed trying hard to speak, "He drank from the cup and handed it back to me with a smile. He whispered, 'Thanks dear' and lay back. He just closed his eyes and that was it. He has gone."

I don't think that I ever cried like I did then. It was as much as anything, the state of my mother that affected me. That and the finality of it conjured up by the three words she had used – "*He has gone*". The thought that I would never see my grandfather up and about ever again was unreal. I could not bring myself to accept it.

As I have already said, I never really knew my grandfather. We had little to do with each other. He spoke of me as 'the little shrimp' and at times offered to help my mother deal with me, "Dosia, would you like me to thrash him for you?" Mercifully help that my mother never took him up on. Many years later, when we had been talking about him she spoke of a darker side, "You know Patrick, when father was in the Dardanelles with the British forces during the great war of 1914–18, if there was to be any corporal punishment meted out, he used to volunteer his services. He would have been a young man in those days. He must have derived some sort of satisfaction from inflicting pain on others."

Another thing: he could stand pain in the extreme. I recall once he had to have one of his toenails either partially or completely removed. The doctor who had come to the house to attend to him was surprised when he declined local anaesthetic, choosing rather to endure the pain. What ever the explanation for these peculiarities, he was an honest God fearing man. Those who knew him best said he never spoke ill of any one. His favourite adage was, "If you haven't something good to say of someone, it's better you hold your tongue"

He loved to recite poetry, especially "Casabianca". A favourite in Victorian schools. It's appeal to him, I believe, must have been the way it invokes selfless devotion to duty: another of my grandfather's strongly held principles. The poem better known as "The boy stood on the burning deck" was about Casabianca, the 10 year old son of Admiral Brueys, commander of the French man-of-war L'Orient that was set on fire in the Battle of the Nile. The poem, by Felicia D Hemans was inspired by this battle in 1798 when the English fleet under Admiral Nelson inflicted a great defeat on the French.

> The boy stood on the burning deck
> Whence all but he had fled;
> The flames that lit the battle's wreck
> Shone round him o'er the dead
>
> He called aloud: "Say, father, say
> If yet my task is done!"
> He knew not that the chieftain lay
> Unconscious of his son.
>
> With mast, and helm, and pennon fair,
> That well had borne their part;
> But the noblest thing that perished there
> Was that young, faithful heart.

With the passing of my grandfather William Henry Rickards, my uncle, took on the family mantle. The little I knew about him then, as a child, must have been what I had heard from my mother. He had been to a prep school at Arnside in the Lake District. He himself had later on spoken to me about the place – "Miserable school, I learned nothing there. As for the headmaster, all he was interested in was lining his pockets. An objectionable sort – he was an out and out rotter."

From Arnside, the young William went as a boarder to Llandovery College, Carmarthenshire in Wales. He was there in 1912 as a 16 year old. It was not until some years later, when I was due to come to school in England in the summer of 1945 that he told me things about Llandovery. He spoke very nostalgically and with great feeling about the place. I now believe that he did so out of a deep sense of grief. More than that, with the benefit of hindsight, he must have been heart broken to have left. Especially as it appears to have been without good reason. I will explain later.

"Patrick you can't imagine the pride I have felt all through my life to have been to Llandovery. It was considered a fine seat of learning, probably the best school in Wales. Like the ones in England it was of course a public school. You know, Llandovery turned out more bishops and archbishops than any other school in the realm"

I listened intently, unable to ask questions or make any worthwhile comments, as I knew little about what he was telling me. I was still in the lower classes of the Gazi Pasha primary school in Mersin. I had never heard of Arnside and at the time it was difficult for me to pronounce 'Carmarthenshire'.

"It is true; the school did encourage the study of Welsh literature and history. Boys whose parents wished them to could attend classes to improve their knowledge of the Welsh language. Because of this there was a notion that Welsh Nationalism was being actively encouraged at the school. I don't subscribe to these allegations."

It was yet again my mother who revealed the incident that she believed had led to young William's early departure from Llandovery. He had apparently been invited to the Carrs – famous for the water biscuits of the same name. On arrival at their home, he was met by Mrs Carr. Hearing his Welsh pronunciation she is said to have exclaimed, "Oh, William what a dreadful accent!"

According to my mother, the upshot was that William found himself in London, a dayboy at Battersea Grammar School. In the capital city, he soon acquired a taste for the theatre, ballet and the arts. All the cultural offerings however failed to keep him there for long. William, still under age, volunteered like so many others to join the British expeditionary force in France.

As I look back to the winter of 1939, familial memories are hazy. Some were passed on to me by my mother whom I recall had the habit of telling me things that I might well have not been consciously aware of. I had little to do with either of my two grandparents and uncle who were the sum total of my immediate family. My mother having no choice but to return to her family home had at times to put up with disapproval from my grandmother. My grandfather had a condition known as 'petit mal' a benign, mild form of epilepsy. There was a dread in the family that my exuberant and noisy behaviour might upset him, causing him to have a fit. I recall how demanding he was, expecting everything to be to his liking, and above all on time. I can almost hear him now making one of his typical reproaches to my grandmother if lunch was the least bit late – "Miriam, you know I like my lunch on time at 12.30. It is now 12.35. How much longer, my dear?"

My mother sought solace by calling on her aunt and tearfully unburdening herself. Sometimes, she would retreat to the bedroom we shared and weep quietly. Not wishing to grieve me, she rarely told me what had brought on her upset with my grandmother but seeing her distress caused me also to cry. Somehow it seemed the only thing to do. She would wipe her eyes and put her arm around me, hugging me tightly. I remember a heart-felt wish that she frequently came out with on these unhappy occasions. Two short sentences that would have been life changing for us both, "One day Patrick, we will have a little place of our own. I always hope and pray for this."

I cannot say whether the passing of my grandfather made life any easier for my mother. She continued to share that big house with my widowed grandmother and uncle approaching his mid 40s and by then a confirmed bachelor. Though depleted in numbers they were seen at least nominally as the Rickards family, still the only permanently settled British residents in Mersin. Such socialising as there was befell my mother. Though my uncle had taken over the Rickards family reins, he was not one for cocktail parties and small talk. Unlike my mother, he rarely attended any of the consular social functions.

The British Consul for the South Eastern region of Turkey in the four years or so leading up to WWll was W.D.W.Matthews. He was based in Mersin for the greater part of the year, but in the summer months, he transferred to Trabzon on the Eastern shores of the Black Sea. A married man, he was accompanied by his wife Luna and daughter Anne Hope.

The Consulate was in the centre of the town by the Yoghurt Bazaar. It comprised a large, two storey building with a red-tiled roof. It was in the centre of a well tended garden surrounded by a high wall. Located between two streets that ran parallel to each other, there were two entrances – one for official business the other for private callers. The top floor was private, for the use of the Matthews family. It was here that Mrs Matthews entertained their visitors. There were several things about the place that stuck in my mind – the masses of geraniums with their distinctive rather peppery fragrance, in the house the linoleum that covered the wooden floors in the reception rooms, and the strong aroma of Mr Matthews' pipe tobacco drifting up from his ground floor offices.

Mr Matthews, graduate from Cambridge, was a career diplomat and linguist accomplished in several languages of the Middle East. He was fluent in Turkish and so was his wife, who had taught at the English High School for Girls in Istanbul. I accompanied my mother on visits when Anne Hope entertained us with her Irish jigs. We were more or less the same age.

The most memorable occasions were picnics at Pompeopolis and other ancient sites along the coast. On these excursions, we were driven in the two Consular horse drawn, open carriages by Fevzi and Mahmut, the '*kavas*' who were uniformed guards. They were both Turks; Fevzi a slim fair skinned man with pale blue eyes, a Laz from the Blacksea, Mahmut was a big man with dark skin and jet black hair, a local from Tarsus.

Mr Matthews' next posting was elsewhere in Europe. He and his family departed from Turkey in the early part of the War. My mother, an accomplished correspondent, kept in touch with Luna Matthews through the war and afterwards for many years. She used to read extracts of the letters she received to my grandmother and uncle. I particularly remember one that she received from London where Mrs Matthews was helping the War effort doing voluntary work in the canteen at the BBC. I have never forgotten the words my mother read out slowly and deliberately from that particular letter, "Dosia, there I was in an apron, my sleeves rolled up above my elbows. I had been bent over an enormous sink, for ages. I was washing up! My back was aching and the skin on my hands was wrinkled through being submerged constantly in hot soapy water. I was confronted with what seemed to be a never diminishing pile of dirty plates, dishes, cups and saucers."

My mother had the habit of reading and re-reading passages from letters she got from some of her old friends, people she had not seen for years but with whom she continued to correspond. Knowing what was coming, she had paused to wipe her eyes. With undisguised emotion she continued to read aloud to my grandmother and uncle, "As I washed up, I began thinking of my life in Mersin. The halcyon days as the wife of the British consul, I was waited on hand and foot! The very thought of those happy, prosperous days compared with my plight in the BBC canteen kitchen – a skivvy, no less, started me laughing. I felt drained, light headed. I could not stop myself laughing. I must have become hysterical, my laughter turned to sobbing. I was crying as never before. Some of the full time BBC staff who had been near by came to my assistance. They sat me down with a cup of tea. I thought to myself, how very British! This set me off laughing again."

My mother's voice broke as she read. My grandmother and uncle were also affected. Mrs Matthews' quip about the cup of tea amused my uncle who laughed, briefly. It was my mother who broke the silence. "Poor Luna! I can imagine her state. I wonder how Matthews himself would have felt had she told him. Do you remember how he got upset about her shopping at Woolworths?" My uncle laughed, saying as he got up to leave the room,

"He was gifted and a brilliant Consul, but, a snob. He must have felt it was demeaning when his wife shopped at Woolworths. How times have changed! They will never again have the life they lived out here. This war will change things like nothing that has gone before."

I kept in touch with Anne Hope. Her life when they came back to England was very different from her childhood in Mersin and Trabzon. It was in February 2004 that she sent me a letter that my mother had written to her father. It had been kept on her father's files, a relic of some 66 years. I found it interesting but also a remarkable revelation. An insight into my mother's thoughts about me as an eight year old in 1939. The contents of the letter are set out verbatim below:

Mersin. Oct. 12th 1939

Dear Mr Matthews,

I am taking the opportunity of writing to you so as you'll get this while in Istanboul.

There is no one who can help me in this matter but you so please forgive me troubling you again. It is about Patrick's schooling. I should be so happy if you could arrange for him to be taken at once at the English High School at Nisantasi. I am willing to pay up to TL300[2] *per annum. If you will exert your influence with your friends at Istanboul I am sure that something can be done for me. Patrick isn't a girl, he's at an age now when he needs some one more than a mother to train him as an English boy should grow up. I am leaving it entirely in your hands. You have always been a good friend to us and will not fail me now.*

Father's been very ill for the last fortnight with dysentery and at one time we nearly gave him up. You wouldn't know him now he has got so thin.

We all look forward to seeing you three very much and hope this letter finds you all well. Love to Mrs Matthews and darling Anne Hope. Thanking you in advance dear Mr Matthews.

I remain,

Yours very sincerely,

Dosia Grigsby

I was nine years old. In the early New Year of 1940, my mother and I were on the "*posta treni*", mail train heading for Istanbul via Konya, Afyon and Eskisehir. Though the route was described as a main line service, the train made frequent stops, being a "*posta treni*". At every station there would be the usual commotion as passengers, mostly villagers, got on and off with their belongings. A monotonous and tiring journey of a day and a half, 40 hours to be exact. The train was

[2] The TL300 per annum that my mother mentions in her letter needs to be explained and put in perspective. After the War in 1945, the £ Sterling was worth 5 TL. The Government in Turkey took the bold decision in January 2005 to change the Turkish Lira (TL) to the New Turkish Lira (YTL) by dropping Six Zeros. A conversion of a million to one. Before this measure was put in place, the £ Sterling was exchanged for almost 3,000,000 TL.

packed. Many passengers with an incongruous assortment of baggage were standing in the corridors. As we had got on at the start of the journey in Adana we had seats in one of the compartments which was soon full to capacity. We were among the lucky ones.

Once through the Taurus Mountains, the train travelled in a wide arc described by the location of the three major towns on its route across the Western part of the vast Anatolian plateau; a featureless landscape. An arid desert-like terrain in summer and a snow covered wilderness in the winter.

What ventilation there might have been for our compartment was sacrificed in an effort to conserve warmth for it was several degrees below zero outside. The swaying motion of the train as dusk fell had brought on the dizziness and nausea my mother suffered from. A lady passenger offered her some '*cologne*' – the cure-all in that part of the world for most ailments!

The guard, who must have been a kind hearted soul, had got to hear of my mother's plight. He passed by and had a word with her, "*Madam*, if you could just hold on a bit longer, I will open one of the Wagon Lits compartments once we are past Afyon. I have no more reservations for sleepers and the inspector will be getting off the train there."

The guard's behaviour towards a widow, particularly one travelling with a dependent child was not unusual. I had witnessed many other instances of consideration shown to my mother by complete strangers. A laudable side of Turkish culture which ensured that we arrived the next day at our destination less travel worn. From Istanbul's famous Haydar Pasha Station it was a short trip by ferryboat across the water to the European part of Istanbul and the museum-like Alp Hotel.

The following morning after breakfast, a taxi delivered us to the High School at Nisantasi. Not a particularly attractive monolithic block, six storey high building with a playground to its side and contained within a high brick wall. From the gates, we approached the school along a concrete path.

The taxi driver carrying my suitcase accompanied us. We went up a wide flight of marble steps and through the school's entrance doors. Once inside we were received by the caretaker. My mother spoke with him, where upon using a telephone in his lodge he spoke to somebody in English punctuating his sentences with the ambiguous tag *"Sir"*, that I had not previously been familiar with.

"Mr Peach is coming down to greet you. He will not be long, please wait here."

With that, Etem *'effendi'*, as I came to know him, took my suitcase and disappeared with it round a corner, out of sight. We did not have very long to wait. A tall man, his height accentuated by his slimness, appeared wearing a loose fitting brown suit. He descended the last flight of stairs and covered the remaining distance to where we were standing effortlessly.

"Good morning Mrs Grigsby, and Patrick! I hope you had a pleasant journey all the way from Mersin. Do come upstairs, I would like you to meet my wife and our housekeeper, Miss Potter who looks after the younger boys."

Mrs Peach turned out to be small and rotund, a chatty woman. She welcomed us warmly, introducing a very English looking, tall, bespectacled colleague who I recall had her hair in a bun. It was Miss Potter.

I cannot say now for how long I endured life as a boarder at the High School. It could not have been more than two weeks. During this time, my mother was forced to prolong her stay at Mrs.Knock's *'pension'* near the British Consulate General; a widow like my mother, they got on well from the very start. It was to have been for just two or three days whilst I got accustomed to my new life style away from home and on my own for the very first time.

The carefully hatched plans by my mother and the rest of the family for me were thrown into disarray. Quite simply, I was not ready for boarding school! I was not old enough and to make matters worse, being so much younger than the others I was an obvious target for bullying. One particular incident sticks in my mind. Two of the big boys, with the help of others, had managed to dangle me over the six storey stairwell. The strangest thing I can still remember, was the feeling of relief when I was hauled back safely. Indeed, a feeling of gratitude that their escapade had not gone fatally wrong! Probably why I did not mention anything to my mother. At the High School the predicament I was in had been unforeseen, worse still, it was insoluble. I had to be withdrawn.

When questioned by her friends as to my premature reappearance back in Mersin, my mother used to explain things in her own particular way, "It was a trying time for us both in Istanbul. Patrick could not settle. He did not take to the place and felt home sick. Every night in the school dormitory he cried himself to sleep. Thinking about him upset me also. In the end, I decided there was nothing for it but to return to Mersin."

Our unexpected return home would have been a shock to both my grandmother and uncle. I am almost sure that they would have had no prior knowledge of what was going on away in Istanbul. In those days news of this sort travelled by letter or word of mouth. Somebody, most likely a friend meeting my mother and hearing the news, would

have passed the sad tidings on to the family in Mersin. My mother was more forthcoming than she had been to her inquisitive friends in answering my uncle's many questions.
"What was Istanbul like at this time of the year and where did you stay?"

"We were lucky. It was chilly but once the sun had been out for a time it was agreeably warm. Mr Moore at the British Consulate General was very helpful. He put me in touch with a lady, Mrs. Knock who had a *'pension'* near the *'passage'* off *Rue Pera.* Though her husband was English, judging by her appearance and accent she must have been Maltese herself. It turned out that her 18 year old son, George was head boy at the high school but a day boy, otherwise he might have been able to keep a sympathetic, watchful eye on Patrick. Her two daughters Rose and Mary were going to the English Girls' School."

When my mother paused, my uncle commented on what she had been saying about the Knock family. "It was good of the gentleman you mentioned at the Consulate General putting you in touch with Mrs Knock. You know out here, the Maltese who are supposed to be British are seen as second class *'outsiders'*. I wonder whether perhaps her husband might have had something to do with the Consulate."

The empathy that drew my mother to Mrs Knock sprang from their similarities to one another though there were some aspects that my mother might not have readily acknowledged. She would certainly have admitted to mutual widowhood and the need to get by financially. Turning to another subject, my mother continued, "Something that I did not know William. Apart from Mr Peach, there is also a Turkish headmaster, Bekir *Bey*, whom I did not meet. I was told that it is Turkish protocol that demands this. As for Mr Peach, well he is very English and of course so is his wife. She was most welcoming. I gather there are several masters who come out from England."

It was some time later that I found the courage to speak about some of my experiences. Matters that I understood little about and incidents that had troubled me during that ever so short a stay at the high school. I would not then have had the slightest inkling, leave alone the ability to explain my experiences as I am now doing. The fact of the matter is that I was surrounded by older and more mature boys, all adolescents. They appeared to have a boundless capacity for sexual fantasy. They also craved to perform their sexual fantasies. They wanted to initiate me into their ways by describing these practises with much sniggering and ill concealed nervousness.

My upbringing had been unusual, though I suspect not surprising given my widowed mother's circumstances, some aspects of which I have already touched on. Much of her hardship stemmed from the loss of my father. Left on her own to bring me up, her prime concern must have been to protect me. Growing up in my grandfather's home I was subjected to his very Victorian attitudes, passed down to my mother and uncle. Most notably their attitudes on anything to do with sex. I can recall overhearing members of my family talking about two words that had come into common usage, or at least reached Mersin – *'crooner'* as in Bing Crosby and the phrase *'sex appeal'* considered most risqué at the time.

In her efforts to shelter me, my mother had kept me insulated from what went on in the world outside. This inevitably excluded even the most basic instruction on the things I mentioned earlier. I have reason to believe that my mother would have preferred it had I been born a girl, then at least physically I would have been made in her image. She seemed ill at ease with the opposite sex and did once mention some intimacy with my father. It was a garbled, unfinished story of how he got his way with her – obviously told from a female's perspective which I could not have even remotely understood.

However, as time went by I had inevitably mixed with children of my age. However incomplete, I seem to recall we kids had some vague ideas about what went on in brothels, after all, we used to go past the place in Mersin. We saw the females there, all prostitutes. However distorted and even inaccurate these perceptions, one thing that I was sure of, my mother along with decent women would have never taken part in the activities so graphically described amidst much giggling by boys at the high school.

With no parental guidance, I had acquired my 'sex education' off the streets so to speak. Like most of the other kids I mixed with at home, I knew about sex. Our perceptions were slanted towards what we heard went on with prostitutes who were paid by men to gratify their carnal desires – '*sikismek*' in Turkish or 'fucking' as is said in English. In my ignorance I never connected these activities, the stock in trade of prostitutes, with procreation. This was the key to what dismayed me so, for I was devastated to hear that my father had done the unmentionable to my mother.

My informants at the High School breaking this news had gone on to elaborate – "Men away for weeks on end at sea become insatiable. Once back with their wives, they are at it all the time. Your mother must have been well used." All this was what came out bit by bit in revelations I made to my mother when I eventually found the courage to speak out. Looking back, it changed little in hers and the rest of my family's attitudes to this 'difficult subject'.

What made more of an impact when eventually I got round to talking about it was to do with my penis. Up until then inert, it was an object of no great interest to me as it had never made its presence felt. I was yet to experience an erection! In the dormitory, several of the boys had tried to talk me into circumcising it. To be practical about the whole business, one or two of them had popped their circumcised members out of their pyjamas to add weight to their various claims. "You need only take the tip off the foreskin off. It is nothing, really! A single stroke with a sharp razor and it is done."

Horrified, it was my mother who spoke. "They must be mad! Good job you did not try anything crazy like that. You might easily have bled to death. You must not touch it." Looking back now, little did I know then what I was to find out much later! That I was in fact medically in need of circumcision.

On my return from Istanbul all my family still had other worries to contend with. The war was raging on in Europe. To make matters worse, in early 1940 things were not going at all well for The Allies. Turkey, my family's adopted home was neutral. Inevitably the worrying though unspoken query persisted – "Neutral, but for how long?"

Circumstances were very different from those in the First World War So much had changed in Turkey since then. Between 1919 and 1923 under Mustafa Kemal, the country had been transformed. Sweeping reforms had rid the country of its cumbersome apparatus of Ottoman Empire, rebuilding it into a modern secular republic. When *Ataturk* died in 1938, Ismet Inonu became the country's second president. He was steadfast in his intent to uphold the principles on which the Turkish Republic had been founded. Especially, to safeguard its security within the contracted borders that had been agreed at the Treaty of Lausanne. Under the Presidency of Ismet Inonu, Turkey was determined to remain neutral in WWII and not repeat the folly of going to war as they had in WWI on the side of Germany.

The situation for the Rickards family had also changed. At the start of WWI in 1914, William Rickards, then still a school boy in London, had volunteered and found himself in the trenches in France.

His father Henry Rickards, though disabled from infancy, served as an interpreter with the British expeditionary forces in Gallipoli. My grandmother and her three daughters were evacuated to Egypt where they stayed for the duration of the hostilities. This time, when WWll broke out in 1939, my grandfather was spared. He had passed away later that September, the month in which the British Government had declared war on Germany. William Rickards, his only son, was too old to be conscripted. The neutrality of Turkey meant that the whole family could continue to live in Mersin.

My family, long time residents of neutral Turkey in 1939, were to find themselves faced with many compromising situations. A common enough predicament at the time which threatened many individuals and whole families throughout mainland Europe. What follows will give some idea as to the relationships that had developed over many decades between families in the town. Relationships which could lead to dilemmas as the war dragged on.

Earlier, I mentioned the marriage of my aunt Rosie to Riri Levante, the youngest of four brothers in one of the town's notable Italian families. The old man, Emilio Levante had come to Mersin sometime before my grandfather. My mother said to me, "You know Patrick, his wife, Billy's *nona* is a Contessa. They say that one of his cousins was a Cardinal in the Vatican. They are well connected. Rosie did well to marry Riri. As one would expect the marriage and the arrival of Billy brought our two families together."

At one time, there had been many Italian families in Mersin. The Levante family were known royalists though their ex-King Umberto had been reduced to a constitutional façade by Benito Mussolini who some time after accepting his premiership assumed the title of *'Il Duce'* – The Leader, in 1925. Like most European families who had settled in

Turkey, the Levantes were business people. None of the four brothers had been interested in Italy's expansionist ambitions under the Fascist leadership of Mussolini. Like my own uncle, they had not been conscripted.

Mr and Mrs Lochner had been neighbours for many years and friends of the family, particularly of my mother. Mr Lochner used to potter about in their garden, an unusual sight in Mersin but something that I was to see plenty of some years later in the UK. A hobby shared with Germans, for Mr Lochner was one. A man in his mid 50s, he was *'in cotton'*. His wife was a tall, elegant woman. They had two sons, both much older than I was; Ronnie and Itel who was the younger of the two. It was Ronnie that I have memories off. A tall chap, but what I recall best was his Zundapp Z500 German motorbike. A motorbike enthusiast, he must also have been something of a mechanic. He tuned up his bike in a downstairs room of their house with the window open to get rid of the exhaust fumes. The din from the Zundapp when revved up used to impress me. On occasions he gave me a ride on his pillion which always terrified me, particularly on bends when the machine keeled over. As for Ronnie's young brother Itel, I never knew him as he was in Germany and later killed on the Russian front.

Most of our family friends were Christians of Syrian origin. Many at the time had business interests with German companies, not surprisingly they were pro-Germany. The rest were ambivalent, preferring to remain uncommitted whether to the Allies or the Axis.

In view of the short time I had been away from the Gazi Pasha Primary School, the headmaster Ali Fuat Firat accepted me back. I resumed visits to my cousin Jorj after school most afternoons. There were the summers in Gozne to look forward to. It would be another two years before there were any important changes to my settled way of life for me in Mersin.

Chapter 4

Memories of my unhappy experiences when I went to Istanbul with my mother were receding. My spell as a boarder at the English High School had been short lived. Once more back in Mersin, the two years or more that I was destined to spend there were to give me the chance, as I matured, to familiarise myself with its people and my surroundings. The War in Europe continued and the effects it had on Turkey, my family and friends had evolved but caused little serious hardship to us.

Mersin had barely changed; it was still a unique enclave. It was home to a colony of '*outsiders*' who were very different from the indigenous masses living around them and throughout the width and breadth of Turkey. Mersin had been a settlement of émigrés, both Muslims and Christians. The former predominantly poor, ill educated and destined to live in shanties earning their living off the land or as manual labour loading and unloading the lighters that were towed backwards and forwards from the ships anchored off shore. They were known as *fellahin* – the Arabic word meaning '*those who till the soil*', an apt description. As a group, the *fellahin* were looked down on by the indigenous community.

By contrast, the Christians, well educated, enterprising and often already moneyed flourished. Most of them making their fortunes out of import, export and shipping. In spite of this disparity, they and their less fortunate Muslim counterparts did have something in common, they were '*outsiders*'. The earliest of these settlers also shared a common tongue, an attribute which has always drawn people closer to each other. Arabic was the language that their parents or grandparents had spoken and which came to be spoken widely in Mersin. All this had changed little since my English grandfather's arrival in the town some 40 years earlier.

As much as the emerging town of Mersin itself, it was its whereabouts that attracted people, just as centuries earlier settlers had been drawn to that same Cilician coast. The Mediterranean Sea lapping its beaches to the south and the foothills of the snow-capped Taurus Mountains encroaching on it from the north. This made for easy approach overland feasible from the east and west. In either direction, the many ruined remains of human settlements including castles and temples that still stand are evidence that man must have trodden these routes even before Greco-Roman times.

There were no museums but then my family and the other Christian inhabitants of Mersin did not need museums to make them aware of their heritage. There were extraordinary ruins and relics of the past all around them. They were there for the asking, many readily accessible, open to those who knew their way and had the means to get to them whether by car or horse back. Ideal picnic sites especially if there was a source of water near by or a cluster of dwellings. The inhabitants, indigenous villagers, would get their young to pick fresh fruit and vegetables that were in season to augment the cooked food brought for the picnic. Much further away and alas not within the range of out picnic sites was Catal Huyuk. Just over the Taurus Mountains in Anatolia, it is said to have been one of the earliest human settlements, like Jericho, inhabited 8,000 years BC.

I was old enough and I suppose interested enough to listen in to what my elders were saying. I overheard snatches of all kinds of anecdotes. These would be told by one or another of my family's friends or acquaintances. Often picked up by them from strangers. Maybe some fellow passenger on a journey. It was not unusual for people thrown together by chance, meeting for the first time, to strike up conversations. These accounts of the unexpected or down right bizarre would be questioned by some of those present leading to lengthy and sometimes heated discussions. Story telling or mere gossip were the essentials of interesting conversation. As I grew older I got to realise that it was often difficult to separate fact from fantasy. I also realised that farfetched as they might be, mixed into them was some historic fact which gave them a semblance of credibility.

Not surprisingly, in that part of the world, many tales revolved around the spiritual or supernatural. All my family's acquaintances, whether Christians or Muslims, took everything to do with religion seriously. People avoided any form of sacrilege. Looking back, there must have been sceptics amongst them. They were the ones who chose to listen but keep silent. In those days denial was unheard of, for to do so was considered sinful. A fact accepted even by non-believers. The Muslims had an Arabic word for it – *haram*, what Catholics would describe as a *'mortal sin'*.

For most people in Mersin faith was a private matter. However it was quite usual to hear people calling on God or Allah publicly. This was done on impulse, without any hesitation and with solemn intent. Supplications – 'God help us' or 'God protect him' were often heard. The usual prayer – 'God be with you', when bidding farewell to some one about to set off on a journey, and there were many others. There are two Arabic words that are probably the most frequently uttered by Muslims. They are, *Inshallah* – meaning 'God willing' and *Mashallah* – nearest translation meaning 'wonderful' when used to avert the evil eye. Both were in such common use that they had been adopted by the Christians. Allah was never out of daily conversation, it was as though Allah was amongst the people in the streets, their places of work and their homes. To many, God was the very purpose of their existence.

The people I grew up amidst, even the rich of Mersin, had none of today's refinements, not even the things we have come to regard as necessities. This is quite simply because they were not available.

On the other hand for those families who could afford them, there were servants. In homes, cooking was on charcoal, floors were swept with brooms, clothing was laundered by hand, irons were heated with charcoal. The people of Mersin were privileged as the town had an *'ice-factory'* where convenient sized slabs of ice were produced. These were purchased, taken home and placed in an 'ice box', the forerunner of refrigerators. Cooked food was kept in 'meat safes'. Villagers had donkeys or horses to get about on, town's people had bicycles. A few young "townies" who had the means went in for motor bikes.

There was the odd privately owned motor car; one or two belonging to friends of the family. These would be brought out for the picnics. The occasions that my mother was included in the party were always a great treat for me. It was not so much the picnic as the chance of a ride in the car that excited me. I recall just such an occasion. I was in a friend's car on the road to Tarsus. We were on our way to the waterfalls just outside the town where there was a little café serving refreshments. The road was little more than a compacted earth track, the surface of which in summer turned to dust. Part of the adventure for me as we sped along was to watch a cloud of this dust leave a trail suspended above the road behind us.

"Look Patrick, can you see that hill over there?" My mother called out hoping that I would see the distant hill before it slipped out of sight behind us. She must have known that it would have been disastrous to slow down. If a car ever did slow down, the dust cloud created almost invariably caught up with it. The vehicle and its occupants were covered with the talc like dust. I nodded my head. My mother pointing to the hill in the distance continued, "Legend has it that Jonah had a miraculous escape and was washed up by the sea on to that hill."

I had never heard the tale of how Jonah had been swallowed by a whale. My imagination must have taken over. I asked my mother the obvious question, "Jonah! Who was he? Why did the whale get him?"

As always when the subject was of a biblical nature, a discussion would take place amongst the grown up Christians in a mixture of French and Arabic. Everyone present making their contributions. Eventually, there was a general consensus which our host and driver, Edouard Butrous summed up. This is what I can recall of it:

"Dosia, as Jonah appears in the Scriptures, we have to accept the legend in principle. He is said to have set out from Joppa. The sailing boat he was on ran into a very bad storm. The crew believed he had brought them bad luck, so they threw him overboard. The rest is more or less as you told Patrick."

Amongst my family's Christian friends, two of the best informed men in the town were Edouard and his brother Gaby. Whilst on the subject, my mother wanted to clear up several anomalies, "Tell me Edouard, where was Joppa? Also, why do we sometimes connect Jonah with Tarsus?" Edouard smiled. There was nothing that pleased him more than to be asked questions on a matter that he knew something about, "Joppa is the old name for Jaffa. The reference to Tarsus is not as clear cut. The little I know is that in the Old Testament mention is made of place called Tarshish. Some of the ancient scholars identify this place as one and the same as Tarsus in Cilicia. That is to say the Tarsus we all know and where we are now going."

"Amazing! When you think about it, this corner of the ancient world, all the way from The Holy Land is really consecrated ground, eh Edouard?"

"Of course Dosia. We are privileged, all of us – Jews, Christians and Muslims alike to be living in these hallowed parts."

As there are no whales in the Mediterranean, surprisingly none of those present that day questioned how Jonah came to be swallowed by one. I have since wondered what explanation Edouard Butrous might have come up with.

Given what I was saying earlier, you might conclude that the pleasures of Mersin's *beau monde* were limited to idle chit-chat and the occasional

Nomads with their camel train somewhere on Tarsus road out of Mersin – a common sight when I was a child

Tarsus, birth place of St.Paul the Apostle is the next town after Mersin when heading East. The remains shown are of Cleopatra's Gate in the middle of the town that has changed little over the centuries.

picnic at some ancient Roman site. Well not quite, as there were other distractions. Hospitality features large in the culture of the Middle East. The hospitality I refer to involved the sharing of food and refreshments with friends as guests in ones home. What better way to socialise. There could not have been any amongst my family's friends who failed in this pursuit.

The ladies of the Middle East prided themselves on their culinary skills which won them great acclaim amongst their friends and acquaintances. All food was prepared and cooked in the home. Many of the dishes that the region was famous for entailed lengthy and tedious preparation. However many servants and helpers the lady of the house had, on big occasions she always directed operations so that the food bore her very own hallmark. Yet, many were able to pursue the other passion of Mersin's Christian society, gambling!

A casino as such did not exist in Mersin. Several of the town's social elite, on their trips to Europe made up for this privation at the gaming tables of the Casino in Monte Carlo. Thus fulfilled, on their return however, they did not turn their noses up at the modest venue the town had to offer. Most nights, the usual habitues flocked to The Merchants Club to take their chances at the poker tables. There were special nights, most important of which was New Year's Eve when apart from poker, *chemin de fer* was all the rage. *'The Club'* as it was commonly known, catered for the town's nucleus of serious gamblers, both ladies and gentlemen. The so called *'big hitters'* amongst them were the few who would only play for really big stakes. They were able and prepared to sustain serious losses.

It was I suppose no more than my childish curiosity in what grown ups get up to that left these images in my mind. Images not only of *'The Club'* but of the devotion to gambling in Mersin's predominantly Christian and well-heeled society. Though I was not yet in my teens, my mother once smuggled me in when she was invited, "Now then Patrick just sit next to me and don't go wandering about. They have kindly turned a blind eye and let you in as uncle Riri is a member and comes here regularly with Rosie."

Even now I can visualise the scene in what was called the *'salon'* – a large marble floored hall with several gaming tables spread about. The players, middle aged men in suits, the ladies dressed up and bejewelled for this most social of occasions. All looking very tense and intent, grasping their cards close lest they be seen by any one around them. Poker was serious business, though evidently an enjoyable way of spending the evening. No one spoke, for to do so might have distracted other players at the table. Speaking was discouraged, tolerated only in whispers. Their guests, some seated, others standing behind them, formed a crowd that encircled the gaming table. As nearly everyone was smoking cigarettes, a yellowish pall of smoke hung over the table. From time to time, one of the participants made a play, reaching out to place some of their cards on the table. A move made with deliberation. This would sometimes bring the game to a climax and when this happened the relief amongst the players was palpable. Some would leave the table for a break whilst the winners would remain to count their '*loot*'.

I grew to have happy recollections personally of the gambling that the grown ups indulged in and with good reason. On occasions my aunt Rosie used to call me over as she passed by our house, "Here Patrick I've kept these aside for you. You brought me luck, I did well at *'The Club'* yesterday evening." Pressing a thick wad of bank notes into my hand, she gave me a hug and kiss. With her usual infectious laugh she added, "Go and spend them on anything you fancy."

But not me. I would always pass these gifts of money on to my mother. When I once treated myself to *'baklava'* in one of the town's shops, I was told off. It was my uncle who reprimanded me saying, "Don't you get enough to eat at home? You have no reason to go into sweet shops downtown and eat. Don't do that again." I felt hurt but as usual, said nothing.

Not long after one of these visits to *'The Club'* a tragedy occurred which I got to hear about by chance. My aunt Rosie called in to see my mother and I had opened the outside door and was hanging about, "Dosia have you heard about Theodore?"

"No, which Theodore?" My mother asked.

"Theodore Dumani. He committed suicide yesterday evening."

"Good heavens, committed suicide! How?" Looking shocked by the news my aunt had come with, my mother had sat down at the dining room table.

"I was told by one of the Dumani family that he threw himself off their balcony. They say he was overcome with money problems. Their business has been failing just recently. Riri and I were talking about Theodore and trying to understand what drove him to take his own life. Riri knew that their business was shaky. Come to that, the Levante business has not been good either."

"Rosie, it is the war we have to blame. It must be affecting everyone here who has business connections in Europe."

"Yes of course Dosia but between you and me, Theodore was a big gambler. He played for big stakes. Unfortunately for him and his family, he has been having a run of bad luck at *'The Club'*. Who knows how his losses had accumulated, poor chap?"

My mother wiped her eyes and stood up to see my aunt off saying, "God rest his soul!"

Though all these years later I recall Theodore Dumani's suicide, whether the war or gambling losses brought it about remain conjecture. Mersin, like the rest of Turkey was spared the ravages of war but inevitably suffered its consequential effects. Though not life threatening, there were troublesome shortages, mainly of manufactured goods. The lack of certain imported medicines was the most serious. Many non-essentials, things like gramophone needles, baking powder, cosmetics, gradually disappeared from the shops. Needless to say a black market emerged for those who were prepared to pay.

Shortages increased and inevitably, there were those who could not pay black market prices, even for essentials. Worst off were the poor living in the towns. The inhabitants of remote villages had always been accustomed to bartering between themselves using money only when they came into the town. In normal times, this made them virtually self sufficient. Even these villagers began to feel the ill effects of the war. Deprivation that inevitably led to a lack of basic hygiene and a fall in health brought a new danger – typhus. It is an infectious fever spread by lice which are carriers. My uncle heard about this from one of his close friends, Dr Muzzafer.

One chilly winter morning, my uncle had just come back from town and seen a strange sight at the small *'hamam'*, opposite our house. I was standing with my mother by one of the windows to which he had called us. His voice was animated by concern as he explained what was going on. I was to hear a great deal more about typhus as time went by.

"As a precaution against typhus the municipality has started to take steps. They have rounded up these people, from one of the villages and brought them to the *'hamam'* by lorry. That big cylindrical thing on wheels is some sort of fumigator. All their clothing will be put in the cylinder for treatment whilst they are in the *'hamam'* washing themselves. Who knows how long it has been since any of them last had a good bath."

A worrier, my mother voiced her concern, "William, you know how hot all the *'hamams'* are. Won't the clothing be damp after the fumigation treatment? Coming out into the cold, good job they don't all get pneumonia."

"I wouldn't worry. Unlike us, these people are very hardy. I wonder whether the authorities will issue them with free soap. Dr Muzzafer was telling me that cleanliness was one of the factors in combating typhus. God forbid there could be an epidemic."

Not long after this, posters were put up by the Municipality warning the public about typhus. My mother bought camphor crystals which she put into small cotton bags and sewed into all our jackets. She had been told by some friend who claimed to know a thing or two about aromatherapy that the pungent smell of camphor was a sure way to keep lice at bay. They could not stand the smell. I complained that people would ridicule me on account of the strong smell coming from inside my jacket. She was not the least bit sympathetic, saying, "Let them! The lice don't like the smell either!"

My mother, like many of her generation in Mersin was prepared to try some of the pseudo medications and procedures making the rounds. Especially when the genuine were either non existent or difficult to come by. At such times, even a quack would not have been rejected out of hand. What is more, any treatment was worth consideration on the premiss that anything is better than nothing.

My encounter with what might be called alternative medicine came about when I had a sore throat. In my earlier childhood, I had had considerable trouble with my ears, mastoiditis. My mother sent me off to *'muallem'* Jabra. The word *'muallem'* in Arabic means teacher and teachers are much respected in Turkey. A tradition encouraged by Ataturk, who on meeting with his old teacher respectfully kissed his hand. This gesture in public was intended to reinforce the esteem that teachers are held in. Consequently, *'muallem'* carries weight beyond its literal meaning. Indeed it might have been this reverence that permitted *'muallem'* Jabra to dabble in medicine.

I remember *'muallem'* Jabra as a tall dark man, dressed in a black suit and dark tie. A rather sombre figure, worthy of respect. He must have been very old and lived on his own as he answered the door himself. Speaking in a croaky voice he greeted me in English which he spoke well.

"Hello, young Patrick."

"Good morning *'muallem'* Jabra. My mother sends you her *selams* and wishes to be remembered. She sent me as I have a sore throat, and you would know what needed to be done. My mother said she would pass by to see you later."

"Yes, of course. Come and stand near the window so that I can see better."

As he spoke, he went into another room and reappeared with a bottle and a long probe made from twisted wire on the end of which there was a wad of cotton wool. He dipped the cotton wool into the bottle which contained a dark liquid. Getting me to open my mouth wide, he applied the potion to the back of my throat. It tasted like a diluted mixture of iodine and honey.

"There you are Patrick. That should do for the time, *inshallah*. However, should you maybe need a second treatment, you can call back tomorrow at the same time, I will be in. I do not go out of the house much these days. Remember me to your mother, also Uncle William and your grandmother, I hope they are keeping well."

I continued to be very much attached to my mother who was sole mentor and role model in my life. Looking back, this could not have served me well. A situation that my mother, herself was aware of and troubled by. She acknowledged this in the letter she wrote more than a year earlier to the then British Consul begging him to facilitate my entry into The English High School. The ill effect that the absence of a father might have had on my development might still further have been compounded by some of her attitudes to me.

My mother lamented the fact that her only child was born a boy rather than a girl. This was regarded by her as yet another of her misfortunes. She attempted to put right this mishap in several different ways. Looking back, I am sure all done unconsciously as my mother was not vengeful. At the time I could not have been conscious of any of these under currents.

It so happened, much to my mother's great delight, that I had auburn hair. I used to cringe whenever she corrected people who mistakenly referred to it as 'ginger' with the all too familiar words, "It isn't the usual ginger. Its auburn! What wouldn't a woman give for such a beautiful hue?" How often she must have thought to herself, "If only that auburn hair had belonged to a daughter, my very own girl!" It was grown long enough to require hair grips, 'slides', as my mother call them. Things might easily have been a great deal worse for me. For what if it was allowed to grow to shoulder length to the point where there might well have been some ambiguity as to my sex? Thankfully I was spared.

Earlier, well before my failed high school adventure my mother dressed me in romper suits, one piece garments, knitwear. I was alone amongst my contemporaries to be clad in this fashion. I recall never feeling at ease wearing them. I also remember how she used to insist on making me wear a headscarf when going out in winter, "You must protect your ears from the cold or you will end up with earache." What with my 'auburn locks', and the headscarf I felt doubly self-conscious. I would protest saying, "I feel ashamed going out in the street wearing a headscarf like a girl." My mother would deride me saying, "Nonsense! Why do you feel ashamed? It is only shame that would make you ashamed!" I could not at the time, nor ever since work out what she meant by these words.

Returning to the wider stage, the war had spread east across Europe deep into the vast Soviet Union. Much was going on undercover else where in neutral Turkey. Until the war, there had been few foreign visitors to Mersin. For all its charm, it was tucked away in the easternmost corner of the Mediterranean. It was off the beaten track. There was hardly any movement of population worth speaking of in or out of the region. In contrast, Istanbul for centuries had been the centre of culture, commerce and though it had been replaced by Ankara as the capital city of the new Turkish Republic, its influence in politics, intrigue and espionage continued. Between them, Istanbul and Ankara experienced a sharp rise in foreign visitors. Developments during the War brought the south eastern region of Turkey into fresh focus. The oil fields to the south of this region of Turkey among other things made the region of strategic value to the Allies. It was not long before there was an influx of foreign visitors to the town, predominantly British.

Europeans could be easily picked out in the town's bustling streets, especially the fair skinned types who were so conspicuous. I would hear members of my family talking about these strangers who had materialised as if from nowhere. Their work done in Mersin, they melted away just as suddenly, unlikely to reappear ever again. Most of these visitors stayed at the Toros Hotel owned by Joseph Dakkak, a family friend. Some of these short term visitors were in their country's diplomatic service. The rest went under the all embracing and ambiguous description of *'businessmen'*. An ambiguity that suited those with work they did not wish all and sundry to know about. There were the wise old owls in Mersin's society who professed that they could tell those involved in '*intelligence*' from legitimate '*businessmen*'.

One way or another, my family got to meet most of these British visitors to the town. Amongst all these many passing acquaintances, there were some who my family got to know well and mix with socially. Friendship with a number of these visitors to Mersin blossomed as they came to be remembered for their own individuality rather than the size or standing of the organisation which had sent them.

One such person was Arthur Maltass. A bachelor who soon acquired a reputation as an accomplished host, giving small intimate lunch and dinner parties at his artistically furnished flat. He cooked and prepared gourmet meals which he served at an elegantly laid table. It was my aunt Olga who knew him best. She always addressed him in her inimitable way as "Arthur *dahling*!"

I had accompanied my mother on one of these occasions when she was invited to just such a dinner. I can still picture Arthur Maltass, a slightly built man, impeccably dressed right down to the usual button hole. As with all the British visitors who came to Mersin, nothing was known about him other than his employer, a British trade organisation known as UKCC.

As with all these strangers they could only be judged by what they had to tell about themselves. It was left to the listeners, my family included, to make their minds up as to their credibility. I first heard about Arthur Maltass from my family. He evidently set out to create his own preferred image of an upper crust English family; mildly eccentric father and his own privileged childhood in England. The device he used for this purpose was a series of humorous anecdotes with which he entertained his guests.

I was present at one of his parties and remember him coming out with one of his many yarns. It was at breakfast that particular day that his father realised that the cruet was not on the table. His father summoned the butler: "Roberts!"

"You called, sir." Responded the butler as he came into the room.

"Yes. Have a look Roberts, there is something missing from the table?" His father exclaimed. Peering at the table intently for a time, Roberts could not come up with an answer. Indeed he as good as told his master that everything appeared to him to be in order. Still cool, calm and collected, Papa is then said to have told his butler, "Roberts, go and fetch the step ladder from the conservatory."

The increasingly bewildered Roberts returned carrying the step ladder and was instructed by Papa. "Now get up the ladder and have a better look." Arthur Maltass never said whether the butler managed to solve the riddle of the missing cruet set. Cutting his story short he told his audience that the cruet never went missing again. Arthur Maltass was a well practised *raconteur.*

Of all those many British visitors to Mersin that my family had got to know in the years during and immediately after the war, there was one who created a lasting impression on them. Bill Bryce was remembered with great fondness. A young Cambridge University graduate in archaeology, he was an expert on the Hittites. Before I came to school in England, I was given a present by Professor John Garstang, a book he had written entitled "The Story of Jericho" inscribed by him and greatly treasured by me. Professor Garstang was leading an archaeological dig on the outskirts of Mersin. The site known as '*Yumuktepe*' was a mound – '*tepe*' – believed to have been man made. As the dig progressed down, Hittite remains had been unearthed. It was this exciting find that brought Bill Bryce out to Turkey.

Bill Bryce was small in stature. My uncle once told me that he perceived him as Lawence of Arabia. He came from a modest family in Guisborough, North Yorkshire. He was one of nature's born gentlemen. A brilliant scholar devoted to his subject and completely lacking any form of pretentiousness. The amusing anecdote he recounted took place at the Istanbul Hotel he had stayed at on his way to Mersin. His candour serves most eloquently to testify as to the nature of the man.

The morning of his departure from the hotel, the lift boy had called at his room for his luggage. Then as if from nowhere, two chamber maids and another young chap appeared much to Bill's surprise. He knew not a word of Turkish and apparently the hotel staff could not speak any English. They stood there smiling. Knowing no different, he shook hands with each of them.

My mother and uncle with whom Bill Bryce had been talking knew the very common almost mandatory practice of *'tipping'*, which is why any where in the Middle East the word '*baksheesh*' is readily understood.

Realising this oversight was the consequence of his unworldliness, they did not want to hurt his feelings so my mother explained, "But Bill they had come in the expectation of a parting handout, a gratuity."

Bill Bryce did not bluster nor display any form of indignation as others might well have done. In fact, he saw the funny side of things. He laughed and said that he had no idea adding that they must have been disappointed.

It was whilst I was still at school in England that Bill Bryce had come on the scene in Mersin. Getting to know my family there, it was not long before he was a frequent visitor. In time a strong bond developed and he was treated as a long lost son by both my mother and uncle. One day, during his long stay in Mersin he was down town with my uncle. They had gone into one of the banks where the cashier enquired of my uncle, "What is your English friend doing here?"

There was nothing unusual for such personal questions to be asked of perfect strangers. A sign one might say of well intentioned interest. My uncle, accustomed to this, explained, "He is an archaeologist, from Cambridge University. He specialises on the *'Hitit imparatorlugu'* – the Hittite dynasty, which he has come from England to excavate '*Yumuktepe*' near here".

Everyone in Mersin had heard of the place. That wasn't what interested the man in the bank but rather the mention of '*Cambridge*'. By then several others of the bank staff had gathered around. The twin seats of academic excellence in England, Oxford and Cambridge, were as well known as the British Empire itself.

I know my uncle would have been overcome with a feeling of pride. Pride for his young friend Bill Bryce but also the pride of being British himself.

"What do you think of this Bill, not only do these chaps want to shake you by the hand, they would like your autograph? You are a celebrity. The very first man from that famous English University that they have met in the flesh!"

Bill Bryce visited me at Hurst. All I can bring to mind of his visit was a parcel that he had brought over for me from my mother. A packet of dried bananas and a tin of '*halva*' – a sweet made from sesame seed oil. Some time after that I was invited to spend a week of my school holidays with his family in Guisborough. Bill was not there but I well remember his young sister. We used to go for long walks along the ridges overlooking the town.

By far the biggest influx of British visitors during the early part of the war came in the guise of 'civil engineers'. They were based outside the town in what eventually became a large builder's site known locally as '*Ingiliz shantiyesi*', the English camp. No sooner there, but word got round they were employees of an English company called Braithwaites who had come to build roads. Few, if any of them were seen in Mersin, they kept a low profile. The lorries they drove were in tiptop condition compared with the local ones which were in various stages of disintegration. All the Braithwaite lorries and jeeps were uniformly painted beige..

My uncle, thanks to his various business interests, was a familiar figure around the town. As a consequence he got to know much of what was going on in the town and beyond. It was always at lunch that much of the town's intrigue and gossip reached the family. With hindsight, I marvel now at how much of what was supposed to be '*hush hush*' during the war somehow got decoded and passed on. I recall snippets of revelations which at the time were believed to be highly significant – "All these English chaps who have turned up as Braithwaites, to build roads. They have come up from Egypt. All their vehicles still camouflaged for the North African desert. They are obviously British troops, 'sappers' in the Royal Engineers. The Allies want to have good roads in this part of Turkey to facilitate rapid troop movement to secure the oil fields in the east, places like Mosul. You know, somebody was going on the other day that in places, the roads would be used as landing strips for heavy aircraft."

After listening to the disclosures about British activities that my uncle had heard about, my mother brought to mind the German propaganda which was rife in the dark days at the beginning of the war.

"Things are going better now for the Allies, thank God. Do you remember the German propaganda that Gullu once came out with at the start of the war?" – Gullu, our servant had heard some farfetched claims about the devastating effect of Germany's air power. It was of course the Stuka dive bomber that had been given a fiendish reputation.

"The Germans have fitted scythes to the wings of their war planes. They swoop down low out of the clouds unexpectedly. They fly down so fast that the screeching noise they make cannot be heard by their victims until it is too late. They are said to come so low that the sharp blades fitted to their wings decapitate any one unlucky enough to be out in the open." This was an instance of Germany's 'war of nerves' which was spread by propagandists to good effect amongst the poor and the illiterate in towns like Mersin.

All the consequences that the war brought to Mersin provided me with an unparalleled fund of experience. I must have benefited from all that I saw and heard about me, yet with my family, we were spared the real horrors of the conflict. In some ways, all we Christians, privileged as we were enjoyed a constantly changing European presence in the town as never before. There were gatherings at the British Consulate to which known Anglophiles were invited. Cocktail parties and musical socials were well attended and greatly appreciated.

I can recall the time when my friend Fonda Tahinci's aunts Athena and Magda performed as a duet. Both exuberant Greeks, they put on a lively display. One of them singing *fortissimo* and the other giving an energetic accompaniment on piano – topical ditties including *Roll out the barrel*, and *It's a long way to Tipperary*. The audience made up of the Mersin Christians, were equally excitable at the end of the Tahinci ladies' presentation, clapping and calling out repeatedly '*bravo*' and '*encore*'.

The all male British settlement at Braithwaites 'camp' also opened their doors, offering hospitality. As time went by following their mysterious arrival, many of them had become acquainted with families in the town. This provided the opportunity for these relationships to be advanced. My mother and her sister Olga, who was still unmarried at the time, were prime movers. The Braithwaite *boys*, whether mature officers or youthful other ranks were naturally keen to meet the pick of the Mersin's young and unattached females.

Unlike the social gatherings at the British Consulate where not surprisingly, guests were invited for their Anglophile leanings, Braithwaites had no such precepts. Their criterion was to accommodate females, particularly those who were easy on the eye. Turkish conventions at the time were such that local Muslim girls could not be entertained in this manner. So it was that, my mother chaperoned groups of Christian girls invited for soirees at 'The Camp'.

These evenings included a lavish cold buffet and drinks with dancing to a three-piece-ensemble. Olga in the meantime cultivated the officer ranks, enjoying a personal relationship with several from Braithwaites and a British intelligence officer called Doran who was later a victim of the Jewish terrorists attack on the King David Hotel in Jerusalem in July 1946.

All was not entertainment and good cheer. Two incidents that I can remember bring back vividly the hurt and anxiety they caused my family. The first and less dramatic of these involved one of my aunts.

The second and by far the most damaging concerned my uncle. It upset my entire family and had far reaching effects which were never resolved.

The war created unlimited opportunities for those who were intent on trouble making. The ground was fertile so to speak, so that any seeds of malice that were sown would germinate and grow rapidly. No one being any wiser as to the identity of the person or source from which they came. Word had evidently reached the then acting British Consul that members of the Rickards family had been socialising with Rosie and Riri Levante, my aunt and her Italian husband and family. Any incident related to the war became public and spread like wild fire. It was not long before Rosie ran into my mother down town and questioned her. "What is this that I have heard about you and William being called to the British Consul the other day? Is it true and if so what was it all about Dosia?" My mother put her in the picture,

"Somebody had been in touch with the Consulate about us seeing you and Riri. The phrase used by Mr Kay was that William and I would have to stop fraternising with enemy nationals." What my mother said must have sounded surreal to Rosie who typically burst out laughing. She looked at my mother in disbelief and enquired, "Was he serious?" My mother, a very different temperament from her youngest sister was far less able to make light of such a threat, replied, "Of course he was serious. He told us that if it persisted, we could be asked to surrender our British passports!"

I thought no more about the matter, nor was it ever mentioned in my presence again. For me life went on as normal at the Gazi Pasha and after school I was back to playing with my cousin Jorj and his friends. Mother and Uncle William continued seeing their sister Rosie and her husband Riri. They were not called on to surrender their British passports. This has led me to conclude that they might well have maintained a lower profile. Alternatively, the acting British

Consul might have come to his senses as about that very same time a farcical security lapse was being played out inside the British Embassy in Ankara. It came to have the code name 'Operation Cicero' and was made into the film *Five Fingers* starring James Mason as Cicero. Sir Hughe Knatchbull-Hugesson the British Ambassador's trusted valet Ilias Bazda, an Albanian was the master spy Cicero working for the Germans.

The more upsetting war time incident involving my family concerned my uncle William Rickards, who was the victim. The Vice-Consul in Mersin from May 1943 was Denis Wright who moved on in January 1945 to take up a post in the Foreign Office in London. It was during his service that my uncle was relieved of his position as Lloyds Agent in South Eastern Turkey. At the time, I believe that none of my family, my uncle included, had any idea as to why this happened nor the person or persons implicated. It was after the war ended that I recall my mother on several occasions bringing up the subject, "William, now that the war is over, you should go over to England and clear your name. You have never had any explanation from Lloyds as to why they took their Agency away from you. At least get to know what was behind it all."

I remember my uncle never answered my mother. He simply did not want to discuss the incident. As he was of independent means, the loss did not affect him financially. It would have been to address the injustice and erase the blemish on the Rickards' family name that would have taken him to England. I now suspect he did not make the effort for two reasons: an inexplicable fear, a phobia, that if he left Turkey he might not be granted a return entry visa. The second stemmed more from emotion than reason, a dread which he told me about on more than one occasion. I recall the gist of this in his own words, "I have never wanted to return to England. I have always feared that I would not be returning to the country that I knew before the First World

War. I would be disappointed. I prefer to keep the images that I have carried in my head for all these years." I have since pondered on how much more changed England would have appeared to my uncle as the years rolled on beyond 1945.

My mother many years later wrote to Sir Denis Wright to congratulate him on his appointment as British Ambassador in Tehran, Iran in 1963. She did not then have any idea of the part he had played in my uncle's loss of the Lloyds' Agency.

Chapter 5

"Hello misery. I see you're back again."

What a greeting, and memorable too especially as I cannot remember any of the others on my return to the English High School in Istanbul. Remarkably, it was one of the masters who had greeted me thus. Taken aback by the jibe, I failed completely to make any sort of a reply. More truthfully, feeling hurt and demeaned all I could do was withdraw into my shell. I was still at the time a timid soul, maybe why I have remembered that master.

Mr Ergas, for that was his strange name, was a local Levantine; he was one of two junior masters at the school. He and Mr Salvatore were both old boys of the school, though very different from each other in appearance and personality. The latter still played football for the school. He was a natty dresser. It was said that he prided himself on being something of a '*womaniser*'. Mr Ergas, in striking contrast was shy and gauche. This exposed him to pranks by some of the older dayboys who he sometimes supervised in after school detentions. I was present at some of those occasions myself. Hilarious as the banter might have seemed to me as an onlooker, it became embarrassingly clear that poor Mr Ergas was unable to cope with his tormentors. Some of them might well have started at the high school when he was still a pupil there. Seeing him as a victim, made me feel sorry for him.

It must have been in the autumn of 1943 that I made this comeback. By then, age 12, my family must have judged me to have grown up and become mature enough to cope with boarding school life. What is more, I had made the long train journey from Mersin to Istanbul on my own.

On the occasion of my earlier boarding school venture, as I have quite recently found out, my mother had said about me, "he's at an age now when he needs some one more than a mother to train him as an English boy should grow up". From a nine year old child in this intervening period, I had undergone changes in myself. Aware for some time of my pubescence, my mother must have become even more conscious of this need that she had identified earlier. It was I suppose a time when a father is most needed, especially as my mother had made no secret of the fact that she would rather I had been a girl. Not surprising given the loss of my father so early on in their marriage and the manner in which she chose to continue her life as a widow. All this did make for some strange attitudes and behaviour that looking back on now, I realise I was an innocent victim of.

I have absolutely no idea how old I was, nor when it happened. By contrast, I can remember the occasion vividly. It was my very first experience of sexual arousal. It must have been early summer, the weather getting warmer, *siesta* time. I had been lying down after lunch in the bedroom I still shared with my mother, as usual I was in my pyjamas, dosing. My mother must have gone out somewhere early, as I was there on my own. The thing my mother referred to as *'your dickie'* had until then been inert. It hung inactive, occasionally brought out for the sole purpose of a *'wee-wee'*.

As I awoke from my nap, it had appeared out of the slit in the front of my pyjama trousers. It was strangely stiff and I felt a pleasurable sensation. By touching, pleasure turned into excitement. I had never experienced such arousal before. Suddenly, with no warning, it throbbed. With each spasm, a thick fluid was deposited on me. I lay there for a while overcome by a strange sensation, particularly in the lower part of my back. A mixture of pleasure and almost pain but not unpleasant. My *'dickie'* I discovered had gone limp. My whole being felt spent, lacking in vigour. I lay there motionless for a time. I was overcome with guilt, though at the time I could not work out for myself why. I cannot recall whether at the time I voiced these thoughts out loud to myself or not. "What if my mother should walk in and find me in this state?" was the first thought that went through my head. Somewhat recovered, I got up. With some cotton wool I wiped the stuff off myself. It was then that I noticed that it was sticky and had an unusual smell. With nowhere to hide the wet cotton wool, I dropped it through a large hole in the wooden floorboards.

I still felt strange, and apprehensive enquiring to myself "Would my mother or any of the others in the family be able to tell what had befallen me?" To the feeling of guilt, fear was added. Fear of being found out or even suspected. I looked in the large mirror attached to my mother's dressing table. My wide open eyes stared back at me in the half-light, as the curtains were drawn. Apart from that I appeared to look no different from usual.

I remembered something that I had been told by my friend Paul Debbane on a previous year when we children were spending the summer with our families up in Gozne. It concerned an older boy, let me call him Nicco. He was several years our senior.

"Nicco showed us a trick the other day that he performs with his '*bulluk*'. He got it out of his trousers. After a bit it started to swell. As he massaged it, gradually it got bigger and hard. After rubbing it vigorously, it discharged a white substance. There were a number of spurts, all of which landed the other side of a line that Nicco had drawn in the dust to show us how far this white fluid could reach." Paul continued his tale, "None of us had seen such a sight before.

Nicco appeared pleased with himself as be put his *'bulluk'* away in his trousers."

Curious, I had asked some questions to which Paul replied but I cannot bring much to mind, except one, "Oh yes we asked Nicco if he could repeat his performance. He joked a bit, boasting that he could but later told us that he had to be careful. If a man did it too himself too often, it was dangerous – it could make a person blind." Blindness! The very thought added to my fears.

In those far off days, the children I used to spend my time with in Gozne were still some way from puberty, like myself. Even so, there must have been a nascent interest in all aspects of the reproduction process. We did not have a proper understanding of it nor did we grasp its connection with sexuality.

Paul for example got known for his skill in examining chickens. Most of the Christian families in Gozne reared chickens that were kept in crudely constructed coops. They were fed barley and all manner of food scraps to encourage them to lay eggs. Paul, by inserting his finger, could tell whether the chicken was ready to lay. Apparently no one else in Gozne or its environs had Paul's lucky gift. Consequently, children from other parts of the village would turn up with a chicken in the hope that Paul would examine it. He was never known to refuse. Not surprisingly, from these modest beginnings, Paul H. Debbane went on to become an eminent gynaecologist in the USA. In his honour, a street in Hamilton, Ohio was named after him where he had built up his practice and ran a prosperous clinic.

About the time of my first sexual arousal there was another incident. This also involved my mother who had been invited to a party at the small '*hamam*' in front of our house in Mersin. Apart from places where people went to have a good bath, '*hamams*' were also meeting places for socialising. The small '*hamam*' was just the right size for such gatherings. A lady friend of my mother had booked the place for an afternoon and invited my mother. My mother at that time still took me where ever she went. I had been before and enjoyed the '*hamam*' parties as there were liquid refreshments, usually fruit juices and some appropriate Turkish sweet meats like *baklava* and *katayif* as well as fruit. All had been going well until one of the ladies approached my mother and in a discrete whisper spoke to her in Arabic. This lady was under the impression that I was out of earshot. In any case she assumed that I would not understand the language.

"Dosia, forgive me asking you this but how old is your son?" I could not make out my mother's words as she had her backed turned to me. The lady went on, "I asked because I thought that he might have been older. You see Dosia, he appears to be aware of our nakedness. What is more he is enjoying the experience."

Once we got home my mother confronted me, "Patrick, tell me the truth, were you looking at any of those ladies when we were at the '*hamam*'?" Feigning injured innocence, I made some sheepish reply hoping that it would serve to deflect further probing by my mother. I recall how my mother lectured me when I caught sight of her once when she was undressed. "Turn the other way. You should not look at me when I am dressing, it is wrong. You will be struck down!" I recalled later, with some amusement that she had also warned me, "As Lot's wife who looked back, you might be turned into a pillar of salt!"

My mother's best friend, Victoria Atalay I recall remarked when speaking with her on how puritanical she was. Maybe to save me from being '*struck down* ' or turned into a pillar of salt, my mother acquired a screen behind which after that, she dressed and undressed hidden out of sight. It was quite ornamental with pastel country scenes including some brightly coloured birds.

When I had a bath, she used to always scrub my back. She came in to the bathroom unexpectedly once. It was very hot and full of steam. I had soaped myself and was standing up. She peered at me through the steam and accusingly enquired, "Have you been touching *'your dickie'*, you naughty boy?" Thereafter, whenever the notion took her on bath days, she would assert, "You've been playing with *'It'* – haven't you?" Amusingly, maybe in recognition of my growing maturity, my mother had dispensed with the rather childish expression *'dickie'* using instead the more grown up term *'It'*. Sounds almost like some music hall comedy routine when I think about it now! It wasn't a laughing matter then!

My newly acquired consciousness with my penis was what alerted me to the problem. The problem, it turns out was quite a common occurrence. In fact, I was born like that. Not so long ago a dear friend Umit Sukru, himself a doctor, explained the problem to me like this – "due to adhesions the foreskin cannot retract making sexual intercourse impossible." He went on to say, "had this condition been noticed early on, it could have been easily dealt with in infancy." In my case, unhappily for me, it had gone unnoticed. Given the sexual taboos of the time this was not altogether surprising. I have come to believe that my mother had an aversion to my penis. After all, had she had her way and had I been a girl, she would have been spared the problem! In the event, action was only taken after I had left school in England and was about 18 years old. I can well remember the remark that I overheard at home. It says it all, "Well some good has come out of Patrick's condition. It has kept him away from women and having sexual relations with them. Who knows what scrapes he might have got himself into otherwise?" It could be argued that as a teenager, until I was nearly 18, I had been deprived. A form of castration one might say, enforced celibacy.

Unaware though I was at the time of all this, I had become more mature and knowledgeable. I settled happily at The English High School For Boys. I went into the same house, Sherwood, and was chosen to play football in the house team. I excelled in athletics, especially in the cross-country race, coming first in my age group. My academic accomplishments, to be kind would at best be described as modest. I say so with good reason as I cannot bring to mind attending class in any subject other than English literature. Even this feat of memory was due to the choice of set books we had. *Mutiny on the Bounty* and the other, all about the British Raj and a colourful character known as *The Nizam of Hyderabad.* Though I cannot bring to mind the book's title, the subject exercised my imagination.

At this second coming to Istanbul, I was more receptive and eager to absorb some of the history and culture of the place. A location unparalleled in the world, straddling Europe and Asia with water on all three sides. The town itself had a vibrant centre with suburbs that spread right out into the undulating country side. The epicentre spread out from the main thoroughfare which sliced through Istanbul's bustling commercial centre called Pera, later known as Beyoglu. The thoroughfare I speak of was at the time still known as La Grande Rue de Pera, since changed to *Istiklal Caddesi*, meaning Independence Avenue in English. At one end Taxim Square and at the other, the '*Tunel*' said to be the oldest tunnel in the world though only 600 metres in length it has a steep descent down to the famous Galata Bridge and Karakoy at sea level in the proximity of the Golden Horn. This district of Istanbul holds some pleasantly poignant memories of my school days. Places that I had often frequented as a visitor from Mersin. Most notably hotels, restaurants even *patisseries* and cinemas. Comfortable old world style hotels, many of which are still standing to this day, monuments to '*la belle époque*'. Well, at least in my perception.

Most memorable though the least imposing, the modest Alp Hotel where my mother and I had stayed the first time, with its spacious though austere rooms and ancient plumbing. It was claimed that Atat-urk had stayed there. The far grander, six storey Pera Palace Hotel built in1892 for travellers on the Orient Express was patronised frequently by Agatha Christie where it is claimed she got inspiration for her novel *Murder on the Orient Express.* I was also invited for the day to the Tokatliyan where my aunt Olga was honeymooning with her husband John Catton. A short way along towards Taksim was Abdullah's restaurant, renowned for its cutlets of lamb *'that melt in your mouth'* and rice *'pilaf'*, fit for a Sultan.

That main thoroughfare was at its most magnificent at night, when it was lit up. Funny how sometimes the banal, trivial and odd will leave an indelible and lasting impression, I was fascinated by two enormous illuminated signs that in the darkness of the night dominated everything else. I used to look out for them as I walked down *La Grande Rue de Pera* towards the massive gates of Galata Saray and the '*Tunel*'.

One high up on the very top of a four or five storey departmental store – *'Be Ba Bo'*, rhythmic and so catchy – why else would it have stayed in my mind? Not surprisingly perhaps, no one knew what it meant. The other illumination – *'Radyolin'*. which left me intrigued by the absurdity of such an improbable sounding name for a toothpaste! I had no doubt been attracted by the bright lights due to my childish innocence and because I had seen nothing like them previously. I have since come to realise that there were many other fascinating sights on and just off *la Grande Rue de Pera.* That area was Istanbul's heart, the epicentre for all tastes, from sublime to base. The presence of sensual allure was palpable whether on the street, in cinemas, cafés, restaurants or out of the way down the less well lit side streets where there were licensed brothels.

Merely out of curiosity, just to have a look at the goings on, I was tempted to venture down those dimly lit side streets. My fear or discretion overcame the temptation. In fact, I never really had the opportunity. I only ever found myself on *la Grande Rue de Pera* at night when I was occasionally invited out by a kind friend of the family or one of my two aunts. Also, true to its reputation, the high school imposed strict codes of discipline on boarders, especially the young ones like myself. I was to find out for the first time about things like 'detention', 'passes', 'out of bounds', 'getting gated' even 'corporal punishment' during my 'stretch' at the high school.

Of greater importance, I was fortunate to have had the opportunity of visiting many of Istanbul's historic places; its ancient walls and fortifications, the many magnificent mosques. Aya Sofya the famous cathedral which when Constantinople fell to the Turks in 1453 was converted into a mosque. Outside that vast metropolis were other wonders: four inhabited islands in the Sea of Marmara, the archipelago they form known as Princes' Islands. The four are sometimes referred to by their old Greek names. The best known amongst them, *'Buyuk Ada'*, translates from Turkish *'Big Island'*, is often called by its quaint sounding Greek name '*Prinkipo*'. At the time, motor vehicles were not allowed so the only conveyances were horse drawn carriages and donkeys. The carriage horses had a wide sack attached to their hind quarters into which they deposited their steaming hot waste, a novel idea I have never seen elsewhere.

These excursions would have never taken place but for two of the senior masters at the high School. Mr Ellison taught chemistry, however, he was best remembered by a few boarders, myself included, who were marooned on rainy weekends with nowhere to go. At such times, when he was duty master, he would invite us to join him in the chemistry laboratory which was in the basement, to attend his highly entertaining demonstrations. Chemical wizardry and pyrotechnics, which sometimes filled the place with fumes the effects of which caused our eyes to stream as we coughed and spluttered. Mr Ellison himself joined us in the turmoil he had created. Activities of this sort, however entertaining, would long ago have been prohibited on health and safety grounds, the more is the pity! The other senior master, Mr Campbell, had read Archaeology and entertained us in a very different way. He would lapse into the dim and distant history of the sites to which he took us, in what was once known as Constantinople. He was the history teacher at the high school. Both of them were Oxbridge men who travelled out to Turkey and lived at the school during term time, returning to their homes in the UK for their holidays.

Istanbul was no longer the capital city of the new Turkish Republic. Ankara in the heart of Anatolia, for strategic reasons became capital in 1923. All the foreign Embassies moved to Ankara the new administrative and political nerve centre of Turkey. Istanbul however continued to flourish as the commercial and business centre of the country. It was a veritable metropolis, as it remained the centre of activity and was also the spiritual centre for the whole of the Eastern Orthodox world. For all that, the population of Istanbul when I was at school during the war years had not reached a million.

Istanbul it was claimed "has more non-Turks than any other town in the country". This claim would unquestionably have applied to the mix of nationalities at the English High School. The entire school, boarders and day boys combined, had a large complement of Greek Orthodox with frequently heard names like Panayotides, Dimitriades, Athanasatos, Zantopolos and Vasiliades. Next came Jews, many whose forebears fled from Spain with typical names from the Old Testament such as Ovadia, Mizrahy and Gabay.

There were many Gabays, brothers and cousins. This presented a problem at roll call as there happened to be two with the same forename initial 'M'. The problem was resolved by designating them Gabay M 1 and Gabay M 2. Though less in numbers, there were Armenians, Maltese, Cypriots. Not to be forgotten, Levantines whose families two or more generations earlier had settled in Turkey from places like England, France, Italy or from further a field.

The High School for Boys was founded in Istanbul to emulate the English public school. I was to discover when I attended the real McCoy some years later in England that there were some big surprises in store for me. Sure enough, the boys at the school in Istanbul were split up into four Houses.

They were named after four of England's well known forests – Sherwood, Charnwood, Arden and Dean, an expedient dreamed up solely for sports purposes but which nonetheless fostered a team spirit on sports days. There was a head boy and school prefects. The school uniform typically comprised of a school blazer, grey flannels and a school cap. As for ethos, this focused largely on '*respect*'.

The predominantly Muslim Turkish people place great store on what they call '*aile terbiyesi*' – what in our order of things could be termed '*family values*'. In their '*aile terbiyesi* ' they insist on respect and discipline. They recognised that these attributes played an important part in the standards at the high school. It was a gratifying tribute to the English public school system and indeed to the country itself that the high school in Istanbul was so highly esteemed by comparison with the other European schools. As a result it attracted boys from very diverse backgrounds.

Catering for Turkey's cosmopolitan population there were also in Istanbul three French Jesuit schools for boys and a Dame de Sion con-

A rare snap, for there were few cameras around at our disposal in 1943. Desmond Barwell's English parents lived in Ankara. The snap shows us in our English High School uniforms, taken at the school's sports ground at Sisli

vent school for girls, an Italian and a Greek School. The celebrated Turkish Lycee of Galata Saray founded in 1868 is situated half way down the *Istiklal Caddesi* behind a magnificent set of wrought iron gates. Interestingly, classes for most subjects were taken in French, the diplomatic language of the time. French was also the language commonly used in trade and commerce. It had been and continued to be until the end of the war. After the war English rapidly became the '*lingua franca*'.

'*Mamas*' in the Middle East are renowned for pampering their sons. My own mother, or '*mama*' as I sometimes called her was no exception to this rule. Ever since I started at the high school in Istanbul, she decided that when I was back in Mersin for my holidays, I should be well nourished. I was to have a boiled egg for breakfast every day. This was additional to the traditional olives, butter and jam, cheese with cucumber and tomatoes which made up our daily breakfast. Tea was usually taken, never coffee. Bread was eaten at every meal, in large quantities, especially at breakfast. There were different types of bread – in winter the slices of bread were toasted. When we were in Gozne for the summer, we frequently had the '*sach*' bread. This was made from unleavened dough rolled out thin and baked on a large circular, slightly domed steel dish, called a '*sach*'. It would rest on three large stones. The space under it filled with red hot glowing embers.

Thankfully, my mother's plans to nurture me were not exaggerated. The doting mother of a friend of mine, Gabriel Mroue used to prepare for him what she believed to be a truly nourishing morsel. Spleen, cut in half and lightly grilled. Served in a shallow soup dish so that the blood that oozed from it was not wasted. I watched Gabo on one occasion as he cut lumps off with a sharp knife and dutifully chewed his way through his mother's offering. He had always been a good son. Later, he told me himself that "spleen is good for you. It works wonders for our blood supply!". "Well not for me!" I decided to myself. I hoped no one would think of passing the tip on to my mother. Gabo, a clever and studious boy went on to qualify as a surgeon in Canada.

Lest I might have given the impression that I was over indulged, let me dispel this illusion. The entire Rickards family under the tutelage of my grandfather Henry, had been brought up with his Victorian values which my grandmother Mariam had come to share with him. Though my grandmother's family were Syrian Orthodox, she was educated in a missionary school run by Dr. David Metheny and his wife who were American evangelists. Had my grandparents been offered an eleventh commandment, they would almost certainly have come up with something on the lines of *"Don't mollycoddle the child!"*

I recall coming home in the afternoons from the Gazi Pasha primary school with a ravenous appetite. No one other than the servant would be in. Waiting for me on the kitchen table would be *'le goûté'* – on a plate, a heaped table spoon of home made jam and by it a tumbler of milk, left for me usually by my grandmother. I remember what she had often told me, "Patrick, you can have as much bread as you like from the loaf in the cupboard. There is a knife there cut what you want off the loaf. Make sure you wrap the remaining bread in the cloth as otherwise it will get stale."

Had this narrative, been about imagined events used to illustrate a moral or spiritual lesson, it would have been termed a parable. Known, with a touch of glee to my grandchildren as the story about *"you can have as much bread as you like but no more jam!"* it is factual. I feel it is no less a parable for being so. It serves to illustrate my upbringing which was well intentioned however unusual or bizarre it may now appear to some. Though it might never gain the same fame as the story about Marie Antoinette's supposed remark, "Let them eat cake" it is of a similar genre. I hope it makes a worthwhile point.

The term *"le goûté"* like '*siesta*' was common currency in Mersin. It was what all my friends from the other Christian families indulged in on returning from their school each and every afternoon. One of my aunts who had been at a boarding school in Montpellier, told me that for their *"goûté"* they used to be given a chunk of chocolate and an unlimited supply of bread. Bread it appears was indeed '*the staff of life*' in Turkey and France, remaining so to this day.

In those days in Mersin items of clothing with the possible exception of socks and stockings, whether for men or for women, were rarely ready-made and available to be bought in the towns' shops. All were made to measure. I recall, a time when my mother arranged with a seamstress called *Sit Birjow* to come to the house for the day. She would arrive about mid morning to start work in our dining room where she had the use of the table and the family Singer sewing machine. She made underpants, shirts and pyjamas for my uncle and myself, dresses and other garments for my mother and grandmother. Trousers, jackets and suits were made to measure by tailors down town where my mother's uncle Tannus had his tailoring business. The same applied to footwear, both men's and women's shoes were all made to measure. Maybe in Istanbul, with its close proximity to Europe, some of the fashionable shops might have had ready made ladies shoes available, imported from Italy. Even in Istanbul, men's and boys' shoes would have been made to measure.

On my return to Mersin for the long summer holidays from the high school at the end of one of the school years my mother wanted to get me ready for our stay up in the mountains. "Patrick, I want you to come down town with me. I want to buy you some shoes for when we go up to Gozne." I was puzzled when we turned off the one and only main road and headed up a narrow side street to the big covered market.

Entering the market she stopped by the butcher's shop, she was having a word with Ali, the butcher whom she knew. It turned out to be the shop next door that my mother had brought me to. "*Marhaba madam*", the owner greeted. We remained standing outside as there was hardly room for the three of us inside. With the odours of entrails and sheep carcasses receding, I could smell the sheep skins on display where we had moved to. There were several pairs of black leather '*Yemenis*' hanging on either sides of the narrow entrance. In my dictionary they are described as '*a light shoe worn by peasants*', perfectly correct. All the villagers in Turkey wear '*Yemenis*'. As the name implies they originated in the Yemen and must be worn widely throughout the Middle East and beyond though probably called by some different name. It is customary for the backs to be turned down to facilitate taking them on and off, the owner choosing to go barefoot at times.

More to the point, '*Yemenis*' are not for the '*beau monde*' as I tried to convey to my mother without causing a scene, "I have never seen any of my friends wearing '*Yemenis*' even up in Gozne. I will be laughed at." As usual on such occasions, my mother brushed aside my concern with a single word, "Rubbish!"

For those unfamiliar with them, they are the footwear commonly depicted in Oriental scenes, and characterised by the pointed toes. They are crudely stitched without inner sole nor any form of lining. Points that I brought to my mother's notice as I went through the process of trying them on. Once more she was dismissive telling me, "I know they are not finished off and probably uncomfortable, but you will soon get used to them."

My mother settled the issue, "I'll have this pair for my son." having talked the shop keeper into a suitably reduced price. We said goodbye and set off home. On the way, my mother put her case to me quietly saying, "Now listen Patrick, these shoes have cost me half the price of a made to measure pair. Knowing how you get through shoes up in the mountains, I can't afford to keep paying for made to measure ones whilst you are on holiday." I could not help but think that she did have a point there. '*Yemenis*' were a good idea after all!

With my schooling in England in mind, much had been going on during the last months of the war whilst I was still at the high school in Istanbul. I was not aware of my family's efforts, mostly made by my uncle William. He had managed to acquire a copy of *The Public Schools' Yearbook* from England. With the help of this, he had written to several schools in the hope of getting me accepted without my having to take the common entrance examination.

At last, a favourable reply came from a school with the curious name – Hurstpierpoint College. I was home from Istanbul and I can remember the letter that had come on an unusual looking single page, and my uncle saying to me, "Listen Patrick we hope that this is going to be your school in England. It is in a county called Sussex, the school is situated near Brighton a well known town on the south coast within easy reach of London. The climate in that part of England should be temperate."

It is as if it had only recently taken place, my mother and uncle giving me the good news that would open up a new world to me. With hindsight and amusingly, how mistaken my uncle had been in talking about *'the temperate climate in that part of England.'* I would soon find out for myself how very different it was in reality.

The reply from Hurstpierpoint had come on an Airgraph. We were told that conventional letters would have taken weeks to arrive. That fateful letter was to affect all three of us – my mother, my uncle and myself. For each of us the experience would be different. I can now only imagine how my long absence miles away in England might have worked on my uncle. The gist of his encouraging words to me later that day at lunch are still in my mind. "Patrick, you are so lucky to be going to England. It will be the start of a new way of life for you. A better one. You will always think back on your days at Hurstpierpoint, with pride. How I wish I could relive the all too short a spell I had at Llandovery!"

My uncle would get close to reliving his own school days through me. A fact I was to realise much later on. As for my mother, though she said little about this parting, I believe it was elation but also despair. Elation because she was doing the best she could for me, despair because being separated was the price that had to be paid. As it turned out, it was to be a life apart for us both which was exacted almost to the end of her days.

My mother in particular, had so much to see to preparing me for my new life at Hurstpierpoint. As for me, that unusual name continued to be a preoccupation. My uncle came up with the idea that it might be derived from the name of some monastery, possibly with some French connection. With hindsight I can now understand the train of thought that took him down the ecclesiastic route but how he came to include a French connection escapes me. He would no doubt have read in the Public Schools year book that Hurstpierpoint College was the first of several schools founded by Canon Woodard.

Like all foreign nationals living in Turkey, I had what people there referred to as a '*permit de sejour*' – a residence permit. I needed it to travel about in Turkey on my own. I had accompanied my mother to the main police station in Mersin where these identity cards are issued. The police officer attending to us asked my mother for the date of my birth. "The 27th December 1931" she said and to which the official replied, "I'll put his date of birth down as the 1st January 1932. It will be better for the lad, this way he becomes as we say a '32 birth' otherwise he would be a '31 birth' – and just for four days!"

This adjustment would have had the effect of deferred national service had I been liable. Mindful of the police officer's kind intentions, my mother acceded to his proposal with her usual smile of gratitude. I had noticed in the past how my mother was careful never to reject some kind consideration out of hand. She explained to me, "Why cause offence unnecessarily?"

As I would be travelling to England on my own, the time had come for me to be issued with my first and very own British passport. Application had to be made at the British Consulate in Mersin for this. I accompanied my mother to the same place I had been to so often just prior to the start of the war only a few years earlier. Mr Matthews had been the consul then. Our visits then had been social, my mother being entertained by Luna Matthews in their sitting room. Anne Hope and I closeted in the nursery until we were summoned for afternoon tea with the grown ups. On this occasion, our visit being business, we were directed to the official part of the Consulate on the ground floor. I have reason to remember this occasion. The official dealing with my mother was not satisfied with some aspect of her application for my passport and informed her that she would have to return the next day. The incident upset me, as it had my mother. Once we were outside in the street I told my mother, "He was not at all considerate."

"Patrick, you must understand he is doing his job."

"What about when we went to get my '*ikamet teskeresi*' at the police station. Look how helpful that Turkish policeman was!"

"Of course I remember. But Patrick, the British are different!"

Something that I was to become increasingly aware of, the many differences between the two cultures. Some positive and pleasing because they matched up with what I had grown accustomed to.

Others that I yet had to understand and get accustomed to. Either way, they were all part of a culture that I still had to absorb and try to come to terms with.

At the time, just after leaving the Consulate I can remember my mother's words, "Patrick you will soon be in England. You will see things for yourself. The British stick to the rules, they do not let their personal feelings influence their behaviour. This way, every one is treated impartially in the same way, according to the rules. It is the best way."

At the time, a thirteen year old, I had become the victim of my very own emotions. Emotions that at times were to well up from deep down inside me. Even before setting foot in England, this turned out to be the very first of an endless succession of what I can only describe as my internal 'conflicts of culture'. Self induced dilemmas that I have had to struggle with over and over again. Looking back now, most of my family must have been victims of the same conflict even though their responses were often very different.

I remember there was one final assignment, an important one. For some time, there had been concern about my eyesight, often expressed bluntly, "Patrick sit up. You will damage your sight if you continue to get so close to your book when you are writing." After the usual deliberations and many family discussions it was my uncle who set the course to be followed announcing, "I have been talking to one or two of my doctor friends about Patrick's eyes. Dr Hayri is considered by most of them to be the best eye specialist in Mersin. Patrick should see him and have his eyes properly examined before he leaves for England." It was not long after this that I went with mother to Dr Hayri's surgery. I can see us now walking across a dusty open space in what was known as the '*Maronite quarter*' where many of the families who had come from the Lebanon had settled. The small quaint Maronite church was still standing then.

Dr Hayri turned out to be a small man. He received my mother with the usual courtesy, coming from behind his large desk to greet us as we were ushered into his spacious office. Once more sitting behind his desk he spent some time talking with my mother through the haze of tobacco smoke which he had created. Extinguishing the last of his several cigarettes in a large ash tray, he beckoned me to follow him.

My mother remained seated as we withdrew to the far end of the room where there were a number of large pieces of equipment. Dr Hayri got me to sit in a big armchair that could be articulated up and down as well as backwards and forwards. He placed a contraption which was similar to a pair of binoculars on my face and went through the process of testing me with different lenses through which I had to read letters of the alphabet on an illuminated wall chart. Throughout this procedure he had been seated close to me. Once he had concluded the test procedure, he brought his seat right up to me and started to shine a strong torch light into my eyes. In the semi darkness, I could hear and indeed feel his heavy breathing and the strong smell of the cigarettes he had been smoking, "Do you play with it?"

At first I thought I must have misheard him. His attempt to speak quietly had only made his already gravelly voice less understandable. He could not have expected a reply as he carried on speaking in his deep rough voice, still shining that strong beam into my eyes. Mercifully my mother would not have been able to catch a single word of what he had been saying.

"If you play with it, you will go blind."

I hardly spoke to my mother as we walked home. Intrigued by what Dr Hayri might have been saying to me, I feared she would start to question me. I knew that I was not much good at making up stories, leave alone one that would be plausible enough for my mother. My main preoccupation of course was the threat that now hung over me. I kept thinking of the incident in Gozne that Paul Debbane had told me about. Nicco was right about the risk of blindness! I had just been told the very same thing by Dr Hayri. Something else, Nicco wore spectacles. He also must have been at sometime to an eye specialist. It might even have been Dr Hayri himself! To my dismay, it all added up.

As luck would have it I had other preoccupations just then. My forthcoming trip to England and the new life that my uncle had forecast all served to put Dr Hayri and his forecast of doom and despondency right out of my mind. Well at least for a time!

Chapter 6

The long process of preparation and waiting was over. I knew not whether to be relieved but sad or expectant and wildly happy. Thinking back, these few words do describe my mood swings in the weeks preceding my going. When I awoke that morning in July 1945, the very day of my departure for England I was overcome by something different which submerged all else. A clearer realisation of what I was in for got home to me causing uneasiness and foreboding. From the moment my family had taken the decision to enrol me at Hurstpierpoint College, the countdown to my departure had started. In a way I was relieved, the waiting was over. The die had been cast, I was committed, there could be no turning back. Perhaps more than anything else, it was the inevitability that gripped me.

I had awakened early. My mother was still asleep in the matching wooden framed bed next to mine. I lay on my back gazing intently at the ceiling, trying hard to think of something other than my departure that afternoon. Try as I may, I could not dispel that feeling of inevitability. I realised, it was also fear that welled up from the pit of my stomach. Fear of my journey into the unknown and once more the inevitability that swept through me. So many thoughts that went round and round in my head.

Unchecked, fear can turn to panic. For me, the only response had been to give in to the inevitable. Total resignation and trust, in the hope that I would come out of the ordeal unscathed. I must have also prayed. It was a habit passed on to me by my mother; it helped. I might not then have been able to explain my thoughts and emotions as I have now, but I was experiencing them sure enough. Nor had I consciously sat down and worked out the remedy. No, the solution must have been instinctive, unconscious reaction to let the inevitable happen. In short, resigning myself to my fate and living in hope.

When I speak of my family, I have in mind not only my mother and Uncle William but my grandmother also, the sole occupants by then of the Rickards' house where I had grown up. It was the three of them who in equal measure would be financing my schooling in England. I am glad that I knew even then. My family discussed the matter openly in front of me, they treated me like they would an adult. It was part of the culture I had grown up with and it had become commonplace to me.

That day of my departure, the morning routines of my family remained as they usually were, unchanged. My grandmother, up well before the rest of us would have gone down town to the market. She returned with a porter carrying all her purchases in a large wicker basket strapped on his back. I had sometimes caught sight of her walking briskly in front with her handbag gripped firmly under her arm. My uncle also had his own daily morning ritual. As there was no hot water on tap, he would have boiled himself a kettle for his shave. He used the hot water also to wash in a basin that rested on a marble topped stand in his bedroom.

My mother and I were always the last to rise. She must have been relieved to be alone with her thoughts as she busied herself in the kitchen preparing my boiled egg. It had been difficult for us both to cope with the separation whilst I had been at the high school in Istanbul. Then, I used to return to Mersin for all the end of term holidays and we had adjusted to the situation. Now, with me away in

England, things would be very different being on an entirely bigger scale in terms of time and distance.

That morning several of my mother's friends called, bearing appropriate gifts, in keeping with local practice. They came ostensibly to wish me '*bon voyage*' but in reality it was to see her and give her their support. Those of her friends who spoke Turkish or Arabic offered her the usual comforting words '*Allah kavustursun*' which roughly translates as 'may God bring you both together'. My mother wiping tears from her eyes would respond '*Inshallah*' – God willing!

Many of the visitors would be moved to shed some tears. These interludes of collective grief numb the senses and blur conscious thought, permitting escape from the unhappy realities of the moment. Besides, unlike the comfort some folk get from drinking, crying costs nothing!

The most moving moment for me came as we were finishing our lunch. My uncle, as I have mentioned earlier, was the nearest thing to a father. He had already done a great deal for me especially when it came to my schooling. In his well intentioned way he had been extolling all that would be awaiting me for my new life in England. When moved emotionally, he appeared ill at ease, awkward. He stood up abruptly, and patted me on the back. With great affection, as I moved to stand up, he put his arm around my shoulder. As I faced him, he kissed me on my forehead. It was his usual way of expressing love for those he most cared for, especially my grandmother. He had tears in his eyes as he addressed me. His sentences were clipped, speaking rapidly in an effort to overcome the emotions he felt, "I shall not come to the station. I don't like seeing people off. So, Patrick this is my good bye, now! Have a good trip. You will be seeing your aunt Olga in Egypt, give her my love. Write to us. I will be so interested in what you think of England and your school. We all love you. We will miss you. I know you must be feeling miserable. But, it is for your good. Bye, bye Patrick."

His few words were said with such sincerity that they have remained indelibly etched in my mind for all these years.

This was his way of parting. He had said what he sincerely believed and also hoped it would be of help to me. With that, he turned abruptly and left the room. I heard him walk from his bedroom to the front door of the house and down the outside stairs. Shortly after, the heavy garden door slammed shut, and he was gone. Though I did not realise it then, that was to be the last time I saw my uncle, mother and family until my first trip out from England three summers later.

That afternoon, my journey commenced at Mersin's railway station on the eastern fringe of the town. All trains left the station heading east towards Tarsus and Adana. I must have passed through the place a score of times going and coming to school in Istanbul. Now at the end of the war, it still remained a small, unpretentious place with few facilities. There was of course the ticket office with its single counter and service hatch. The ticket clerk, poorly paid and with few prospects issuing the tickets did his best to deal with passenger queries. The adjoining waiting room, bare but for its two uncomfortable wooden benches. There were the usual malodorous toilet facilities. You would have to be pretty desperate to use them!

There were a number of lofty eucalyptus trees near by. They cast their shade on the small red brick building of the station. I liked to see that scene as I approached from a distance. That solitary terracotta coloured building took on a rustic allure surrounded by those giant pale green eucalyptus. It had been so often my very first and also very last glimpse of Mersin and thankfully it remains one of the only views of Mersin that has not changed over these many years.

As it was a branch line terminus, the locomotive with two or three carriages would almost always be waiting. Passengers and their friends seeing them off would board immediately, they had purchased tickets so that those travelling could find seats of their choice. This gave the added advantage of sparing both passengers and their friends the discomfort of having to wait in the station waiting room.

My mother supervised the handling of my cabin trunk on to the train by the driver of the horse drawn carriage that had brought us there. That done, she sat down next to me. We spoke for the sake of speaking to hold back our thoughts that were by then in disarray, "Good job we came in good time, you have a nice corner seat facing the engine. Let's hope you do not have a long wait in Adana for the express coming up from Bagdad. Tomorrow like now you will be in Ankara. *'Inshallah'.*"

We were both on edge. "Don't worry *Mama*, you will have plenty of time to get off before the train starts to move. We will hear the guard's repeated blasts on his whistle and the usual commotion. There are others seeing passengers off who will also want to alight. Sit a bit longer, please"

So she stayed, repeating what she had already told me, "Mr Sutherland is going to meet you when you get to Ankara. I hope the train is not late. His wife had a baby not so long ago. Their first! It is very kind of them to have you to stay with them." I chipped in,

"When will I get a flight to Cairo?"

This was unpredictable my mother explained, "I have been told that even when you have a ticket, the seat could be taken by some Military VIP as they have priority. As a school boy, I suppose you would be a low priority. Much will depend on circumstances at the time. Anyway, once in Egypt Aunty Olga will look after you until there is a ship to England. Don't worry things will get sorted out."

My mother wiped her eyes once more, soon she would have to get off the train – "You know Patrick, the British Council have been so helpful. All thanks to Mr Tomlin." That was the last thing she said.

People parting, tearful send offs, frantic whistle blowing and even the engine's shrill hoot all added to the cacophony so typical of the start of a long journey on Turkey's railways in those long forgotten days of 'steam'. As for me, I was on my way into the great unknown that stretched out endlessly ahead. We must have embraced. Strange, I cannot remember.

I recall little of the Sutherlands and my stay with them in Ankara. By contrast, it was the mode of my departure, master minded by Mr Sutherland himself, that left an enduring impression. I can still picture him. A tall slim chap who smoked a pipe, bespectacled with thick fair curly hair parted to one side. He wore a tweed suit, a handkerchief casually protruding from its breast pocket. As for his French wife, predictably she was slim and dark. As my mother told me, they did have a baby, a recent arrival. It cried a great deal. They lived in a quiet, leafy residential part of Ankara in a flat.

My mother had taken English classes for adults, sponsored by the British Council since the start of the war. She knew Mr Tomlin who at the time was the head of the British Council in Turkey and through him others who had come to Mersin and been entertained at our home. It was as a consequence of this that she was being given help with my trip to England. I can recall what she told me about Mr Sutherland, "He must be one of the youngest men in the British Council. A rising star. He is a Cambridge man and public school boy though I do not know which one he went to. Not only is he looking after you up in Ankara, he has also assumed the responsibility of getting you to Cairo. How I hope one day you will turn out to be like these men." My mother held both in great esteem!

Due to my low priority on flights to Cairo, my stay with the Sutherlands went on for longer than had been hoped. I took the opportunity to meet up with some of the English boys I had been at the high school with. We went on a cycling trip to '*kavakli dere*' a beauty spot where we had a picnic. The name of the place translates into 'poplar valley' the brand name of Turkey's most popular wines. When I got back that evening Mr Sunderland had some news for me, "We are still not having any luck with your flights Patrick. I have been in touch with the Americans who might be able to sort this out. I have arranged to see the man who deals with their air transport first thing tomorrow morning. I want you to come along with me." With that, he put his arm around me in a gesture of encouragement.

Next day I accompanied him to the American air base. We were shown into an office. Its very starkness made it look big and spacious. The wall facing us was covered with maps. Seated with his back to this wall at a wooden desk was one of the Americans, a large cigar in his mouth. He was talking on the telephone. A haze of bluish cigar smoke hung around him. He half rose and greeted us with a friendly smile, but still managing to smoke and talk on the telephone. We sat down. I gazed idly about me.

The large fan set to run at its maximum was moving the warm cigar scented air but hardly cooling the room. Our host was perspiring visibly. Not surprising as he was a giant of a man. His bright ginger hair was cropped short all the way round the sides, leaving a flat tuft on the top of his head. Clean shaven except for a matching ginger moustache, he was dressed in beige trousers and a matching short sleeve shirt. Sweat had darkened the fabric of his shirt under both arms. From time to time he lay back in his swivel chair, resting his heavy boots on the corner of his desk. He was the very first American officer I had ever met. So different from their evangelist missionary teachers at the American college in Tarsus.

Once off the telephone, it did not take him long to get everything fixed up with Mr Sutherland. I was to be transported on a USAF Dakota transport plane from Ankara to Cairo the very next day! I never knew in what capacity I made the trip. I did not have a ticket, boarding pass nor any other document. Nor can I now recall going through passport control before boarding. For all I know, I might even have been treated as cargo!

That was the first time I had flown. What is more, it was not as if I was flying by some run of the mill passenger airline but by courtesy of the United States Air Force. I have since found out that the Dakota was one of the most famous of WWII military aircraft.

Next morning, there it was sitting on the tarmac like some big bird of prey with outstretched wings that appeared to droop under the effect of the blazing sun. As the USAF jeep that I was in got closer, it took on the form of the giant hulk that it really was. Painted in a dull greyish green camouflage, I wondered where it might have seen its active service. I looked intently in search of some battle scars, before I clambered aboard, but I could not spot any. The heat on the runway was intense and it was not much less once inside the plane's hold. I remember my excitement and anticipation of taking off and climbing up into the azure sky above Ankara.

I was travelling on my own. More to the point, I was breaking new ground not only for myself but for my entire family. None of them had ever been up in an aeroplane. Come to think of it, few people I had ever heard of in those days had travelled by air. It was not just a bit of a spin that I was going on. It was to be a long haul to Cairo, a non stop flight of some four hours. Cairo lies due south of Ankara, once clear of Turkey's Mediterranean coastline, the flight path would be over the sea. What an experience, sitting high up there in the clear sky. There was no sensation of speed. There we were to all intents and purpose motionless, thousands of feet up above land and sea.

All I can remember is being in the near dark bay of the plane. There were no portholes, or very few of them if indeed there were any at all. I was not able to look out of the Dakota and see the landscape below. Had I been able to do so, I'm certain it would have been one of the images I would have carried with me. I was conscious of a continuous tooth chattering vibration from the close proximity of the powerful piston engines in both wings.

The noise from them though continuous appeared to rise and fall. I was on my own most of the time. There were no other passengers. Members of the crew appeared to come and go from time to time, they were speaking between themselves, but due to the noise and vibration, I could not make out what they were saying. The compartment I was in must have had some rudimentary canvas or webbing seats. Failing that, I might well have sat on my cabin trunk, it was becoming something of a travelling companion.

Once airborne, some of the novelty must have worn off. With little to occupy me, I lapsed into a period of home sickness. I sat there on my own and wondered what they would all be doing at home in Mersin. They would have had lunch and retired to their bedrooms for their usual '*siestas*'. Then it would be time for afternoon tea, it had always been my uncle who prompted my mother saying, "Aren't we having tea Dosia? It's gone four o'clock!" A custom handed down to him from my grandfather. Neither of them ever made the tea! After tea, my uncle would go off on his habitual daily walk, usually with his English newspaper which he would stop to read before returning.

These thoughts brought to mind what my mother had told me – "Keep your passport and wallet in the inside pockets of your jacket and don't ever take the jacket off. When you go to bed, slip them both under your pillow and sleep on them". Instinctively I felt in my jacket's inside pockets to be sure my passport and wallet were safely there. The jacket was given to my mother for me by her youngest sister Rosie. It had belonged to her husband Riri. Uncle Tannus who was a tailor turned it inside out and altered it as necessary to fit me. Of course in the process, the button holes instead of being on the left ended up on the right! An unfortunate peculiarity that did not go unnoticed later on.

Dusk was approaching when we landed at some airport near Cairo. I was back in Egypt, the place of my birth, after an absence of just over 10 years.

By the time I was out of the airport and on a bus for Cairo town centre, it was getting dark. Few passengers from other destinations accompanied me from the airport where the Dakota had landed. I was still experiencing the after effects of the powerful vibration and the loud noise from its engines. I gazed out through the side windows of the moving bus at the ever changing street scenes. I found myself in a different world from what I had been used to in Turkey. Most strikingly, all the men were wearing the traditional Arab headdress – '*keffiyes*' or the more urban '*tarbooshes*'. Many were dressed in the robe-like '*galabiyes*'. In Turkey the '*fez*', had been banished in a move to Westernise the country.

The still night air was hot and humid. Egypt like South Eastern Turkey where I had come from grew cotton, they had similar climates. As the bus went through the suburbs approaching the centre of Cairo, I became increasingly aware of an all pervading odour, enhanced by the warm dank atmosphere. I had never experienced the likes of this strange though not entirely unpleasant smell. It was my aunt, later during my stay at Ras-el-Barr, who identified its source as the sweet aroma of ripe mangoes. A fruit that I was yet to taste.

I alighted from the bus at the Carlton Hotel in the heart of Cairo where I had been booked in to stay. The lobby, as it is now called, of the hotel had a polished marble floor. There were several swarthy men in dark coloured uniform jackets, collars and ties, working behind the reception desk. They all wore '*tarbooshes'*. A young boy, also swarthy, in a uniform the jacket of which had a buttoned up collar appeared from behind the reception desk. He carried a small open topped paste can and brush in one hand. In his other hand a bundle of colourful labels. He also wore a '*tarboosh'*. He proceeded to affix the labels to every item of luggage belonging to the newly arrived guests. Applying the glue with practiced dexterity, he stuck the labels rapidly. The colourful label on my trunk bore the words '*Carlton Hotel – Cairo'*. The label's illustration was of a river with sailing boats, palm trees bearing bright yellow dates, and in the distance the pyramids. What else could it be but a scene of Egypt? Rather proud of it, I made sure it survived on my trunk, for many years!

The bedroom I was given turned out to be at the back of the hotel. It had a small narrow balcony just big enough for a chair that I could sit on. When I returned after dinner, I discovered that I could see the film being shown at the open air cinema across the road. The film was in Arabic, a love story which I decided to watch.

Next morning at breakfast, I was to meet by chance one of the senior masters from the high school in Istanbul – none other than Mr Campbell. Sitting at my table, I happened to glance up and caught sight of the tall, bespectacled slightly balding figure in an open neck shirt and casual light weight suit walking between the tables towards me, there was no mistaking him.

Thankfully he did recognise me, "Patrick Grigsby from Mersin, fancy meeting you here." He eventually sat in the chair facing me and asked,

"So what brings you here all on your own?" I told him of my family's plans for my schooling to continue in England. As we talked it emerged that he knew the Sutherlands as there were several boarders at the high school who had been sponsored by the British Council. Hearing of my flight on a USAF Dakota arranged by Mr Sutherland jokingly he said, "The Sutherlands must have been desperate to see the back of you."

On his generous invitation, I went around the Cairo Museum and also the zoo with him. It was like the times at the high school when he was duty master on weekends and took a few of us on excursions. An archaeologist, turned history master one could not hope for a better informed person to guide us and tell us all about the happenings in the dim and distant past. That was the very last time I saw him. We parted at the Carlton Hotel as I stayed my last night in Cairo with an Italian family prior to my train journey the next day. I was bound for Ras-el-Barr, to stay with my aunt who was sharing a summer chalet with her cousin Ceza Nabarawi and daughter, Hoda.

It was through my mother and snatches of family conversations at home in Mersin that I got to hear how my aunt Olga came to be in Egypt. Her marriage to John Catton, early in the war when he was acting British Consul in Mersin had been short lived. My mother put the whole thing in a nutshell as follows: "I don't know what she expected from him. At the end of his working day at the Consulate, I suppose he wanted nothing more than to come home for some peace and quiet. Olga filled the house with her gambling friends, most of them local Syrians with whom her husband would have had nothing in common. When he got home, the last thing he wanted was noise and no where that he could relax in his own home."

They both left Turkey and moved to Egypt only months after their marriage. The war was still raging in Europe. Egypt had always been a popular destination for Italian nationals who settled and prospered there. During the war, British internment camps were set up for them in El Mansura, one for men and another for women. John Catton an ex-Major in the British Army was in some way the architect of their eminent appointments as Commandants. He of the men's camp and my aunt Olga of the woman's camp. Her only child, Peter Mary Lindsey was born there. It had also brought my aunt into contact once more with her Egyptian cousin Ceza Nabarawi.

I went to Cairo's railway station in a '*gharry*' accompanied by my cabin trunk. The journey to Ras-el-Barr was slow with many stops. Though uneventful, it was a novel experience. The countryside in the Nile delta was flat, wet and fertile, its monotony being relieved with clusters of trees amongst them the distinctive palms. Very different I thought from what I had been used to travelling between Mersin and Istanbul. The arid, featureless plain that was central Anatolia contrasted sharply with the majestic rocky outcrops of the Taurus Mountains.

The train line cut across many small tributaries of the Nile. These were divided over and over again for irrigation. Most of the land was cultivated though there was hardly any evidence of mechanisation. Scenes of human activity everywhere. '*Fellahin*', men and their womenfolk tending the vast acreages of vegetables that grew in such abundance. All the men wore the traditional '*galebiye*'. The women working with their heads and part of the face covered.

As we travelled along, there were other distractions, amusing ones! Young boys in their '*galebiyes*' would line up to greet the passing train and its passengers. As if by some pre arranged signal, they all raised the front of their '*galebiyes*' to reveal their genitals. With undisguised glee, they waggled their penises at us with one hand, whilst waving with the other. This display, a new form of entertainment for me, caused some righteous indignation amongst some of the elderly in my compartment.

Travelling North from Cairo, the train I was on went through Benha, Tanta and El Mansura on its way to the coast. My final destination, Ras-el-Barr, where my aunt was spending the summer was only some thirty miles from El Mansura where she was living at the time. Most interestingly, soon after my arrival there, I found out that Ras-el-Barr was a creation that came to life for the summer season only. For the greater part of the year it was a featureless sand flat, part of the Nile Delta that stretched to the waters of the Mediterranean.

The very fabric of Ras-el-Barr was recreated afresh for the start of each summer season. All the dwellings, rented out to visitors for the entire summer season, are fashioned from reeds and rushes that grow in great profusion in the wetlands of the Delta. Floors are wooden except in kitchen and bathroom where they are concrete. It is this rebirth that gave the place its unique *cachet*. Nonetheless, Ras-el-Barr conformed to what is expected of a summer resort in that part of the world – sunshine throughout the long days and mercifully cool nights. Ras-el-Barr had water and fresh air in abundance, the two things that the Egyptian actress Leila Murad sang about in her 1940s film about another of Egypt's coastal resorts.

The reed and rush constructed summer residence my aunt shared with her cousin was spacious. Accommodation comprising several rooms built to form an inner quadrangle open to the sky. On at least one side of this inner yard, there was a large veranda. A common feature in such a hot climate. It served as a shaded cool living space through out the day and in the evenings for meals, entertaining guests, and gazing up at the stars.

It was during my stay that my aunt introduced me to mangoes. These and other fruits could be found in great abundance in the open air market. Fish was on sale within a very short time of being netted in the Mediterranean, large sole were my aunt's preferred variety. I spent much time on the beach and we also went out in sailing boats. The evenings were spent with friends and sometimes at the one and only open air restaurant where the holiday residents gathered to socialise. I may well have been a month or more in Ras-el-Barr waiting for a ship destined for the UK.

At long last, came the dawning of the day. It must have been at breakfast that my aunt gave me the glad tidings. My aunt, as only she could be, not only sounded but actually appeared exuberant with joy, "Patrick your long wait is nearly over. I have just received confirmation that you are booked on a ship sailing from Port Said for England early next week.

You lucky boy, you will have a berth on the *SS Franconia*, one of Cunard's trans-Atlantic liners. Somebody I know travelled to New York on her before the war. They were in raptures about the trip".

I have no recollections of my departure from Ras-el-Barr. Sadder still, no images of Port Said, where I was born. Nor any flash backs of my first glimpse of the *SS Franconia.* My aunt might well have accompanied me to Port Said to see me finally embark on the last leg of my odyssey.

I did not experience quite the delights that my aunt had portrayed when she told me that I had "a berth" on the SS Franconia. For a start, the liner's New York service was brought to an abrupt close when in 1939, she was converted into a 'troop ship'. I was to share her austere facilities with the entire regiment of Lancashire Fusiliers who also boarded in Port Said. My 'berth' turned out to be a hammock. One of several hundreds. They were slung high up to permit free movement on foot beneath them.

I was to find that to get into a hammock required a degree of agility which I could just manage the first time. What I am unable to remember is how I ever succeeded in locating my own hammock among a sea of them strung out in successive decks descending into the bowels of the ship. Only salty sea water was available to wash in. We were issued with special bars of soap that gave a modicum of lather with the salt water. Hardly what my aunt's friend would have termed 'fabulous' had he been accompanying me after his New York cruise, and there was more to come.

The final affront for my aunt's pre-war passenger friend, had he had the misfortune of accompanying me on the *SS Franconia* would have been the indignity of a luncheon or dinner shared with me. I recall the almost endless queue. When I finally got to being served, I held the tray as steadily as I could. Designed specially for use on '*troop ships*', it was a stainless steel pressing. It comprised dished compartments shaped to accommodate a three course meal – soup, main course, pudding. As one can imagine, an over generous helping could easily find its way into an adjoining compartment. Worse still, a sudden lurch by the ship and the pudding's custard would end up with '*meat and two veg*'!

The *SS Franconia* only called at Naples. I recall being anchored in the bay of Naples maybe for two days. No one from the ship was permitted ashore. I have an abiding memory of two things whilst anchored there. Firstly, the bizarre sight of masts sticking up out of the water and below out of sight in the murky waters the ships and other vessels that they belonged to. The war having just ended, clearing up operations had not as yet been put in hand. Secondly, a human tragedy right there in front of me. The sight of many young boys, children, diving to retrieve the scraps of food, mostly bread, thrown out from the ship's galley.

The *SS Franconia* docked in Liverpool on or near the 11th September 1945 to a great welcome for the Lancashire Fusiliers. Bands playing continuously, families on the shore who had come to greet their *'boys'*, Union Jack flags being frantically waved as we disembarked down the gang ways.

Two months or more after saying good bye to my family in Mersin, I had at long last set foot in England. I still had to find my way down to London and from there to my final destination – *Hurstpierpoint College*, which my uncle had spoken to me so much about.

Chapter 7

The sea had never held out any charm or attraction for me. When the *SS Franconia* finally docked in Liverpool, I must have been relieved to disembark. The journey from Port Said had been uneventful except for the short stay in Naples. I had struck up a friendship with three of the soldiers on board returning to their homes in Lancashire – Knocker West, Ginger and William Morgan. Given the disparity in our ages and maturity, it might be more realistic to say that they took me in as adoptive parents would. I have a large hardcover scrapbook that I started soon after the Christmas holiday of 1945. At the start of this, I have a snapshot of Knocker West and his mate Ginger both in their army uniforms. Judging by the swarthy character wearing a '*tarboosh*' peering over their shoulders, it was taken in Egypt. I have another picture souvenir which is inscribed on the back "A friend named William Morgan". It shows him in swimming trunks outside a building with a sign that reads "D Company Store" though there is nothing to say where this location might have been.

Once more it was to be a commonplace episode that remains in my memory and reminds me of my three army friends. I had been given a present of a bicycle one Christmas. One of the stunts I had perfected was to ride it fast and make the rear wheel skid on loose dust lying on the asphalt road surface. I had never cycled on an icy road, yet I refused to take their word that a skid on black ice was more likely. I was to discover the truth soon enough for myself. It was then that I realised the tolerance they had shown towards me. An early object lesson, which served me well and has remained with me. I have from time to time looked at the two photographs in my scrap book and pondered as to what might have become of Knocker, Ginger and William Morgan.

Onboard were some dozen or so youngsters who must have boarded the ship earlier on its return journey to the UK. Sons of British colonial settlers being sent, like myself, by their families to schools in England. They kept very much to themselves, none of them ever spoke with me. I had come to the conclusion that they considered themselves to be a rather superior lot. My upbringing had taught me that their likes are best "left alone to get on with it!"

There was also a group of coloured men, Africans, who kept together. They spent their time gambling with dice non stop. Engaged in this way, they had wads of banknotes in their hands. Early into our journey, a voice came on the public address system, to make an announcement starting with the words "There are sharks on board." There was stunned silence and for a while, you could have head a pin drop on the deck. This changed to a roar of laughter as the voice continued – "I must caution these certain gentlemen that gambling is not permitted on this ship!" more laughter and this time some cheering and clapping of hands by troops and other passengers sunning themselves on deck. The coloured '*gentlemen*' still did a bit of dice throwing, keeping out of the way and without the conspicuous display of banknotes.

Once I was off the *SS Franconia* on Liverpool's terra firma with my cabin trunk my whole purpose was to get on a train for London. Curious about everything I saw around me and through the window of the speeding LMS train, the journey passed rapidly. As if by a miracle, I was met at the station by one of the Hurstpierpoint College masters. I recall how he asked the taxi driver to make a detour "for this young man who has just arrived from Turkey to get a glimpse of some of London's sights!" Still intrigued by all I was seeing, we boarded the Brighton train at Victoria Station, alighting an hour later at the small prim station in Hassocks, so different from my memory of the one I knew so well in Mersin. A touch of homesickness swept through me briefly.

Arriving at the school by taxi, we had turned left off College Lane, we approached the school buildings across the spacious outer quadrangle. The taxi pulled up in front of the main entrance. Car rides had been rare experiences for me. I had never before heard the sound of tyres rolling over loose gravel. A distinctive sound that on later occasions has always reminded me of my arrival at Hurst. Almost the entire school front could be seen from where I had alighted.

The walls were uniformly grey. The front aspect of the school impressed me by its stark unadorned plainness. Grey, I was to discover like the English autumn and winter weather. There was absolutely nothing the least bit welcoming about that first experience. Standing there in front of the main entrance I can still recall my immediate feelings. In a state of despair and dread, my one thought was of my family in Mersin. A voice within me was calling out *"I want to go back home."* Though I had not uttered the words, that was my heart felt plea. I can now best describe the place that I had then gazed at as bold, bare and monastic.

In spite of the set backs and resulting delays in Ankara and at Ras-el-Barr in Egypt, I had arrived at my destination a couple of days before the start of the Christmas term. Not a bad outcome given the post-war travel conditions of the time. Thankfully, even though the school was not open, I was to be put up by one of the masters and his wife in their married quarters. This turned out to be a small flat within the main school buildings. All this had been explained to me by Mr Tregonning, who had met me in London and on arrival at the school had introduced me to Mr and Mrs Mason with whom I would be staying.

Hurstpierpoint College – the first of the Woodard schools. A view of the front of the school taken from what were known at the time as the South Woods. A scene that I found daunting when I first set eyes on it in Sept 1945

Mr Kenneth Mason, I was to find out was the house master of Fleur de Lys and the senior history teacher at the school. I had been enrolled into Red Cross, whose house master, Mr Robert E Bury was a close friend of the Masons but would not arrive until the start of term. I recall being in their sitting room. A lively log fire made the room cosy and welcoming. It was mid September in Sussex, the chill of the early dusk was a sign of the fast approaching winter. We had just finished the corned beef sandwiches and salad prepared by Mrs Mason who had done her best to make me feel at home. We were rounding off the evening with a final leisurely cup of tea.

It was Mr Mason who addressed me, "So you have been at an English boarding school in Istanbul before coming here. How good is your written English?"

Without waiting for an answer, he had got out of his seat and reached for a book off one of the shelves, continuing to address me as he busied himself thumbing through its pages, "I think it would be a good idea for us to find out."

I could not understand why he had used the word 'us' as if inviting me to join in some fun. The last thing that I had expected or was prepared for was to be tested so soon after my arrival. I realised that ready or not, I had no choice in the matter. He went on to explain that he would test me out by dictating a short passage from the book for me to write down. Looking back now and with the benefit of hindsight, he had my best interests in mind and genuinely must have wanted to assess whether I would be able to keep up with the other boys. Noticing my look of apprehension, he even tried to put me at ease saying, "Don't worry, I will not rush you. Tell me if you find it difficult to keep up".

Well, this impromptu "test" as he had called it was to be a revelation for him. He had set forth reading from the book at what he judged to be a steady speed at which the average English boy out of prep school could write. He must have soon realised his error of judgement. After several long pauses and repeats, he gave up, calling a halt. He took the paper that I had been writing on from me.

Glad to be relieved of it, I was able to turn my full attention to him as he studied it. Mr Mason was a stocky man with thinning hair and fair complexion he appeared prone to blushing. Watching him intently I realised that his heightened colour was brought on when he got upset. As he studied the sheet, his colour had turned to almost puce. He was also grimacing, shaking his head and muttering to himself, "Dear, oh dear!!" over and over again as he puffed on his pipe. Finally looking at me he said, "My dear boy, your spelling is simply atrocious. Didn't any one ever bother to correct you?"

"Yes, sir." A conciliatory reply that I had hoped would calm him down, but it did no such thing.

He gave me a look of utter despair. He seemed to smile, though it turned out to be more of a pained grimace. These glances at me were accompanied by a flow of heavy sarcasm. I was to be told much later that Mr Mason was well known for his sarcastic outbursts in class. It was his way, though apparently done without malice.

Mr Mason still looking at me, went on to ask in his rather mocking way, "Yes – no one ever corrected you. Or, yes – they did! Which judging by your singularly pathetic performance, I very much doubt".

I must have just looked blank as I tried to work out the conundrum he had set me. Impatient, he did not wait for an explanation, "Now that you are here, I don't know what we are going to do with you. I shall have to have a word with Mr Bury, before the start of term. I should get yourself off to bed now, it is getting late."

Thus dismissed, I was mercifully spared further humiliation. In such a short time, he had left me with a lasting feeling of utter despair. Getting up, and relieved to get away, I said goodnight. Mrs Mason followed me to the little room where I had slept the previous night. Pausing in the doorway she smiled, asking me if there was any thing I needed. I shook my head mumbling my thanks. She came out with some words of motherly comfort, ending with that most corny of clichés, "Don't worry, you'll be alright."

As my luck would have it, the little room I slept in was just under the Chapel tower. Its big clock chimed on the quarters. I did get off to sleep eventually. The room barely big enough to accommodate the narrow single bed was like an icebox. Not surprising as I could neither see nor, more to the point, feel any means of heating. The metal window frame with its leaded glass was the source of the chilled air that found its way in through its many chinks. I had spread out the spare grey blanket that Mrs Mason had offered me the first night. For a while my imagination raced wildly as I kept pondering on Mr Mason's words, *"I don't know what we are going to do with you."* I mulled them over in my mind. I had only just arrived. Would they really send me back to my family just because I spelt English words phonetically, the way words are spelt in Turkish?

At the time I am speaking of, Hurst which was to be my home from home and catered for a total of some 220 boys of which only 10 were dayboys. Founded by Canon Nathaniel Woodard in 1849, it was a church school with a clergyman head master and also a chaplain. The chapel was sited centrally and connected the main buildings of the school. It featured daily in the school's life. The school buildings were in the form of an 'H', the cross bar being the chapel. The uprights of the 'H' accommodated four of the school's Houses on ground floors and first floors. The House *'day rooms'* were on the ground floor and dormitories on the first floor which included changing rooms, showers, washrooms and toilets.

Cloisters ran through all the buildings at ground and first floors. There was a fifth House in a separate block administered by the headmaster. All the outside walls of the buildings were clad in flint stone, a traditional feature in many of the county's ancient buildings. The school celebrated its centenary with pomp and ceremony in the summer term of 1949. It was also to be the year I left Hurst for good, though with very different feelings from those I have described on my arrival.

At Hurst, the school's day to day administration was attended to by the house masters of each of the five Houses. Each House had a junior and a senior *'day room'* with a boy in charge. Every House had a *'rooker'* – a study which served the house captain and three or four house prefects. Discipline throughout the entire school was entrusted to prefects who reported to their respective house masters. So much for the social order in each House.

At the top of the administrative pecking order were the school prefects and the captain of the school. The most visible of their privileges was the sharing by them of the high table with the house masters at dinner in the big hall. Rewards for achievements on the sports field were kept quite separate. Apart from team captains and vice-captains, honours were periodically bestowed on team members in the form of *'colours'* of which there were several rankings.

As a *'new boy'* in Red Cross House, I was trying to understand and absorb the *'English public school culture'*. There was a great deal of it to digest. How very different from anything that I had come across before in my schooling including the English High School in Istanbul which was supposed to have been based on it. The House system in particular was to have significant implications. It became apparent almost from the start that our free time was to be spent within the confines of our own Houses.

So much for the '*bare bones*' of the House and school structure or skeleton. Far more important was the '*system*' itself the '*modus operandi*' if you like, the way Hurstpierpoint College over the many years since its foundation had come to have its operating '*system*'. It was the way of life I had embarked on as a '*new boy*' at the start of the Christmas term in 1945.

A visit by a boy from another House was to say the least most uncommon. Permission had to be obtained from a prefect of each of the two houses. Though fraternizing between the houses was not actually forbidden it was thus made difficult and in the process discouraged. Each house had its own '*house tie*' worn at all times. This isolation created and encouraged a sense of '*belonging to a house*' or at least an awareness of it. House masters in turn imposed their characters and ways on the boys in their house. Within the school in all sports, there were inter-house matches and competitions which fostered a strong '*house spirit*'. Not surprisingly then that lasting friendships tended to be formed between boys from the same House.

There was an occasion I recall with some amusement. I was sitting in my '*horse box*' like the rest of the Red Cross juniors – it was my very first '*morning prep*', after which we would disperse for lessons to '*the Huts*'. The head of our day room, Peter English called out in an authoritative voice, "Grigsby and Gilmore-Ellis, both of you '*courts*'." I stood up in my '*horse box*' transfixed wondering what I was supposed to do – "Yes, and you Grigsby, '*courts*' and get a move on!".

Still perplexed, I hastened after the boy Gilmore-Ellis and caught up with him down an ill-lit passage way which lead to the outside of the school buildings. We had reached a yard with an open air urinal and a back to back row of toilets – juniors one side, seniors the other. Inadequate as they were, these facilities served the entire school. None of them had doors. Boys waiting their turn, patiently standing outside in the open, chatting. Some of them getting impatient. Some maybe even desperate, I heard one of them plead, "Oh! Come on Jones you constipated ass. Get on with it."

I waited at a discrete distance in the open yard for Gilmore-Ellis to finish peeing at the makeshift urinal; a bare expanse of wall at the base of which was an open gully. The wall was painted black with bitumen to a height of about 4 feet. There was a water pipe at this height running the length of the wall. Water gushed out occasionally through the holes that had been drilled in it to swill the wall, gully and anyone unable to get out of the way in time.

"What do we do now?" I asked as Gilmore-Ellis did up the buttons down the front of his trousers. He looked at me and started to giggle. I persisted –

"Do we have to change into our gym things before we go to the '*courts*'?"

"No, for heaven's sake man!...These are the '*courts*'! ... Come on Grigsby we better hurry back, English will be wondering where the hell we've been."

As we hurried back, I must have thought to myself, odours aside, at least in the Turkish schools the toilets were a touch more private. They had doors! No wonder, put off from using the '*courts*' I suffered with chronic constipation. I became one of Sister Berry's regulars at morning surgery when I used to call in for my dose of Petrolager.

I was settling down well to my strange new life at Hurst. There was still plenty more of the unexpected in store for me; what was termed '*fagging*', a custom unique in English Public Schools and oddly something my uncle had omitted to brief me on. I was to find out for myself. One day I was in the junior day room, there was a loud bang on the wooden partitioning wall with the '*rooker*'. "Grigsby – get around to the '*rooker*' post haste."

In the absence of English, who was head of the junior day room, his responsibilities were automatically assumed by the next most senior of the boys present. Whoever it was had already figured out that I was the most junior present. It therefore befell me to attend to what ever was required by the prefects. I went out into the cloister and round to the first door on the left. I knocked and waited. "Come in." shouted someone from inside the '*rooker*'.

I opened the door and peered in. All I could see right there in front of me was a newspaper spread wide open. Who ever was reading it was hidden out of sight except for his hands which held the paper upright. The legs of the person reading the paper appeared from under it. They were resting casually on an adjoining chair. I could see the soles of his shoes facing me. With out bothering to even look at me, a voice from behind the newspaper spoke, "Take my shoes off and give them a good polishing."

In a flash, I thought to myself "*The arrogance of it! Who does he think he is ordering me about like that?*" I made no reply. I backed out silently through the half open door behind me. Once in the cloister outside, I closed the '*rooker*' door quietly and made off. My departure from the scene was short lived. It wasn't long before I was traced and found myself standing in Mr Bury's study facing him. He was not in the least happy with what those responsible must have told him about my failure to do what was expected of me in the line of '*fagging*'.

"I will not have you disrupt the smooth running of the House. What do you think would happen if every '*new boy*' got it into his head that he would not conform with the accepted practices of this school? I will take no disciplinary action this time. '*Fagging*' might be new to you. You will have to get used to our ways. Just think you might be a prefect yourself one day. Off you go."

'*Fagging*', a well established custom and one of the pillars on which the public school way of life has been founded was open to abuse. So much depended on the character of the prefect, who benefited from such a custom. I am loath in this context to bestow on it a semblance of legitimacy by using the word '*tradition*' to describe it. Viewed another way, if a senior boy is arrogant and a bully by nature, when promoted to prefect he will use his many privileges as instruments of power. Through them, he will express his arrogance and bullying, seemingly with the establishment giving him their full support.

The shameful revelation of my poor written English was never raised by Mr Bury. He might well have been told but had decided to let the issue rest. Over the years, as my house master, I was shown a great deal of patience and consideration by him. I had never been told by my mother that at some stage he had taken on the responsibility of acting as my guardian. This only dawning on me long after I had left Hurstpierpoint College. An omission that has played on my conscience as I was never able to thank him, as I would have liked.

The first day of term, in company with all the other new boys I was put through a screening process, the purpose being to determine the subjects that I was to study and at what level. We new boys were I recall given several options. The one that I can bring to mind, oddly enough was the option of either taking Latin or biology. My uncle's words rang loud, "Patrick, if you have the opportunity, try and get into a class in which they will teach you Latin. It will be a great help with languages."

The upshot for me of the screening process was fairly predictable. I was placed in the lowest set of the beginners' class known by the strange name Shell 'C'. Not a scholar by nature nor inclination, I did however try my best with all the subjects I was taking. As the weeks rolled by, I felt increasingly uneasy with my lack of progress in Latin. I took to sitting at the very back of the class to escape questions or be asked to make some contribution to the lesson. Latin made no sense to me and worst of all, I was taught by Mr Bury.

I took it on myself to make a few enquiries with the boys in my set. This revealed that they had all done Latin in their prep schools! That was good enough for me; I discussed the matter with Mr Bury and was switched to the alternative subject, biology. I had wasted several weeks. It was to be an invaluable object lesson. In future however well meant the advice, I would be the judge of my own circumstances and act accordingly.

Classrooms known officially as 'th*e Huts'* were away from the main school buildings and were used solely for lessons. They were in fact exactly that, wooden huts! Seen from outside, they looked like the long narrow pre-fabricated sheds for battery hens. Inside, they were partitioned into rooms with doors and windows and a corridor that ran their entire length. The assembly was raised off the ground on a brick base. Inside each classroom there were individual desks each with a chair. Facing them a raised desk with a high stool for the master. A blackboard was fixed to the wooden wall behind. They were all identical. Heating was by means of a 4 inch diameter hot water pipe, raised a few inches off the floor that ran through all of '*the Huts'*.

The numbers in classes were small, no more than 10 or so. As these rooms were used by classes in different subjects, the desks were always left empty. All textbooks, exercise books, pens etc belonging to each boy were kept in the House *'day rooms'* where each boy had his *'horse box'* for the purpose. By contrast, the physics, chemistry and biology rooms were appropriately equipped and the walls were covered with charts and visual aids.

The early part of my first school year was packed with novel experiences.

It was of course the immediate post-war period in austerity Britain. Hurst in common with most if not all Public Schools was single sex, boys only. Age old practices like corporal punishment and *'fagging'* flourished where today they would be considered by parents as inappropriate or even barbaric!

Adversity and even deprivation were then espoused as *'character building'*. The cloisters that linked all parts of the school and overlooked the inner and outer quadrangles were protected from the elements by glass. However, they were not heated. There was precious little heating in the dormitories either. When temperatures dropped in winter, we were encouraged to keep ourselves warm by wearing our overcoats at all times throughout the day. The staff, just as vulnerable to the bitter cold did the same.

Every opportunity was taken by headmaster and school chaplain to teach the recognised Christian standards – *'it is better to give than receive'* – *'turn the other cheek'* – *'do unto others etc….'*. Not so long ago, a very old friend, himself a public school boy, quite out of the blue said to me, "How things have changed – if you are honest, if you have manners – if you show consideration, you are now looked upon as a *'loser'*!"

When I first started at Hurst, many masters were still away in the Forces and the school had relied on old masters drawn out of retirement. One such master was Mr L.C Evans who travelled in from his home in Brighton. He taught English. He had a way of making lessons entertaining. I can still picture him; a rotund figure in his blue pinstriped suit complete with a gold watch, its gold chain hanging from his matching waistcoat. His round face, set off by ruddy cheeks radiated his good nature. He had a habit of peering at us over the top of his rimless spectacles. Wisps of white hair persisted around the sides and back of his otherwise bald head.

I now feel ashamed to say that his good nature did not deter us in Shell 'C' from having our fun. After all, boys will be boys! Nearing the end of a lesson, probably through fatigue, he dropped his guard. He had been telling us how things had changed in Brighton compared with happier days he had known before the war. He complained particularly about the lack of service. He had been experiencing difficulty getting his shoes repaired. Seizing this opportune moment, one of the wags raised his hand and asked, "Please sir. How often do you go to the barber?"

Mr Evans, without the least sign of outrage at the impertinence of the question smiled benignly and replied, "Oh! well!.... Mrs Evans attends to that." With a touch of humour pointing to his head, he added "It is hardly worth a visit to the barber!"

"Well done sir." The whole class called out in unison.

"Now, now boys do try and keep your voices down. Noise travels so easily through these adjoining walls and we do not want to disturb the other classes. Do we?"

"Absolutely not sir."

We had come to realise that Mr Evans was absent minded and also hard of hearing. Failings that did nothing but encourage the antics of most, if not all of us in Shell 'C'. It would be no more than the truth to admit that what many of us lacked in brains, we more than made up for in classroom banter. I must also admit that we had got to know the teachers who tolerated our jocularity and how far we could go with our antics!

On another occasion two of the older boys in my set had brought a radio into class. They were both seated at the very back of the form with the sound turned low listening to a county cricket commentary. Low though the volume was, it was still audible to the rest of us.

"Has somebody got a radio on at the back there?" Neither replied, keeping their heads down pretending to be writing. When asked again by Mr Evans, one of them looked up in surprise and said, "A radio sir? Ah, I can hear something now sir – it sounds like that noisy bunch next door." Keeping a straight face, as the rest of us were desperately trying to suppress our mirth, the other wag put his hand up and enquired, "Sir – would you like me to go round and ask them to tone their voices down so that we can get on with our work?" Mr Evans, who very often must have been well aware of the ribbing, chose to ignore that helpful offer!

Our attention sometimes focused on the class *'swot'*. The academically gifted boy, especially if he was honest enough to make it obvious that he preferred books to cricket or rugby. I recall one such boy, Coles.

Just when Mr Evans was about to enter the classroom, two of us heaved Coles up as high as we could. He instinctively gripped a steel tie-bar, part of the internal roof structure at the back of the form. We let go of him and made for our seats. Coles remained hanging helplessly and terrified, his feet dangling 2 feet or so off the classroom floor. By the time Mr Evans made his entry, all of us were seated at our desks with our backs to Coles. We stood up and greeted him with our usual spirited "Good morning sir".

With us all standing, Mr Evans had not immediately noticed Coles hanging from the ceiling. Once we were seated, he became all too obvious. His arms stretched with his unbuttoned jacket pulled up above his shoulders he looked like some giant bat. With a pained look on his face Mr Evans, still standing exclaimed, "What on earth is that boy up to?"

"Which boy, sir?" We asked, feigning surprise.

"There, behind you chaps."

We all turned round in surprise at the sight of Coles by then looking most uncomfortable and desperate to be relieved from the plight he was in.

"Oh! It's Coles sir. He takes every opportunity to draw attention to himself. He is a proper show off. Just ignore him sir."

"Oh come on boys, we can't just leave him there. Get him down." Mr Evans instructed us as he took his seat in readiness to start the lesson.

Mr Evans was not alone, there were other masters who succumbed to our antics. I might have given the impression that they were victims. Not at all! Knowing where I came from, I for one used to be picked on by teachers, "Oh dear, oh dear! It's that infidel Turk again!" I recall other boys also being singled out for ridicule – "Come on you silly ass." or "Don't just stand there like a constipated cow, answer the question." Stunts like the one played on Coles were not considered bullying. Had bullying been deemed to have occurred, the perpetrators would almost certainly have each been given '*six of the best*', the polite term for a good flogging. Capital punishment was meted out by the house masters or they sometimes delegated the task to one of the house prefects. I never heard of one who declined the opportunity!

My start at Hurst also coincided with a number of sweeping changes that I would witness and in some cases be affected by. Teachers who had been in the Army were returning, including Mr Bury. During the war and until my arrival at Hurst, the headmaster had been a layman, Mr Walter S Dingwall who was about to retire. The school governors must have seized the opportunity to return to the school's early tradition of having a clergyman as headmaster by appointing the Reverend R C Howard.

The school which had been kept ticking over by old teachers brought out of retirement had itself lapsed in its standards of discipline. It was, I recall about to receive a resounding shake up from the new headmaster, who was quietly making his presence felt. I have already mentioned some of the hardships of the times. In contrast to them, I recall when I was first at Hurst being served at meals by waitresses. Young things they were, and many of them pretty too, clad in their black uniform dresses. I remember seeing notes being passed to them by boys as they were being served. I thought no more of it.

Rumours about sexual encounters brought the note passing back to mind. As the gossip grew and spread, tales filtered down to reach even the new boys. The tales brought titillation but also trepidation – the innocent judged guilty for merely knowing. The reality that emerged was that boys were sneaking from their dormitories, along the dark deserted cloisters, in the small hours of the night to the girls' sleeping quarters. A long running practice that had been going on whilst the war occupied peoples minds rather than such moral issues.

The purge, when it came, was uncompromising. It eventually led to the wholesale sacking of the female domestic staff. Several boys who had been involved with the girls were removed by their parents, or expelled from the school. Even the captain of the school was not spared. The Reverend R C Howard had made his mark in no uncertain way and remained a formidable patriarchal figure thereafter. He was a big man. I can see him now, in his flowing gown and mortarboard squarely on his head striding down the middle of a cloister. What made his progress so memorable was the way boys parted company to the left and to the right to leave a clear passage ahead of him.

With our waitresses gone, and never again to be replaced, the boys themselves had to serve at meal times. It was no surprise that the burden fell on new boys like myself. It was a chore that disrupted our meals on the days that we had to perform this new and unexpected service.

There was a gallery above the entrance to the big hall and a raised stage at the opposite end. At dinners, the masters took their places at the long refectory table set on the stage. Conceived in this way, the big hall also served as the venue for the school plays and for speech days, both equally well attended by parents. We had our meals at heavy, bare wooden refectory tables, seated on equally utilitarian wooden benches placed either side. Five rows of these ran the length of the big hall to accommodate the five Houses, each having a compliment of some 45 boys. At lunch, it was customary for different masters to join us at the head of one or other of the tables.

For our afternoon tea in the big hall, we were provided with thick slices of white bread. I was mystified as to how the loaves were all exactly the same square oblong shape and size. The loaves were nothing like that where I had come from in Turkey. I found out that this was because in England, an exact amount of dough was placed in identical metal moulds in which it was then baked. It did not register at the time that this might well have been an early rudimentary form of mass production. As I recall, the loaves must have also been ready sliced judging by their uniformity.

At Hurst, the slices were referred to as '*chunks*' by everyone and how very appropriate a description. Matron supervised tea as masters were not present. She dished out the jam or spread, a heaped spoonful being the ration. Most of the other boys with parents or guardians in the UK had well stocked *'tuck boxes'*. I also had one but it was usually empty and being so, did not merit a padlock. Some of my contemporaries in Red Cross taking pity on me, occasionally called out, "Hey! Grigsby send over one of your chunks" – on to which they deposited some of their tuck. A generous act but one that left me with a slice of bread covered with all manner of spreads.

I had found out that a chemist in the village stocked jars of Radiomalt. A malt extract with cod liver oil. What is more, they were not rationed. Thick and syrupy it was difficult to spread but I was not deterred. I kept my jar in my *'tuck box'* down in the chapel crypt where every body else kept theirs. Though it had no padlock, my jar of Radiomalt tempted not a soul.

There was a mid-morning break from lessons. We returned to our Houses for this when we each had a third of a pint bottle of milk and a currant bun. These were delivered to each of our Houses by Charlie Chart, the school porter. As you might guess, with an unfortunate sounding name like '*Chart*', he had long ago acquired his lewd nickname by which he was known around the school. The tray of buns and the bottles of milk were placed on the wide wooden window ledge in the cloister just outside the Red Cross junior day room.

One morning a boy from Chevron made his way over to where I was, "Grigsby, we have a new boy in Chevron. Like you, he comes from abroad. Actually his home is in Egypt. Would you like me to bring him over to meet you?" I must have shown willing. A few minutes later George Hill returned with the new boy he had spoken about. "Grigsby, I would like you to meet Hazzan. He comes from Egypt."

The introduction over, Hill returned to his House at the other end of the cloister. Little did he know that he had set in place a life long friendship. Geoffrey C.Hazzan, late of Victoria College in Alexandria, tells how once we were left on our own I confided in him saying, "I feel I must tell you. *I do not like Jews!* There is no reason though why we should not be good friends."

I cannot recall this claim. Yet, I have to admit that I might very well have said what Geoffrey quotes me as saying. Even though we were in different houses, nothing deterred us from mixing with each other contrary to the school's customs. Furthermore I was most happy to practise my Arabic. In the process I added to both my vocabulary and also acquired a string of jokes and sayings, the likes of which could only have been dreamed up by Egyptians.

It was long after I had left Hurstpierpoint College that I came to realise the purpose of that unique way of life that I had lived through and become part of. With some variations, it was typical at the other public schools, certainly at the 200 or so who belonged to The Headmaster's Conference. The purpose was quite simple. To turn out young men who could be sent off to all four corners of the world to run the Empire. Well trained, trustworthy administrators who would conform with the accepted practices of the British Establishment. Like peas in a pod, they would have come out of the same mould, their *Public School.*

They would have been most likely taught by masters who themselves would have been through exactly the same process. Taught the unquestioning acceptance of authority. Team spirit rather than individualism. Taught to accept and embrace privilege by striving to one day attain it for one's self. Encouraged to bond with their own kind. An order put in place by men who had this vision that would safeguard this country's possessions overseas. It was an incredible system. Though I came to be all too aware of its flaws and eccentricities, I considered myself nevertheless privileged to be a part of it.

It made me also realise that unorthodox and independent minded school leavers turning up in some distant colony with their radical ideas would have created chaos. They would have been a threat to the conventional smooth running of the place. They would have '*rocked the boat*'. The last thing that the administrators of the Empire would have wanted. Things of course have changed since 1945 with the beginnings of the demise of the Empire. I have already touched on some of the consequences of this change.

Immersed as I was in it, I was getting to grips with the public school way of life. It was certainly unique. It took a while to come to terms with. Longer still to get used to it and maybe even accept it, especially as a new boy. I was also, whether I realised it or not, an *'outsider'* though certainly not the only one at Hurst. I had not had the benefit of being acclimatised first at an English preparatory school. I was lucky though in having a house master like Mr Bury. I have since thought about what was going on and convinced myself that he had taken special pains to help me. To guide me through what he once described to me himself, as *'the mine fields of public school life'*.

Looking back now, most of my contemporaries complied with the system. I did make my own protests to begin with. *'Fagging'* and some of the so-called privileges were things that I particularly took issue with. Realising that on my own, I would have been no match for the system to which the vast majority in the school subscribed, I relented. I like to believe that I had instinctively realised that conforming, in favour of a quiet life, was the sensible thing to do.

Not being in his House, I heard little at the time about Humphery-Moore and what had driven him to rebel openly against the school's established authority.

M.C Humphery-Moore was a contemporary of mine but at least a year ahead of me and in the 'A' stream. He was without doubt an intelligent lad but rapidly getting to be branded as *'mutinous'*. Given what I have already said, it could only have been his appearance rather than anything else that I am able to bring to mind. He was not striking physically, very average. His unkempt hair hung over his horn rimmed spectacles. This and a slight stoop made him look furtive as he scurried around – he did have an odd gait. Seemingly always in a hurry, he was taciturn and when he did speak it was with a gruff voice. He had outgrown his trousers and given his scruffy attire, I wondered about his family circumstances and what bearing this might have had on his rebellious behaviour. In his rapid rise to infamy, he had gathered several impressionable boys around him. They were a veritable bunch of malcontents.

On the day of his choosing, Humphery-Moore and his sidekicks broke into the school armoury. With the rifles and live ammunition that they misappropriated, they went into hiding in the South Woods just below the school's outer quadrangle. They were apprehended quickly and without incident. No one seemed to know nor was able to surmise what exactly he might have planned on doing. The headmaster immediately ensured that the entire incident was snuffed out by issuing a notice banning all reference to the matter. I believe that Humphery-Moore was expelled and as far as I can recall, that was the end of the story.

I had forgotten the Humphery-Moore escapade. Then, some years ago when I switched on the television, I happened to tune into a 1960s black & white film entitled *IF* with Malcolm McDowell. *IF* is described as a bizarre drama set in a fictitious though authentic public school. The story moves from intimate scenes of life in a boy's world, through fantasy and farce, to a violent climax of mayhem. A classic film of its type. It would be interesting to those who like me went through public school in the 1940s. But maybe even more gripping for recent school levers. Some might well be relieved at the passing of some of the old practices. Not so long ago when I called at my grandson's public school I spotted a notice on one of the boards. It was headed "A Pupils Rights". I was intrigued. I thought it might be some light hearted leg pull. I started to read it and realised it was in earnest. In fact so earnest that it verged on the hilarious – times have changed, indeed!

IF brought back to me some of the pervasive atmosphere of Hurst that I had experienced. It evoked in me some of the feelings and emotions that I had myself experienced. The latent menace of prefects' authority, *'fagging'*, lack of privacy, outside toilets – euphemistically called *'courts'*, austerity, unappetising food and the uncomfortable strangeness of sex. Malcolm McDowell, in the roll of 'Mick' Travis, the rebel in the film though nothing like Humphery-Moore in appearance conveyed the same mixture of intellect and rebellion. They both shared a quick witted sense of humour. This anecdote, one of many about Humphery-Moore, told to me just recently serves to illustrate the fellow's wit, "One day when Mr A.J.Hill was taking his geography class, he was speaking about wildlife on Dartmoor and the odd variety of birds that were found there. Quick as a flash, and pleased with himself, Humphery-Moore volunteered that they must be *jail-birds*!"

Looking back on Humphery-Moore after his expulsion from Hurst, it would be unwise for me to claim that he could not adapt. For others might well disagree. They might say that it was rather his failure to change the system he was rebelling against that brought about his departure. I have no idea what became of Humphery-Moore following his hasty removal from the school.

I knew of just one boy who indeed could not adapt to the public school way of life at Hurst. He was in the same House as myself. Interestingly he had absolutely nothing in common with Humphery-Moore. An Australian, his name was F.W. Brooks and he was at least two years older than the September 1945 intake, like myself. In spite of his age and academic maturity, he was put into the junior dormitory and day room. An error of judgement maybe! Yet it might have had little or no bearing on his departure. His exit from Hurst was devoid of the slightest bit of drama. He simply walked away into the night.

It was Cherrington, with his Australian connections who put me in the picture, "Brooks will not be returning to Hurst. I had expected him to run away. He had slept in his bed but the following morning it was still unmade even after breakfast. He had disappeared during the night and no one appeared to know anything about it. Speculation was rife not only in Red Cross but throughout the whole school about his overnight disappearance. Well the fact of the matter is, the way of life at Hurst got him down. He could stand it no longer so he took off during the night. He walked all the way to Shoreham where his guardian lived. He was a tough Aussie but he could not take it!"

Given his origins and up bringing he was probably not one for towing the line and falling in with the English public school way of life. I can imagine his reaction to being instructed – "Hey, you! Take your hands out of your pockets".

I remember this as one of the aggravations that new boys had to put up with. One of the many petty rebukes that the over zealous senior, hell bent on exercising his new found authority, was permitted to dish out to his juniors. This was another thing that I came to realise, that Hurst was a microcosm of the world at large. It prepared the young *'new boy'* fledglings for what was to come. Unlike Brooks the Australian, most new boys must have worked out for themselves a way of coping as one has to in the real world outside.

At Christmas, more than at any other time of the year, the chapel became the very hub of life at Hurst. Friends of the school, parents and any '*outsider*' who chose to attend were welcomed to the Sunday services the year round. Leading up to Christmas, even the short daily evening services lasting 15 to 20 minutes took on a festive feel. It was high season also for our chaplain, the Reverend R H Bowyer Yin possessed of a charismatic presence.

The chaplain was very popular, affectionately known as 'The Yin', though probably not by the other masters nor the headmaster. A slim, lithe figure with slick jet black hair, his skin had a dark mellow hue to it. I can never recall seeing him without his dog collar and black cassock. I was in his class for scripture. It was his custom to turn up for his divinity lesson with an armful of Bibles. He proceeded to launch these at us like missiles, a less than reverend manner of distribution. He did make up for this lapse in his own inimitable way. Any boy who fumbled his catch and allowed the Bible to land on the floor was for it – "Butter fingers!... you dropped it, you blithering ass!" This tongue-lashing was followed immediately by 'The Yin' giving the unfortunate boy's ear a sharp and painful tweak or two.

It was once more my friend from Kuala Lumpur, or as he used to say 'KL', who with the benefit of an Australian father and Malay mother had put me in the picture as to the real identity of 'The Yin'. Charles Arthur Cherrington and I, whose families lived abroad, found that we had much in common, and as a consequence we had become good fiends. I recall him asking me, "Have you read any of Leslie Charteris' novels?" I had to admit that I had not. Come to that, I had only read one of Sapper's 'Bulldog Drummond' novels and a bit of Rider Haggard. Others were mostly cowboy adventures by Zane Gray with lurid titles such as *Hash Knife of Canyon Trail.* Charles was eager to pass on to me the entire story about 'The Yin' that he had heard from his parents out in Malaya.

"Our chaplain, 'The Yin' as we now have come to know him, is the true to life embodiment of Simon Templer the criminal hero character created by Leslie Charteris in his novels. In them, Simon Templer is also referred to as 'The Saint' a unique nickname that I am certain will endure. There is an uncanny similarity between 'The Saint' and 'The Yin' in appearance and in character. Something the new headmaster must have come to be aware of with considerable displeasure!"

Thinking about our scripture classes and some of the antics that 'The Yin' got up to, I smiled. Charles' comment about the headmaster's considerable displeasure had tickled me. It was also to prove prophetic.

"Leslie Charteris is the pseudonym adopted by Leslie Charles Bowyer Yin, the real life brother of our chaplain. Born in Singapore, the sons of an English mother and a Chinese father. Both brothers were educated at Cambridge University, our chaplain's brother went to the USA and started his writing career. His parentage explains why 'The Yin' has a distinctly oriental appearance."

I suppose anxious to prove all he had told me, Cherrigton ended saying, "You should read 'The Saint' novels, they are really gripping!" Out of sheer curiosity, I did read one or two of 'The Saint' books. Sure enough, 'The Saint' was the very embodiment of our chaplain minus his dog collar and cassock who leapt out of the pages of the books. After that first term, Charles and I were destined to spend several holidays together in the South of England, arranged for us by Mr Bury.

With the benefit of hindsight, Charles' great interest in The Yin and the author Leslie Charteris' famous character that appears in his books known as 'The Saint', is not surprising given Charles' own mixed origins. I had come to realise that my friend Charles might well have passed himself off as a lookalike for either with his unmistakable Malaysian colouring and the features he must have inherited from his mother. Like most of the Asiastic population from the Pacific countries, he had that slim, lithe build which got him into the school swimming team. A natural swimmer, he was also an accomplished diver.

As the end of our first term approached, my thoughts inevitably turned to Christmas. Apart from being my first one in England, it was also the very first one spent away from my family.

During the years I was at the English High School in Istanbul, I had always returned home for the school holidays. Living as we were in a predominantly Muslim country, there was no sign outside our home of Christmas. However, due to the strong influence of the Catholic and Orthodox churches in the town, it was Lent and Easter that were celebrated rather than Christmas. My family were the exception. I remember, we always had a Christmas tree and my mother saw to its decoration. She also made the traditional Christmas plum pudding. For lunch on Christmas day there was a turkey, stuffed with rice, and also chestnut stuffing. But, there were never any Christmas cards, no decorative wrapping paper nor crackers to pull. No holly or mistletoe.

Pondering the progress I had made that first term at Hurst, my thoughts went back to my short stay in Mr Mason's flat. A good sign, as I had become blasé about that written English test Mr Mason put me through. Quite indifferent. I had dropped Latin for biology, a subject that I enjoyed and was doing well at. I felt settled in Red Cross House thanks to Mr Bury. I was selected to play rugby in the School Colts team as a wing forward. I had also been enrolled into the school OTC – Officers Training Corp as it was known – and been issued with a uniform. Even more to the point, I had been having target practice at the '*butts'* as I came to know the shooting range.

One of Hurst's traditions was a mystical ritual known as '*The Boar's Head Feast*' celebrated by the school choir in the big hall. With the lights dimmed, they could be heard chanting as they came up the stone steps from the crypt. The first candle-lit glimpse of them as they entered the big hall, I felt was quite inspirational. They processed around the big hall in their full-length white cassocks chanting as they went. The focal point of the procession was a real boar's head on a large platter carried by two members of the choir at shoulder height. The boar's head was made all the more spectacular by flames that flickered about it.

Then there was the carol service. Held on the very last day of term, it was so well attended that the chapel was full to overflowing. The overflow being accommodated under cover but outside the chapel. The school prided itself on its choir. Mr Tregonning, who had met me off the Liverpool train in London, was music master and organist. It was his hard work and devotion that was responsible for their excellence. This closing service was made the more memorable, as many of the traditional carols were sung in Latin. At the end of that first term, I was showing due respect and adherence to tradition. Things that my family, but my uncle in particular would have been overjoyed to know.

The Christmas holiday approaching, I was preoccupied as to how I would be received by these strangers, the Osmonds in Leatherhead and the Hergas in London. The former family connection went back to my grandfather's early days following his arrival in Mersin in 1890. The latter was more recent, it had been my mother who around 1910 when at Marlborough college in Buxton had become a life long friend of Gwen, the Mrs Herga with whom I would be staying first. I could not help but wonder how I would fit in with these English families. These were to be testing occasions for me.

I have been often accused, as if it were a crime, of living in the past. I can see no reason to make any apologies for this. It has occurred to me though, that this way I have, must go right back to the testing times I have just been describing. For surely it is when one is faced with some form of foreboding that one's mind finds relief in casting back to the comforts of the familiar. So it was then that memories of Christmas in my beloved Mersin came flowing back to me.

Contrary to what might be expected, those Christmas memories were both transient and I have to say mundane. They were, however, what

I had grown up to be familiar with; they made me feel at home. I can bring to mind the dark ill lit and at that time of the night deserted cobbled street where my mother alighted with me from the horse drawn carriage. We were in the main street outside the Catholic church. The strong welcoming smell of *'bahour'* incense once we entered. Everyone knew everyone else. The respectful quiet, almost inaudible words of greeting, hand shakes and many embraces. Later on, Juliette Saad's familiar voice singing '*Minuit Chretien*', '*Ave Maria*', adding a celestial dimension to the deeply devout aura of the church and its people.

The next morning, Christmas day, at breakfast my mother, grandmother, uncle and I exchanged hugs and kisses, wishing one another 'Merry Christmas'. In the town, it was no different from any other day. If it happened to be a week day, everyone was at work as usual. We did always have a turkey, stuffed and roasted, and to follow, one of my mother's Christmas puddings for lunch. Sometimes, when the family had guests, we would also have wine though if the guests were locals the chances are they would have preferred a glass of *'raki'*, the local *'fire water'* or '*lion's milk*' as some of the habitues would say.

My mother always managed to find some one who for a few Liras would chop down a pine tree. This would arrive at the house under cover of darkness on a horse drawn cart hidden under some makeshift camouflage, for to cut down trees growing in the wild was '*kachak*', illicit and illegal. An offence subject to a serious penalty, if caught. A calculated venture my mother took each year to celebrate my birthday on the 27th December. It had become a tradition but it also gave my mother the opportunity of inviting her friends to a buffet party of her own.

Running the risk of falling foul of the Forestry Commission, the *kachakci*' always cut down a big pine believing I suppose that he might as well '*hang for a lion as for a lamb*'. A way was worked out to secure the tree in a large container filled with earth which took the *kachakci*' and a helper to haul it up the outside staircase and into the hall. So it was that the handsome pine dominated the hall for a few days before Christmas exuding a strong aromatic scent of pine resin.

The waves of the Mediterranean lapped the shore only a few metres from the front of our house. Even in December the climate was mild, semi-tropical, yet no one ever ventured into the water as I had heard they did in the Serpentine, breaking the ice to do so.

These were some of the thoughts and so very many more that went through my head making me realise *Turkey and my people, just then were so far away.*

Chapter 8

"I will meet you under the clock at Victoria station."

I wonder if it still is where people meet. It now sounds to me rather old hat, even amusing in a nostalgic sort of way. It is in fact, what Mrs Herga wrote to me in her letter. Strangely the only bit of her letter that I can remember word for word. She had written inviting me to Rosecroft for the first half of my Christmas holiday and I have no doubt that she included a few words by way of introduction. No telephoning in those days. People had to express themselves by writing even in unfamiliar, tricky circumstances. To endorse her welcome, she ended her hand written letter with the words 'Aunty Gwen'.

I had also received an invitation from my mother's other friend who lived near Leatherhead. In her invitation, Mrs Osmond had asked me to spend the second half of my school holiday with her. I never knew whether these holiday arrangements were brilliantly planned by my mother, or whether it was providence that looked kindly on me that first Christmas.

Returning to my newly acquired 'Aunty'. My mother had met Gwen Francis, as she was then known, at Marlborough College, a girls' private school in the spa town of Buxton. As my mother would have been about 17 years old, the school must have also been some sort of finishing school. Gwen, my mother told me, was older than her and was at the school in some working capacity as some sort of '*assistant*'. They became life long friends. The Francis family were from

Merthyr Tydfil, an industrial town in South Wales. Other than this, I had no idea what the lady that I was to meet at Victoria station would be like.

Mrs Herga, whom from the very start I was to know as Aunty Gwen turned out to be a smartly dressed, animated female who immediately put her arms around me in a warm greeting, "I could tell you were Theo's boy as soon as I caught sight of you. Let me give you a kiss. Now we must get to the underground before the rush. Come along, this way. We can talk once we are on the train. I hope you had a good trip up from Sussex."

A most outgoing, sociable woman, she liked to talk and encouraged me to do the same in reply to questions she kept putting to me. She spoke fast with pauses as if to get her breath back. She smoked, always using a cigarette holder. Once on the underground train, smiling she said to me, "It is quite a long trip to South Woodford, I usually have a little snooze, you won't mind will you Pat? We will have plenty of time to chat when we get to Rosecroft and don't worry, I will wake in time." With that she promptly dozed off leaving me to my thoughts.

I had a brown suitcase made from what was known as a '*composite*' material. Unlike one made from leather, it had the practical merit of being light. It was big enough to hold the few things that I had brought away from Hurst for the holiday, including one of the two piece suits that my mother's uncle Tannus had altered to fit me. I was wearing the light brown one. My mother had reminded me to keep the dark blue for best as it was more suitable should I be taken out during Christmas. One or two of the boys at school had poked fun at the fact that the button holes and buttons were on the wrong side. Teased for being different did not particularly upset me.

It was my very first experience of travelling on the London Underground. So very different from the '*Tunel*' in Istanbul but then, the London Underground was not the oldest of tunnels in the world. The last time I had been in London was when Mr Tregonning had met me off the Liverpool train. That was less than three months ago and so much had happened since. The compartment we were in was almost empty. As the train sped along rocking rhythmically from side to side, I could see our reflections in the glass windows facing us. My gaze settled on Aunty Gwen's small, rounded shape sitting next to me. In her snooze, she had tipped over slightly so that she was supported by the glass partitioning by the sliding doors. Though closed, I knew she had pale blue eyes and her hair was tinted a smoky blue colour, she was always perfectly groomed with a stylish pair of spectacles that sat on an ever so slightly hooked nose. How different from my mother. Another thing, everyone called my mother Dosia yet for some reason she had referred to her several times as Theo.

That day, as we made our way to Rosecroft, the home in South Woodford of Dr and Mrs E.E.Herga, though I did not realise it, I was being transported into a completely different way of life from the one I had been accustomed to with my family in Mersin. Nor would I have guessed that with the demise of Aunty Gwen and her generation, that very way of life would itself be coming to an end in England. What I am referring to is the English middle class. It was during that Christmas holiday that I was to get my first glimpse and insight into that fast disappearing way of life. Albeit seen then through the eyes of a school boy. This first holiday serves to contrast family customs and attitudes in England with those I had been accustomed to in my home in Turkey, the telling of which I hope will be all the better with the benefit of my maturity.

At the time my sole purpose was to enjoy the change from the rigours of boarding school. I was keen to get to know my hosts, their families and friends. I would show my gratitude by being attentive. If the opportunity arose to repay their kindness, I was ready to do so. I was also able to converse with my elders yet show deference. I was fortunate to have been brought up in a culture that placed great store on respect, especially for elders. I owe a great deal to my family and teachers in Turkey for this.

* * *

On arrival at Rosecroft that afternoon, the very first person I was to meet was Kathleen, the live-in maid to whom I was introduced by Aunty Gwen in the kitchen. A good deal older than myself, she might have been in her mid twenties, a small, seemingly timid female she was dressed in some sort of uniform and head dress. Nobody else was about in the house at that time of the day.

"Now then Kathleen. This is Patrick the son of a dear friend of mine, we met when she came to my school in Buxton. She now lives in Turkey. Patrick has just started at boarding school near Brighton and is spending Christmas with us."

I cannot recall whether I shook hands with Kathleen. I doubt it, as in those days in England, as I seem to recall, shaking hands was not done very often. Kathleen had smiled back at me when we were introduced but had not spoken. Aunty Gwen having made the necessary introduction, turned towards me continuing to talk in that spirited manner that I was getting used to, "I feel Kathleen should address you as Master Patrick. You are still far too young to be called Mister. I think that would be the right thing …don't you?"

As she finished speaking, Aunty Gwen continuing to look attentively at both Katleen and myself tilted her head to one side for a reply. My guiding instinct kept me silent. Her words though seemingly addressed to me, were in fact instructions which Kathleen recognised as such. Having heard her mistress lay down the style in which she was to address me, she replied, "Very well, madam." A response that I was to hear often.

My introduction to the maid in the kitchen was a first time experience for me. To my knowledge nothing like that had ever taken place in my family circle, nor would it have been remotely likely any where in Turkey. Most significantly for me, and what stuck in my mind, was the manner in which it was played out. It was to be a fore taste of many other occasions on which Aunty Gwen, went about her business and those she had to deal with. She was a stickler for etiquette and always made sure that whatever needed to be done was done as convention demanded. A dictum that she herself followed and one that called for fair-mindedness and diplomacy.

I was told that it was customary for overnight guests to hand the maid of the household a tip at an opportune moment before their departure. Aunty Gwen I remember briefed me on this the night before I left Rosecroft, "Now then Pat, I have some thing to tell you. I'm sure that Kathleen has looked after you. I know that when I have been up in town, she has served you afternoon teas. Here is what I believe would be an appropriate amount for you to give Kathleen thanking her at the same time before you leave tomorrow. Even though you are still a school boy, it is a good thing to get used to these customs."

Kathleen had been in service at the Hergas since leaving school. During that time, she had got to know her mistress and her ways. Their relationship, though reserved and formal, was warm and friendly. Each behaving towards the other with consideration but within a framework that had evolved through usage over the years. I was to hear many years later that Kathleen, though unfortunate in not having been able to continue her schooling, was self educated and she had aspired to good taste in music. In her later years classical music and ballet became her great passion. She never married and after leaving the Hergas moved to Chelmsford where she still lives, now well into her 80s.

I mentioned earlier how my grandmother used to get up very early and go down to the big market in Mersin to buy all the vegetables, fruit, bread, meat, fish and so forth. She would return with a '*hamal*' in tow, all her purchases in a large basket slung on his back. Aunty Gwen went about this chore in a very different way. Some days, immediately after breakfast, she would make several telephone calls. She was in the habit of shopping this way from the comfort of her sitting room. I recall an instance when I overheard fragments of her conversation with Mr Whiting, the fishmonger on George Lane:

"What have you got today Mr Whiting? I'm having some guests and I want something special for them." Mr Whiting, whose voice on the other end of the line I could not hear must have come up trumps judging by Aunty Gwen's instructions, "That sounds nice, you did say North Sea halibut didn't you. Very well, send me two and a quarter pounds." Delivery would be made in due course by one of Mr Whiting's delivery boys on his bike. She had similar arrangements with the butcher, grocer and wine merchant – both she and the Doctor enjoyed their regular daily pre dinner tipple – two or three '*gin and its*' as Aunty Gwen used to call them. None of my family, nor any of the other families they mixed with in Mersin had the habit of pre-dinner '*aperitif*' in their homes. Even the odd few who had European affiliations or the benefit of education in French schools did not have this drinks culture.

She used to say to me, *"I like a little flutter"* – I had no idea what she was talking about the first time she came out with it. "I'm just going to ring my bookie, I've been given a tip by some one who knows what she is talking about for the three o'clock at Epsom." I must have looked quite vacant standing there because she went on to say – "Horse racing, Pat. It is the sport of Kings."

Once more, all this made me feel separated from my past by an eternity. She had become my mentor in every sense of the word – "You need to know these things Pat" she used to say and then go on to tell me. I remember her reeling off the names of what she told me were '*the Classics in the horse racing calendar*'.

It wasn't until the early evening after finishing his patients' rounds that Dr Herga was heard parking his black Daimler saloon and entering the house that we met and I was introduced to him. Strangely I have no recollection of this introduction. I always addressed him as 'Doctor', he would occasionally call me 'Pat me boy' but more usually just Pat. He was a tall man always dressed in a dark pinstriped three piece suit and a matching rather sober tie.

Every evening when he got home he used to spend some time before dinner in his usual arm chair by the side of the fire in the sitting room engrossed in what he described as '*writing up my books*'. Sitting the way he did, balancing the ledger he was writing in on one knee, he never looked comfortable. In the process, his suit got crumpled and as he smoked incessantly, it was covered with cigarette ash. "Oh Ernest darling look at the state you've got yourself into!" Aunty Gwen would say in anguish as she reappeared from the kitchen looking her usual radiant self, glass in hand ready for a refill, "Another one, just before dinner?" she would enquire. Impatient, she never bothered to wait for a reply, she reached for his empty glass. He was never known to decline another of his wife's generous '*gin and its*'. On occasions he would get up and serve himself whilst his wife safely out of sight could be heard talking to Kathleen. Glancing at me, he would wink, putting his finger to his mouth and say, "Not a word to Gwendolyn, hush, hush!" Any refills he thus managed were additional to his wife's customary two or three '*usuals*'.

Aunty Gwen had a brother and sister. Her brother Howard Francis was a school master in Wales, married to Blanche. Over the years, I met them just the one time. Gladys her younger sister, was a most glamorous female. Her husband was also a medical man. Dr McElroy was a good looking, suave and rather reserved sort of individual. I cannot remember ever speaking with him. He was a striking contrast to the easy going informal Australian, Dr Herga. Much to his wife's dismay, it was most evident that he had made absolutely no effort to take on the guise of London culture and sophistication. She herself had progressed up the English middle class ladder on the strength of being married to a *'professional'* medical man, leaving her modest Welsh roots behind in Merthyr Tydfil. Earlier in her life, she had been captain of the ladies team at the local golf club and an active supporter of the local Conservative party. In her later years, she had switched her competitive talents to bridge which she played regularly in London several times a week.

Even as a young school boy brought up in a very different environment, on later stays at the Herga's I became conscious that there were sweeping socio/political changes taking place in Britain. I got to know that Dr Herga like his brother-in-law, Dr McElroy had opted to stay out of Atlee's Labour Government's newly formed National Health Service. He kept his panel of private patients who paid for his services including medication prepared by Miss Dewhurst, his pharmacist. She came daily on her bike. There was a side entrance to Rosecroft. This permitted access to the kitchen and down a flight of stone steps to the cellars, one of which was the laboratory where Miss Dewhurst prepared the different medications. Dr Herga had his morning surgery at the house. When I was troubled with constipation, he examined me once in his consultancy room. It was at the back of Rosecroft, an identical room to the large sitting room. Both rooms looked out onto the garden. It was big and secluded. As all my stays were during the winter, I never ventured into the garden. A gardener called John used to come and tend it.

The Hergas had a son and daughter. Tony at the time of my first stay at Rosecroft was still in the Army. He was doted on by his mother, the apple of her eye. The day after my arrival, she took me down into the cellars and showed me a Raleigh bicycle that was leaning up against the wall, "I got John to give it a good cleaning last week in readiness for you. It's Tony's bike, though I don't suppose after all these years he will want to ride it again. He is still with his unit out in the far East. He's a Captain you know, with the 9th Jat an Anglo-Indian regiment. You can ride it any time you want Pat."

I did meet Cicely later when she came down from St Andrew's where she was at University. She was slim and dark and I seemed to think she resembled her mother. If Tony was the apple of his mother's eye, then Cicely was her father's favourite. They had both been to public schools, Cicely to St Felix near Southwold and Tony to The Leys in Cambridge. The Doctor had gone to the trouble to explain to me that he had chosen The Leys as it had a reputation of preparing boys for a business career, "Cis is the scholar. Tony is not, and I felt it would be best for him to be groomed for a business career."

True to my mother's prediction, I did have occasion to wear my dark suit several times. It was evident that the Hergas were habitués of London's theatre land. I accompanied them to two shows – *The Winslow Boy*, and the other a drama, the title of which escapes me. It was billed as a hitherto taboo subject involving black on white violence and sex. I seem to recall one of them was at the Savoy. Funnily enough, I had heard of the Savoy and the Ritz back in Mersin, bywords of luxury. I also saw a pantomime. *Cinderella*, my very first experience of a typical English *'panto'*. In it the part of Prince Charming, surprisingly was played by a female. An attractive one clad in tights and shorts designed to show off her legs to advantage. Characters in *Cinderella* kept up a dialogue, often frenetic, with the children – an early form of *'audience participation'* I was told.

Both Dr and Mrs Herga were prominent socialites within their circle. He had links with The London Hospital in Whitechapel, and with other medics socially and professionally. He partnered his wife in bridge in spite of having to put up with her fault-finding when they lost. She was conventional and a stickler for etiquette, things he had not much time for. When she chided him, he would adopt an injured demeanour and as if to gain some sympathy he would say, "Pat, take my advice. Never get married and teach your children to do the same."

One of these people who never did anything by halves, she did excel at bridge. She travelled up to '*town*' several times a week where she was a member of Crockfords, described to me as a '*gambling den*'. It was patronised by top British bridge aficionados, professionals like Harrison Gray and Terrence Reece, whose autographs she got for me in my autograph album. Her best haul was Bob Hope's on a Crockford's letter head which I still prize.

Woodford had the distinction of being Winston Churchill's constituency. The Hergas were members of the Conservative Association, so were many of the other families they mixed with. As a consequence, Rosecroft was an '*open house*' to their friends during the festive season. Down from St Andrews, their daughter Cicely used to entertain young friends of both sexes which made my stay all the more enjoyable.

Cicely had prepared some party games to entertain their guests after dinner. One of these was a quiz. Illustrations cut out of newspapers were assembled on a board to be identified. One was a picture of the newly elected Labour Prime Minister, Clement Atlee. He bore a more than passing resemblance to Dr Herga. The entire Herga family, their relatives and friends were naturally all diehard Conservatives. One of the guests who might have had a '*tipple*' too many, cried out, "Why, if it isn't Ernest himself!" The irony of this resemblance led to some amusement and light hearted banter. Ernest with his '*Aussi*' manner put on his usual nonplussed look. Not so Gwen! She was not at all amused.

In the Herga household, even when there were no guests, dinner was always formal. It was a family occasion and the one time of the day when everyone would get together. I used to look forward to these dinners. Primarily to hear more of the Doctor's stories about Australia and what he called *'the outback'* and the Aboriginals. Some of his humorous, if indelicate yarns about the *'Abos'* might well have caused offence even then. Thankfully, the term *'politically correct'* had not been coined, nor had it become part of our culture.

Like my uncle he had been in the mud and shit of Flanders, though unlike my uncle he was commissioned to the rank of Lt.Colonel in the AMC. He spoke often about his batman, Bert whom he described as "*a cockney sparrow*" – a little chap, but so resourceful. "I tell you, Pat he could get hold of anything that I needed. My horse sadly became a casualty of the war. She got killed. A stray shell got her. Bert found me a replacement by the next day. It wouldn't have surprised me if he had snaffled it from behind the Jerry lines."

There was one dinner party I remember well. It reinforced my notion of what it was to be *'outsider'*. Conversation had got around to how I came to be staying with the Hergas and of course my own family origins. One of the guests, a charming lady, had taken particular interest in the matter, enquired of me, "So why did your family send you all this way to England for your schooling?"

I explained how I had been to a Turkish primary school in the town of Mersin then when old enough, I was sent as a boarder to the English High School in Istanbul.

This led her to remark, "That must be why you speak such good English!"

She may well have intended a compliment. Yet, her remark made me feel demeaned – "I always spoke English with my family at home." I countered, almost by way of retaliation.

Comprehension lit up her kind face. She beamed, "So your parents are not Turkish!"

At this point, one of the other guests who had been listening chipped in, "But Gwen had told us that your mother was born in Turkey!"

It was occasions like this that made me aware that I would always be perceived as different, an '*outsider*'. The awareness of this led me to the following way of reasoning – *I am not in the least ashamed of my family's mixed origins. The sooner I reveal them the better. This will dispel ambiguity. The ambiguity that led to the misunderstandings that I had experienced.*

It was, I recall my mother and to a lesser extent my uncle who as I grew up impressed on me that I was '*British by birth*'. I will explain the significance of this. Born though I was to British parents in Port Said, I have an Egyptian birth certificate. Most importantly however, my birth was registered at the British Consulate who issued my parents with my British birth certificate. This carries the same authority as any birth certificate issued in the United Kingdom. I am reminded of how my mother taught me to describe my British status as she and her two sisters and brother must have done in their time, "You have to tell them that you are British *by birth*, don't forget. It is very important – *by birth*!"

I recall a family who came to Mersin during the War. The father had been posted to Turkey, where his wife and their sons joined him. Even though they had British passports, they were treated as second class citizens by colleagues from Britain. As soon as the war ended, they left to '*start a new life in Rhodesia*' as they put it. I now believe that people like that who have not been able to come to terms with their origins have exposed themselves to untold grief for not doing so.

It had been a magical time for me at Rosecroft that first Christmas. I was fortunate in being destined to spend the subsequent ones there whilst I was at Hurst. It proved to be very different from the less eventful Christmas times in Mersin. The Herga family and their friends had so much more activity to keep them occupied socially than my own family and their friends. Living as they did in London, public entertainment of every imaginable type was there for the taking.

There was one thing though that I did miss. That was accompanying my mother to the big Catholic church to attend the Mass '*du Minuit Chretien*', as we always did. Though I could not follow the ritual, my senses were moved especially by the strong scent of the frankincense and the '*Ave Maria*' that was always sung. Then after the service everyone stayed behind to have a few words with the old priest, '*Pere Paul*' who had served the Catholic community for so long, before dispersing.

I have no recollection of how I got from South Woodford to Mrs Osmond's home, near Leatherhead where I spent the rest of my first school Christmas vacation in England. Known to my mother as Tinta, she had been her childhood friend in Turkey all those years ago. Her father, Colonel Massey served as British Consul in the South Eastern region of Turkey.

The lady I met for the very first time that Christmas, Mrs Osmond, was what I came to recognise thereafter as typical of the upper crust English '*county set*'. She was tall and slim, always dressed in a tweed suit and cashmere twin set with the usual string of pearls. She had fine features, her face was freckled and she wore spectacles. She had a Pekinese dog. A vicious little beast that tried to bite me.

The Glade where she lived with her husband, Colonel Osmond stood in its own grounds right out in the Surrey countryside in a locality known as Tyrrells Wood. It must have been quite some distance from the town of Leatherhead to which we never went. I recall taking walks on my own down the deserted country road that went past the house. Everything was covered with snow and it was freezing cold. Walking back up the long tree lined drive there was a free standing garage that housed their motor car. I never saw it as Colonel Osmond must have driven off early each morning. He worked at the War Office in London. The house itself was a large rambling place with a vast red-tiled roof. There were several chimney stacks. I could see plumes of smoke coming out of a couple of them which spurred me on to get back to the warmth in side.

I have few recollections of the surroundings nor of how I passed the time. With little to do, I had tried to engage with the Pekinese but it would not respond in a reasonable manner. As a last resort, I embarked on reading *Gone with the Wind* which I managed to finish before returning to Hurst. Not a mean achievement considering my more usual literary tastes.

The next time I stayed with Mrs Osmond was when she had moved to a very much smaller property in the town of Steyning. I expect The Glade must have become much too big for them after their two children had grown up. It was also so remote. Their new house was a picturesque cottage in Steyning. It was painted white and had a thatched roof. A long established creeper spread itself over much of the front wall. I deduced that it must have been a vine as the property was called Vine Cottage. Nanny was still her companion.

Chapter 9

That first Christmas of 1945 in England became the benchmark for all my future ones. The build up to this religious observance day, when I was a new boy at Hurst and when I returned to England in 1950 for my apprenticeship in Lincoln was different from what it has now become. I remember those times as less glitzy with less emphasis on the '*must have*' culture. Neither was there then the compulsive urge each year to go '*one better*' than the previous. I can still conjure up the feeling of wonder and anticipation with which that Christmas had approached. It was the mood of '*collective expectation*' that seemed to sweep the whole of the country, young and old alike, that got home to me on the run up to Christmas in 1945. As a schoolboy at the time it seemed interminable. Even when it was over and I returned to Hurst, I felt the festive spirit had lasted the full two or so weeks of the school holiday. It struck me then that many of the Christmas traditions were uniquely English

One of my abiding memories of the last day of term had been RT Ottley, a boy in Star House. A big rumbustious lock-forward who had just been awarded his Colts XV rugby colours. There he was revelling in the occasion. The extra long black and white Colts XV scarf was wrapped several times around his neck yet both its ends touched the ground. His mother must have burned the midnight oil to get such a long scarf knitted in time. Long scarves knitted to order with school colours were all the rage. Just before being collected by his parents, I spotted the tall figure of Ottley wandering around saying goodbye to his chums and masters. By then he had also acquired a trilby to match the loud check tweed jacket he was wearing for the occasion. Greeting a master he would ceremoniously doff his trilby leaving them with little will to tell him off for not wearing his school cap.

With the benefit of hindsight, two things have occurred to me about that Christmas. For Britain at large it was an opportunity to cast off the burden of a war that had gone on for almost six long years. There were still many shortages and it remained a time of austerity. All foodstuffs were either rationed or could only be acquired '*on points*'. Either way, mothers would have endeavoured to save the family's meagre rations to put on a '*good spread*' for the whole family to enjoy over the festive days of Yuletide. For me personally, it was the never before experienced novelty of the occasion that has endured.

Growing up with my family in Turkey, I was aware of their two religious feasts or '*bayrams*'. 'Eid' in Arabic. The dates varied as each year they were 10 to 11 days earlier. At the end of Ramadan, the month of fasting, there was the three day long '*Ramadan bayrami*' also known as '*Seker bayrami*' which translates into the '*Bayram of sweets*' due to the custom of sweets being offered around. The town's many Christians visited their Muslim friends to wish them '*Bayraminiz mutlu olsun*' – may your Bayram be a happy one. The other religious celebration was a four day long festival when sacrificial sheep were killed and the meat distributed to the poor and needy appropriately known as '*Kurban bayrami*'. Apart from the usual good wishes, it was customary on this particular occasion to say '*Allah Kabul etsin*' – '*may God accept your offering*'. In return, the response would be '*sag ol*' – just two short words but they are intended to convey much that is lost in translation – '*I wish you a long life*'. From an early age I had grown up hearing these and similar common place protocol both in Turkish and Arabic. Intricately voiced social exchanges, set rituals, courtesies for every imaginable occasion. A custom founded on respect and empathy which might at times appear to those who had not grown up with it, theatrical and maybe even exaggerated.

These niceties were not one sided. Muslims would call on their Christian friends in the town to wish them well at Christmas and Easter, bearing in mind that both Jesus Christ and the Virgin Mary are recognised in Islam. Christ is always spoken of with due respect as '*Hazreti Isa*' – '*Jesus, the exalted.*' or Messiah using the Arabic term – '*Hazreti Mesih*'. The Virgin Mary is respectfully spoken of as '*Mariam anne*' – '*Mother Mary*'. Christmas is '*Noel Bayrami*' and Easter '*Paskalya Bayrami*' or for those who might have difficulty remembering or pronouncing the word, a more practical alternative '*Yumurta Bayrami*' in which '*yumurta*' translates into '*egg*'.

This latter form was the version my childhood friends and I used as we went about on Easter morning vying with each other to see who had the strongest hardboiled egg. Losers had to give up their cracked egg to the winner, who made short shrift of it. I recall we kept our stock of hardboiled eggs in a cotton bag. We also made sure we had a supply of salt to flavour the eggs which we hoped to win. It was a busy morning especially for those who succeeded in cracking the most eggs.

I grew up with this widespread empathy which will have existed back to the times of my mother, and further back to my grandparents and doubtless earlier still in Mersin. Oddly enough, in spite of these harmonious relations, there was a boundary line, a demarcation that was rarely, if ever, crossed in deference to their religion, by Christians and Muslims alike. The demarcation that I refer to was '*holy matrimony*'. It was a custom that both Christians and their Muslim brothers and sisters subscribed to. By common observance therefore, there were no mixed faith marriages in Mersin nor probably any where else in Turkey in those days. Proof, if proof were needed that it is not differences that are the problem but rather the inability to respect the differences and be able to live harmoniously with them.

At the English High School in Istanbul the end of the Christmas term was no different from the end of the other terms. More than anything else, what I looked forward to was the return to my family and friends in Mersin. There was also my heightened excitement at the prospect of the long, and often eventful train journey across Anatolia.

In the immediate post war Britain, I had little opportunity to be aware of the harsh realities of life. In those days a boarder in a public school was insulated from the outside world. Nowadays it would be difficult to imagine such a state of existence given the enormous leap forward in electronic technology in the past 50 years and the spread of its use. This technology now provides a continuous flow of information both sound and visual from across the entire world. An incredible resource now available to the youngest of school children. By contrast, I recall how I had been impressed by one of the boys in my House who had what was known as a '*crystal-set*', an early form of radio receiver. Amusingly, getting it to work depended on a cat's '*whisker*'!

Cloistered life at Hurst was further exacerbated for me, by my not having my family or even a relative near by. Consequently I was unable to get away from the school's cloistered seclusion at weekends, except on rare occasions, and then just for the day. This inevitably reduced my chances of meeting and mixing with the '*average man and woman in the street*'. Thus, I heard and saw little of the real austerity Britain from across all social classes. Where they were visible to the eye, I did manage sometimes to take stock of the harsh realities of that post war period.

Most memorable were the bomb sites, large areas in the middle of London's West End from which the remains of bomb-damaged buildings had been cleared. Where the devastation was removed right down to the foundations I could see from the street above a plan view of what must have been standing there. Over time these sites had started to return to nature with shrubs, weeds and brambles springing up. They reminded me of the many remains of Greek and Roman settlements along the coast line wilderness of parts of South Eastern Turkey. There also, much of the walls had been cleared away over the centuries by local villagers who made good use of the masonry to build their own houses. Back in London, where access could be made for vehicles, some of these sites were kept from returning to nature. They were turned into money making car parks providing adequate parking for the small numbers of cars on the roads during that time of austerity.

Rationing was in force and continued into the 1950s. I remember obtaining an identity card from the National Registration Offices at the bottom of Lindum Hill in Lincoln. I still have that identity card issued on the 12th December 1950. With that I then acquired my ration book which I had to hand over to the Lindum House Club where I was staying at the time. Strangely, fish and pork pies were not rationed, yet bread was. Luckily, there was no shortage of bread at Hurst.

Petty black market operators known as Spivs abounded. The black market affected availability in shops on the high street and I recall was condemned as '*unpatriotic*'. Spivs, I was once informed '*are a bunch of swine, up to every shady trick in the book*'. However deplorable they and their practices might have been, Spivs endured. I heard of groceries, even poultry and some meat products being available '*under the counter*', yet this was deemed acceptable. People could eat out as restaurants could serve meals provided the cost was under five shillings. In such times, a degree of ambivalence must have been inevitable. One way or another, it served to make Britain's austerity a little bit more bearable, at least for those who could pay.

Coming as I had from a small town in south eastern Turkey, rarely visited by Europeans, I had been greatly impressed by the boys in my House at Hurst. It was their knowledge of motorcars and aeroplanes, which I was so lacking in, that had intrigued me. They could identify cars by make and model and even reel off performances in a most knowledgeable way. As for aeroplanes, war time fighters and bombers, not only the British ones but also American and even some of the German machines. A handicap that I must have been sufficiently troubled by to have discussed with my housemaster. I can recall Mr Bury's words which were intended to give me some consolation, "Now then Pat, in other ways you are more mature than boys here who are of your age or even older. You have the benefit of a wider horizon having grown up surrounded by people of so many different nationalities and back grounds."

Mr Bury's words set me thinking as I never had before. Thoughts passed through my mind about people from the many different and unusual places who had come to Mersin. It was then that I started taking stock of the many other facets of my upbringing. One aspect of my early childhood came to mind. It was about our summers spent in the primitive village of Gozne tucked away from civilisation in the Taurus Mountains. There were all manner of perils such as venomous spiders and scorpions that shared the house with us and beyond there were snakes and the occasional hyena, foxes and even wild boar that ventured into the village, under cover of darkness.

Though much of it had been eradicated, malaria was still a peril. We had to sleep under mosquito nets which also served to protect us from other *'creepy crawlies'* like centipedes, horseflies and the harmless though fierce looking scarabs. I don't suppose there would be many in my House who would have heard about, leave alone shared these, or similar experiences.

Even in Mersin one had to be alert to danger. Rabies was common and a great threat as it could be transmitted even by a lick. Many animals could be carriers. I recall seeing a uniformed official chasing a rabid dog through the streets. It was foaming at the mouth. Once he had it cornered, he shot it dead with the rifle he had been brandishing.

During the Christmas holidays that had just gone, I was presented with a handsome black leather bound "Five Year Diary" for my birthday on the 27th December by the Hergas – "Now then Pat, Ernest and I thought you would like this. It will cover your entire stay at Hurstpierpoint as it goes right through to the end of 1950." I did think it was a most handsome gift true enough, although I failed to make use of it, lacking in the self discipline needed to have sat down every day and kept a meticulous record of what I had done.

At the start of 1946 with the Christmas holidays behind me, I was back at Hurst eager to pick up from where I had left off at the end of my first term. There were changes, the effects of which were at the time, hardly perceptible to me. The Reverend R C Howard, the new headmaster who came to the school at the same time as myself was the prime mover. He appointed S C Simmons, an outstanding scholar and also a sportsman, captain of the school. For all that, at the time it had struck me that in choosing Simmons, the headmaster had gone back on what he had said to a close friend I had made from amongst my contemporaries. I can still bring to mind word for word what he confided in me. I have no reason to doubt its veracity. "The headmaster told me the school was a Church of England foundation. He intended to curtail the influx of any more Jewish boys. In short he did not want the likes of me in the school."

* * *

Since my arrival in England, my reminiscences are of my first term at Hurst and the Christmas holiday. However, some of the novelty had worn off and in its place school life had become routine as I embarked on my second term. My progress was summed up by Mr Bury in the Lent term of 1946.

> "P.C.N. Grigsby:
> He has done very well again this term in the House and has quite settled down. He showed a lot of ability and determination in the school sports. He is still apt to say he cannot do things before he has really tried but I think I am coaxing him out of this. He also tends to take certain subjects in form too easily – a tendency which must be discouraged immediately." R E Bury

* * *

Away from home and having no relatives in England, I lacked the usual support that a youngster of my age would have needed from his close family. Worse still, I was in the throes of adolescence and starved of parental love and affection, the consequence of which started to affect me emotionally. My problems will unfold as I continue the narrative of my ensuing years at Hurst.

Our chaplain, the Reverend R H Bowyer Yin did not come back to Hurst after the Christmas holidays. My friend Charles had implied as much when he told me all about '*The Yin*' and his alter ego 'The Saint'. No explanation was given in the Hurst Johnian of July 1946 for his sudden departure after so many years. However, interestingly further on in the same Hurst Johnian, there is a lengthy and touching tribute to him, prepared by boys in Maths VI.

* * *

Appropriately fitting though this tribute is, it omits to make any reference to 'The Saint'. That name evidently too notorious to be spoken! A clear sign that the new headmaster had not approved of the chaplain he inherited from his predecessor, Walter Dingwall, a layman. '*The Yin*' was replaced by the Reverend John Ridley who turned out to be an unfortunate soul, who for some reason became a figure of ridicule in the school. He moved on after only a term or two.

'*The Yin*', appeared to have vanished into thin air. More than half a century later, in the school's magazine of July 2000, I came on a brief entry about him. He had returned to his birthplace, Singapore. Approaching his 90th year, he was said to be enjoying life to the full! Many of my contemporaries I am sure will still remember him with great affection.

Even if school life had taken on a common place aura, every start of term if nothing else, brought a fresh lot of fledglings – *new boys*. Returning to Hurst for the Easter term, I still had part of the winter ahead of me and of course the Summer term which would see me through my first full year at Hurst. I was just 14. To some I might have appeared older, more mature, given the unfamiliar experiences I had been through since leaving Mersin some four months earlier. Significantly, I was no longer a '*new boy*' in Red Cross. Things had moved on, as they do. All four of our house prefects, including R H Mason the House captain, had left. All of them were well into their 18s, and had been members of the School's 1st XV. Red Cross had an intake of four new boys to perpetuate the eternal cycle of '*fags*' who would take over the chores that my contemporaries and I had performed for our House prefects the previous term.

To add to the austerity, I had to contend with the bitter cold and snow. Conditions that transformed the entire country side into a white snowscape. Hurst was indeed a solitary outpost, isolated deep in the Sussex farmlands. The nearest villages some three miles away. The school buildings themselves were stark, small leaded windows were set in the flint faced walls devoid of any timber that might have given the place a less chilling effect. From the outside, the place could be mis-taken for some rambling soulless institution. It was thanks to the clock tower above the chapel that persuaded one to believe that it must be after all, a monastery. I was to discover that it was indeed monastic on the inside also. I had endured heavy snow falls when I was at the Eng-lish High School in Istanbul. Circumstances there I well remember were different. For a start, the high school had efficient central heat-ing. However cold the outside world, and in winter Istanbul could be very cold, we were warm inside the school. Not so at Hurst.

Dormitories, like the day rooms and '*the Huts*' where classes took place were heated by a single 4 inch diameter steel pipe, through which hot water was circulated, as some generous spirited person once said, "it did at least take the chill off." There must have been about 20 of us in the Red Cross junior dormitory. As luck would have it, my bed was immediately under a skylight. This could be opened and closed by a pull cord that dangled down behind the tubular steel head frame of my bed. Whenever I had the opportunity, I closed it in the hope that the meagre heat from the 4 inch pipe would be a bit more effective. It was a forlorn hope.

"Grigsby, open that skylight."

That was English, head of the junior day room. I had no option but to comply. It was only the previous term that Mr Bury had admonished me following my '*Rooker incident*' – '*dissent*', was what he had called it. His words had stuck in my mind, "I will not have you disrupt the smooth running of the House."

Situated as my bed was, under the skylight, most of the incoming snow settled on me. Earlier I had tried to reason with English on this account, but to no avail. If it was for fresh air, that the skylight had to be opened, plenty of it was already finding its way in through the many windows. There were several steel windows set back in the deep recesses of the thick walls. These were always held ajar by a sliding lock device. This way everyone in the dormitory had an equal share of the Sussex winter air.

It was after this that I began to wonder whether the school's hierarchy were at all prepared to see sense. Rather, they struck me as more concerned with upholding some strange rationale that they had created in the cause of '*character building*'. The one that comes to mind – *"theirs was not to reason why but just to do and then to die!"* Good high minded stuff but hardly justified given the particular circumstances. Not surprisingly, English thus encouraged, appeared to take pleasure enforcing his will regardless of the discomfort it caused, me in particular. Looking back, I wonder whether there might have been a hint of malice in this sort of behaviour. I did even ponder at the time whether the system, however well intentioned, was not encouraging in the likes of the boy English a degree of '*bloody mindedness*'.

"I do not want to find that skylight closed when I wake up in the morning."

"But when the skylight is open and it snows, it all comes in." I pleaded as I had done so often before. English glowered at me from across the dormitory, "Get it open Grigsby, now!" He snapped and then in a change of tone he announced, "Lights out in five more minutes."

English, still strolling about in his dressing gown was always last to get into his bed at the top end of the dormitory. A position always reserved for the senior boy. Several boys were still reading books or magazines, some just chatting to their neighbour in the next bed. They were as always, taken by surprise when English, the five minutes up, turned the lights off. A half rebellious chorus of "Oh! Damn." was met by his customary response,

"That will do! No more talking."

In Red Cross House when we got up in the mornings, tradition had it that we remove our pyjama tops to wash in the unheated, glacial washroom before returning to the dormitory to get dressed. Many of my contemporaries used to remove their entire top garments in one, when getting undressed for bed. Next morning, they were able to slip in to their vest, shirt and pullover in one deft movement. Even the house tie was in place only requiring the front stud in the stiff collar to be fixed in position. This way, the most accomplished of these '*quick change*' artists could be dressed in a matter of seconds with minimum exposure to the freezing conditions of the dormitory.

Philp, a boy a term or two my senior, had the strange habit of wearing an airman's leather helmet in bed. He claimed it kept him warm. Before lights out, he used to wander about the dormitory in his dressing gown wearing the thing. Head entirely covered, part of his face obscured in the tan leather, he made a bizarre sight. Over time my contemporaries and I had got used to seeing him in his eccentric get-up. It emerged some time later that the airman's helmet had belonged to his father, a pilot in the RAF shot down in the Battle of Britain, leaving Philp to be brought up by his widowed mother in Portsmouth. This probably explained why Mr Bury, took no notice of his seemingly odd habit of behaviour.

Mr Bury never failed to make an appearance in the dormitory every night. His entry was preceded by whispered calls of "KV"by those who heard his slow deliberate approaching footsteps on the bare stone floor in the cloister. Not long demobilised from the British army with the rank of Captain, he was a small man, with sharp features, sun tanned – he bore a striking resemblance to 'Monty', hero of the time Field Marshall Lord Montgomery of El Alamein.

Smoking his pipe as usual, he would stop for a brief moment framed in the doorway. I have wondered since whether this bit of stagecraft might not have been the latent actor within him. I say this because it was he who produced, to great acclaim, the school play each year – always one of the works of William Shakespeare. Having taken stock of the situation in the dormitory, Mr Bury would then go round having a light hearted chat with those of us whom he might have picked out. It was the prerogative of the head of the junior day room, at the time English, to put the lights out. Mr Bury would have timed himself to make his exit, on queue, before the lights were extinguished.

I have already mentioned that by special dispensation, we were permitted to wear our overcoats when there was a particularly cold spell, this indulgence applied even in chapel! Boys like Dick Ottley entitled to wear knitted scarves in the School Colts XV and 1st XV colours, a small privileged minority did so. Everybody else not thus privileged had to make do by turning up the collar of their overcoat, a further indulgence as this practice was not normally permitted. In spite of all these measures, I still remember the headaches I got on account of the unrelenting cold through out the school. Thankfully I was as yet unaware that the even worse winter of 1947 was yet to come.

Apart from the entitlement of wearing scarves that I have just mentioned and the privilege of turning up overcoat collars, there was an array of privileges, some of which I can still bring to mind. Any one, even the lowly new boys could put their hands in their jacket pockets at anytime, anywhere. Putting ones hands in trouser pockets was strictly forbidden, unless privileged to do so. House prefects could, but only within the confines of their House. School prefects could, through out the school!

In a similar vein there were also numerous tenets. Some times they were, referred to by the boys at Hurst as traditions. I prefer to avoid the use of the word 'tradition' as I believe it should be reserved for matters of some greater substance. The following few examples should, explain my reasoning:

In the dormitory – the top button of pyjama jackets had to be left unbuttoned. Pyjama jackets were not permitted to be tucked into the pyjama trousers. Having knees up in bed was strictly forbidden, even after lights out. Of the many petty regulations, some dreamt up by past prefects, this last one must surely have been the most ludicrous. Apart from not being quite sure of its purpose, I could never understand how it was to be enforced. However stupid or frivolous, at least these practices were not harmful.

There were other ways open to the few opportunists who wanted to assert themselves. The most commonly used being the pecking order or as it was known at Hurst '*seniority*' – a suitably vague, indistinct notion that could be easily manipulated. As a new boy, I was often told to *'switch-off'* or *'turn-off'* for no better reason but the fact that a boy *'senior'* to me chose to speak to me thus. Choosing to ignore the rebuke by not replying, I was then told, "*Grigsby don't be so damned cocky!*" All this did teach me something that served me well in later life – self control and passive defiance. What better way to deal with authority that is devoid of reason and completely unassailable.

During that cold winter, the one place where I felt reasonably warm was the House day room shared by about 20 of us. We all gathered there for morning and evening *"prep"* it was also where we spent our limited free time. There was one place I knew of that was even warmer, the study or *'rooker'*, shared by the House prefects. One of them had brought a powerful electric heater from home which must have made all the difference. When I was at my coldest and most miserable I used to think to myself "*Rookers*! Now, there is a worthwhile privilege."

Having got into the swing of things during term time, my thoughts turned to the school holidays, especially the long summer holidays that I was to spend in England before my first trip back to Mersin in the summer of 1948. The places where I was to spend all these holidays were arranged by Mr Bury. As luck would have it, I was paired up with Charles Cherrington for several holidays at various locations in Devonshire.

Charles and I spent the first of our holidays together near Okehampton. It must have been Easter, when we stayed at the home of Mrs Walker in the heart of the Devonshire countryside. She was the widow of a senior Naval Officer, left with two daughters who lived away; she must have been very lonely as she spoke incessantly about them. They had unusual names – Charmian and Phyllida. Staying on holiday with us were three school girls – Barbara Black and her sister from Singapore were at one of Hurstpierpoint's sister schools in Taunton. The third, Mena Stapleton had come to Cheltenham Ladies College from Egypt. My mother knew of her family who had settled in Port Taufik at the Southern end of the Suez Canal. It appears they had major interests in cotton. Like me she was born in Egypt, and interestingly, she was named after the first king of Egypt.

As a consequence of Mrs Walkers' close chaperoning, Charles and I hardly ever found ourselves alone with the girls. We both rather liked Barbara. She was confident, and mature though she liked to appear coy and demure. We had both come to the conclusion that she was anything but. She used to wear tight jumpers. By constantly pulling them down and throwing her shoulders back, she emphasised her maturing bust. She had striking black eyes and dark brown hair which added to her other charms. We had also decided that she was sophisticated. A view that was reinforced when she declined to join us on our bus trips to the local cinema. Put off probably by our choice of film, usually Westerns. All this served to encourage Charles and I still more in our quest. This was not surprising given that she was the only girl we had met, even if it was just to talk to, once liberated from our all male incarceration at Hurst.

To stave off our boredom, Charles and I used to mow Mrs Walker's lawns. It was hard work as she only had a hand mower. We were both undaunted. In fact we turned the task into a form of display for the benefit of Barbara in particular. We had both convinced ourselves that a display of strength, agility and endurance by us would win her over. It didn't – so we resigned ourselves to the reality that she was just playing hard to get!

Finding ourselves at a loose end, with nothing better to do and rejected by Barbara, we vented our disappointment on Mrs Walker's pets – a Jack Russell which we called 'JR' and Siamese cat, Suki. We had noticed that JR was frequently in a state of arousal. As his only prospect was

Suki, we tried to get them interested in each other. Our best endeavours came to naught with Suki escaping from the attentions of JR by trying to scramble up the chimney. This led to an unusually grave looking Mrs Walker interrogating us, "Have either of you boys any idea how Suki came to be covered in soot. It has never happened before."

We both managed to look suitably surprised, even concerned in our efforts to put Mrs Walker's mind at ease, "No Mrs Walker, we have seen nothing unusual. Don't worry, we will keep a look out and let you know if we come upon anything strange."

JR's personal problem remained unresolved. The only change was that Suki eyed him with suspicion, and tended to settle near one of the doorways for a fast exit from the sitting room. Charles and I made no headway with Barbara either. When we parted at the end of the holiday, she let me have a small photo of herself and I recall writing letters to her in Singapore. As for Mrs Walker, neither of us were to see her again as Mr Bury arranged for us to have our next two holidays in Fuge.

The remote cluster of three or at best four dwellings in a steep sided ravine was reached by a single track that terminated there. The first of the dwellings, a stone built house, was where the Butlers lived and where Charles and I spent two summer holidays. For some reason, these dwellings were separated from the settlement proper, known as Fuge. Looking back, the strangest thing about the place was that we never saw any inhabitants and even at the time Charles and I used to speculate on the property nearest the Butler house being haunted.

With nothing else to do and as we were both adventurous and even a bit wild, Charles and I frequently headed down what might have been a bridle path leading to the sea. The Butler's dog, a young Airedale always chose to accompany us. Tireless and eager to please, he made an ideal companion. Even on the hottest days, the big trees and the abundant vegetation kept the strong sun out, cooling the surroundings. We picked our way carefully on the rough track that snaked along one bank of the ravine. There was a faint smell of humidity and decaying wood. This was the first time since coming to England that I got a sense of adventure. I was reminded of the many mountain walks I had been on near Gozne in Turkey but without the blazing sun and the snakes. We kept the dog busy by throwing lumps of branches down the side of the track. Nothing got the better of him provided he could get a grip on it with his strong, vice like jaws.

These memories and many more remained with me. It was to reawaken the past that I wanted to revisit Fuge. Through out my life, there have been places to which I have had a compelling urge to return. Some times places of no great consequence, maybe even places that I had got to associate with a not particularly pleasant time of my life. This longing to return somewhere however strange is real for me. It is a compulsion that when accomplished leaves me with a great feeling of satisfaction.

Before my retirement we had a timeshare flat in The Marine Quay at Salcombe from where we used to set off on excursions. Quite by chance on one of these occasions, I found myself driving on the coastal road in the vicinity of Start Bay and Slapton Sands. It was here by a pub, famous for its fish and chips, that a World War II tank had been mounted on display. It made me recall the stories and rumours I had heard about a war time incident out at sea when US troops on an amphibious exercise had come under a surprise attack themselves by the real enemy, the Germans. The unexpected encounter left large numbers of the Americans dead or seriously injured. This was one of the haunts from my school holidays with Charles Cherrington which we used to come down to from Fuge.

I had never forgotten Fuge. It was where the Butlers had lived and I managed to bring back to mind that it was some way inland from the village of Strete. Accompanied by my wife, Beryl, we eventually found our way to it. We went past the settlement, still devoid of any shops or pubs on the narrow single track road. We started going down hill, the house that had belonged to the Butler family was still there on the steep, tight bend. The other house, that I vaguely remembered beyond, had become well and truly derelict. The whole place was as remote as I could recall it to have been. It was even more closed in by the same enormous trees that had grown in the intervening years even bigger. Though it was a bright sunny day, it was cold and shadowy where I stopped the car. The air about us smelled musty. I managed to turn without getting stuck on the muddy grass verge. Driving off, I experienced that strange sense of satisfaction. My visit had awakened so many memories; in particular of my school friend and holiday companion Charles. My curiosity well satisfied, I was sure as we drove away that I would not be revisiting Fuge.

Mr Butler, before his retirement, had spent his entire life at sea. He had ended his career as a ship's purser. He took pleasure telling us about his hard life at sea and especially about his boxing exploits. He had been, he would have us believe, something of a boxing champion. He was a smallish man with a ruddy, weather-beaten face. The thick horn-rimmed spectacles he wore did nothing to diminish the pugnacious air he had about him. He strutted about as I suppose an ex boxing champ would have got in the habit of doing. Neither Charles or myself liked him.

The tricks of the trade he had acquired as a ship's purser had evidently not deserted him in the retirement work he and his wife had under taken, that of providing board and lodging for boarding school boys from overseas. He prided himself on matters of discipline and running '*a tight ship*' as he put it. His wife and son were noticeably cowed by some of his domineering ways. It was Mr Butler, himself who presided over the table at meal times.

"Do you boys want any more bread. Speak now or for ever hold your peace?" He would declare wielding the bread knife as he stood at the head of the table. He was always dressed in the same brown, thick tweed suit with the check patterned Vyella shirt and usual tie, some sort of club tie it was. I can only remember being served Devonshire pasties probably because he used to insist on telling all present how they originated and how much better he judged them to be than the Cornish ones. "Not bad grub these pasties. One of Mrs Butler's specialities, though I say it myself." He would proclaim and then turning to his wife, oblivious of her embarrassed discomfort he would go on to say, "Very nice they were too, my dear."

In contrast to her husband, Mrs Butler rarely spoke. She hardly had the opportunity to do so even had she wanted to. She was a timid, ladylike person. Slightly built, she had freckles and the ginger hair to match. Needless to say, we preferred her as she appeared to be so much nicer and certainly more refined than her gruff southpaw husband. Because of this, and maybe without any good reason, we both also felt sorry for her. Their son, an only child, as I seem to recall, resembled his mother. He was away most of the time doing his national service in the Army.

Mr Butler had to drive into Dartmouth from time to time in his two seater sports car; as his wife never accompanied him, he used to offer Charles and I a lift. "Battling Butler is out for every penny he can get. I bet you he includes something on the accounts he sends Mr Bury for these so called *'lifts'* into Dartmouth." Charles had once told me. Even so, we never passed up the opportunity.

"Are you ready boys. Come on." Shouted Mr Butler as he let himself out of the front door and as on all previous occasions he gave Chas and I his usual instructions. Mr Butler was a creature of habit.

"I'll pick both you boys up at the top."

We walked the short distance up the steep rise and round the bend in the road. We did not have long to wait, soon we heard the car's engine start up. It emitted a loud crackling noise from its exhaust as it suddenly came into sight round the bend. Battling Butler had as usual donned his cloth cap, muffler and the goggles which he wore over his spectacles for added protection from the cold rush of air. He rarely had the canvas hood up, not in summer any way, even if it was raining. He brought the vehicle to a skidding halt on the loose gravel that covered the surface of the hardly used, narrow road. "Jump in." he yelled above the sound of the engine.

Charles and I used to take it in turns to sit in the passenger bucket seat whilst the other clambered over the side of the open two-seater roadster and slid into the uncomfortable recess behind. This would barely accommodate one person sitting sideways on. As we hurtled along the twisty road towards Dartmouth, it felt as though we were flying – it wasn't that we were going all that fast… just that it felt that way, particularly at the back with no protection from the wind.

Glad of each other's companionship on those holidays in Devon, Charles and I had become close friends, enjoying each others company we had much in common; we were both *'outsiders'*. I had met his mother when she was in England, a strikingly attractive Malay woman. I remember being taken up to London by her in company with Charles and having lunch at the very first Chinese restaurant in Soho. It was also the first time I had tasted Chinese food. After I left Hurst in 1949, I lost touch with Charles. Mr Bury told me in one of his letters that Cherrington, after leaving school, had made the Army his career as a commissioned officer. He was tragically killed when still in his prime by bandits in Malaya. It must have devastated his mother as he was an only child and she doted on him. I had never met his Australian father.

I did spend two holidays in Brighton. The longer of the two, of all places at a preparatory school, Hollingbury Court right out on the top of the windy downs, well out of the town centre. I must have been there for a week, maybe 10 days on my own during one of the Easter holidays. The school was in recess, so consequently unoccupied except for the headmaster, his wife and their son. There were one or two other teachers who put in an appearance from time to time. Like me they must have had no where better to go. We got together only at meal times and for a cup of tea afterwards in what must have been the staff dayroom. The conversation centred on the son, whom I was to hear was an ex Blundells boy, something of a star pupil, by all accounts. He had just been commissioned into the Royal Navy judging by his brand new uniform. Not long out of school, where he had been a prefect he had evidently not yet shed his sense of school boy '*seniority*', taking me for one of those new boy rookies. He did not deign to so much as to acknowledge my existence but then neither can I bring to mind speaking with any of the others.

The men folk, all keen golfers, used to go off to some golf club. My instincts had kept me clear lest I get asked to join them for fear that I would end up caddying. In any case there appeared to be little that might have engaged us in conversation. Thus left with little to do and only the headmaster's wife around, most days I used to walk down into the town centre and if I had the money, go to see a film show.

On one of my excursions into Brighton, I was tempted to buy a Swiss roll. I returned with it on one of the trolley buses that used to go right the way back as far as Hollingbury Court. It was a steady climb up to the top of the downs. I had a slice of the Swiss roll that evening when I retired – it was ghastly, full of what I imagined to be soda but was later told must have been baking powder!

I threw the rest of it away.

My accommodation comprised an entire dormitory at the Hollingbury Court School. I had it all to myself not to mention the run of the adjoining changing rooms, toilets and washing facilities. A questionable privilege once I switched the lights off and climbed in between the cold sheets of my bed. It was the only one amongst a dormitory full of bare steel bedsteads stripped of any trace of comfort as if they were bare skeletons stretched out all around me. Without another soul around, straining hard listening to the silence, I did get off to sleep eventually.

A ghostly dormitory and a duff Swiss roll, the only memories of that Brighton holiday. That says it all! But then, I have since wondered whether many boys of my age in the 1940s would have fared any better. Were not holidays then devised to ensured plenty of the outdoor life and exercise followed by wholesome, if unimaginative meals? The lack of money permitting little else.

There were other holidays that I can remember, happier ones. Usually at Christmas when I was invited once or twice by school friends to stay at their homes. The best remembered of these was a week with Chris Carter who lived in Ealing. Chris, much more so than many of the other boys in my House, was completely unpretentious. He once told me it was because his entire family were all London born and bred. "We're cockneys you know." He had said. Having no idea what he was talking about, I could but take his word for it.

Like me, he was an only child. His mother was a petite, attractive woman whom I thought looked so much younger than many of the other mothers I had seen. It also struck me at the time that his father, a big jovial man treated her with great affection. A notion which was born out by the fact that he always did the washing up. I had never before coming to England known or heard of a man to ever wash up or do any household chores. Chris' father E.L.Carter had also been at Hurst as a boy, what is more, in the same house we were in, Red Cross.

His father, he had told me was '*in business*', he sold toys and games. A room his father used as an office was festooned with a vast array of samples. Curiosity had got the better of us, we could not resist rummaging through the stack of samples. When Mr Carter came on us exploring, he was not at all put out. He was a very sociable person. He used to tell us about some of his experiences '*in the business*' as he termed his work. I remember he appeared to have a great deal to say about Hamley's in Oxford Street and more generally the build up to Christmas, "It's the busiest time of the year. Easter also but not on the same scale as Christmas. Of course, orders have to be in with the manufacturers during the summer. Even earlier if there is 'tooling' to be made, that is where the skill comes in. Then by New Year, things slacken off. It is time then, for me to get my golf clubs out." He would laugh and rub his hands together in anticipation.

With parents like he had, Chris was also a good mixer. He had come across to me as being thoughtful and considerate, traits that one often finds in those who are self effacing. Unpretentious as I have already said. Whilst staying at his home which I believe was off Ealing Broadway, Chris took me along to what he described as a '*Christmas party*', "I want you to meet some of the girls I know around here. We hardly have the chance during term time at Hurst. Mark you they are nice girls, not like the ones that chap Pierman meets in some arcade in Worthing. If his exploits that he brags about are to be believed they must be amateur prostitutes, anyway we will have a nice evening, particularly if the girls out number the chaps!"

Mixed gatherings, the likes of which Chris had been telling me about were unimaginable in Turkey so it was going to be a very new experience for me. The lady of the house greeted us all as we entered and we were soon invited into the dining room. We took our seats at the table, a dozen of us. Whoever had made the arrangements had made sure that there were as many boys as there were girls. There were the usual offerings – sausage rolls, sandwiches, and a vast selection of buns and cakes. Tea was served by the lady of the house who remained until we had more or less finished all that had been put out. The adjoining doors were opened into what must have been a large sitting room where there was a record player and a selection of 78s.

What was to become the *'real party'* started most decorously in spite of the lady of the house who might have acted as chaperone being nowhere to be seen. Earlier at the table, I had noticed the girls were in flimsy frocks chosen no doubt with great care to merit the clothing coupons forfeited. As Chris had told me, they all seemed nice girls. Pretty and desirable too I vaguely recall. The music turned down low served to create a romantic mood, prompting Julie, a curvaceous blond, who had taken over in her mother's absence to call out "Let's play postman's knock." Fortunately my instincts stopped me from blurting out "What's that?" and just as well for there was a unanimous response, "Oh yes, Julie. What a wizard idea." With that, more lights went out and the excuse for a bit of adolescent kissing and caressing was under way. As I cast my mind back I cannot help but think to myself now "Oh, the innocence of it all. With no alcohol, no drugs" – and even more to the point – "No pill!"

As we walked back to Chris' home that evening he did ask me if I had enjoyed myself at Julie's party and of course I would have thanked him and told him how much I had. But to be realistic, I was going to continue to be a victim of my family's ambition for me to have '*the best education in the world, at an English public school*'. Victim because I was to go three years before my first holiday with my family in Mersin, and of course also a victim because I had no roots in England. Nowhere I could call *'home'* to take friends to. I now doubt if I would have been able to express all this at the time. What I do not doubt is the effect, of which I was then not aware, that it was having on me. I never sat down in my moments of despair and had a good cry. Perhaps I should have.

Chris Carter, unlike me, did return to Hurst for a fifth year. I made enquiries about him through the school many years later. I was told that he went to Canada with his family and settled there for good. He was in his very own words '*a Cockney*'. He had been a good friend to me. I have missed his unpretentious spirit wherever it might be.

Chapter 10

It was a bright sunny day with clear blue skies as the aeroplane I was in made its approach to Istanbul's Yesil Koy airport. My seat was by a porthole and I had been gazing out intently. We had flown over water, the Sea of Marmara shimmering brightly. I had spotted a merchant ship which seemed motionless, yet judging from its wake it was ploughing its way along at speed. An island appeared, but I could not tell which of the Princes Islands it was. There were some small boats with their sails filled out by what must have been a brisk sea breeze. Yesil Koy then was not much more than a collection of houses scattered about and surrounded by nature's greenery. The aeroplane by then was close to the ground. As landmarks swept past, we appeared to be going faster. The aeroplane seemed hesitant as it gently tilted first to the right then to the left before it touched down. From the little I could see, the Yesil Koy airport appeared bigger than the one near Athens but nothing as busy as Northolt. After taxiing a short distance, towards the single two storey building, the aeroplane came to a halt and the engines cut out. When the doors were opened, and we all trooped down the steps, the heat was intense, it appeared to weigh down like a hot, damp blanket.

My mother had written telling me that I would have a wait of several hours at the airport before my flight to Adana by THY amongst other things, she told me "Friends who travel to Istanbul have told me that there is a good restaurant. You could go there and have a meal. Stay there until the time comes to board the Adana plane as it will be cooler than any where else." Well, that is what I did. As it was well past mid-day, there were few customers, I had the place almost to myself.

I tucked into the food that the waiter had placed before me with great gusto – a portion of *'imam bayildi'*. Aubergine cooked in olive oil with lots of garlic, onion and tomato, its Turkish name translates into English as 'the imam fainted' – he was over come with pleasure. I followed this with another aubergine speciality, prepared with minced meat and served hot, *'karni yarik'*, accompanied by a nice *'pilaf'*. To this day, I consider aubergines to be the tastiest of vegetables. We often have them as a 'meze', sliced and fried in olive oil with a liberal dressing of garlic yoghurt. I had also got through a great deal of freshly baked bread as one does with Turkish food. Thus satisfied and feeling replete, I finished off with a 'hosaf' of dried apricots, a compote.

That day, back in Turkey after an absence of just over three years, I felt that I had returned home. What better way to celebrate than by indulging myself in some of the dishes that I had missed so much whilst I was in England? I can bring to mind exactly what I had for my lunch at Yesil Koy on that first occasion that I returned to Turkey. In the years that followed, I was to land there often flying in from England. Without fail, on each occasion I revisited that same old restaurant and had exactly the same dishes the memories of which remain indelible in my mind.

The airport now has changed beyond recognition to accommodate the enormous increase in traffic and is now known as Ataturk Airport. The restaurant that had become so familiar to me has long since vanished. In its place global franchisees now cater for the modern travellers preference in fast foods – alas, these do not include my favourite dishes of aubergine.

It would have been shortly after the 12th of July in 1948 that I flew from Northolt which was at the time London's only airport. My journey, which I believe was with BOAC, would have started at the South Kensington Terminus. No queuing to check-in, no crowds, no tension even though it was to be my very first flight on a civil airline. Three years earlier, I had been transported by courtesy of the USAF in the cargo hold of one of their Dakotas from Ankara to Cairo. Then, I might well have been as good as hitching a lift, arranged somehow by Mr Sutherland as a last resort to get me on my way to school in England. On this second occasion, I was a bona fide passenger. I recollect, sitting in a spacious comfortable lounge.

The days of mass air travel, cheap all-in holidays abroad and charter flights were still a long way off. There were no young men with designer stubble dressed in denims, no scruffs in tatty jeans, no beatniks, no backpackers, no young women with bare midriffs showing off their navel piercings. Just the other passengers for the flight, smartly dressed, many smoking. We were all waiting patiently. A stewardess, well groomed and smartly dressed in her BOAC uniform appeared. She read out the names of each passenger from a checklist that she had on a clipboard and asked us to follow her.

On board the plane, in spite of it being a warm day in July, it was cool. The seats were as good as armchairs. Air travel was for the few who were happy to pay for their creature comforts. Apart from any other considerations, passengers were not packed in like sardines. Glossy magazines of the time – *The Tatler, Illustrated London News* and of course *Punch* were passed around. Meals were served as they would have been in a top class hotel, with napkins and proper cutlery.

The flight was scheduled to put down in Rome and again in Athens. Due to some technical problem, the plane was grounded at Rome's

Chiampino airport. All passengers had an overnight stay at the Hotel Quirinal in Rome. I had the good fortune of being invited by one of the passengers, a gentleman, to accompany him on a visit to some friends of his in Anzio. Looking back I suppose he must have felt sorry for me, the only minor, stuck in the hotel with nowhere to go.

As I sat after my lunch in the restaurant at Istanbul's Yesil Koy airport, I felt relaxed after the previous day's experiences in Rome. I had enjoyed the novelty of the drive down to Anzio. Once there, I listened to the conversation which most of the time had been about the amphibious landings that had taken place towards the end of the war. The stop at Athens earlier that day had gone as scheduled. The time had passed quickly enough at the modest airport building with very little to offer by way of shopping or any other form of distraction.

The single terminal building at Yesil Koy in those days, served both international and domestic flights. My flight to Adana in South Eastern Turkey would not be called for some time. With little else to do, I had remained at my table in the restaurant. It was probably the coolest of places thanks to several large fans that kept the air circulating – there was no such thing as air conditioning then.

In a few hours I would be with my family. I find it hard now to believe that I had not seen any of my family for a good three years. I was 13½ when I left Mersin on the first leg of my long trip to England, it had taken almost three months. The only form of communication then had been by letter – telephoning was not an option.

When I had been at school in Istanbul, air travel within Turkey was unheard off. Flying from Istanbul, the THY aeroplane touched down at Adana Airport, a drive of well over an hour to Mersin. Strange thing is I have absolutely no recollection of how I got to Mersin nor of what must have been a very emotional, happy yet tearful reunion with all my family.

Looking back, I am inclined to dismiss the notion that this might have been a bout of selective amnesia brought on by a sense of guilt due to school reports being less than acceptable to my family. It has to be said that I had never quite lived up to my family's expectations. What is more, they often spoke of the academic achievements of contemporaries of mine in the mistaken hope that the news would spur me on. The fact of the matter is my 1948 end of year reports from Hurstpierpoint, whilst not turning me into an 'achiever' did not make me out a 'loser' either.

At Hurstpierpoint, and away from my family, rather than brood over these things I must have instinctively turned to what natural abilities I had. Running came naturally to me, it seemed effortless. From early childhood in Mersin I ran everywhere. I rarely, if ever, chose to walk.

There was little to impede me in those days. There were hardly any motorised vehicles to worry about. There were two roads through Mersin. The back road served the various '*bazar*', produce being brought in on pack horses, donkeys with laden panniers, camels – usually a train of two or more ambling along behind a donkey carrying his master. People on foot were accustomed to crisscrossing this endless flow. There were pavements but walking on them was often impeded by racks of produce from the shops. Then there was the front road, the '*corniche*' parallel to the sea and through the fashionable residential part of the town. It was not cluttered by man nor beast. I recall the occasion when I had just gone past the patisserie on the corner and was making my way diagonally across the main square, as usual I was running.

"Pat…rick! Don't… run!… W…a…l…k!"

The yell, as if through a loud hailer, could be heard clearly over the general hubbub. It came from the other side of the square. I froze, startled primarily by the unmistakable rage in the voice. For an instant I imagined that like me everyone around had stopped in their tracks even though none would have understood what had been called out. It was Uncle William who had spotted me from his Lloyds Agency offices on the far side of the Custom's Square. He beckoned me over to where he was standing.

I recall that I was embarrassed by his very public outburst. I also hoped that none of the people around had witnessed my discomfort as I walked towards him sheepishly. I was a mere child at the time.

"Yes uncle!" I croaked feeling humiliated and also frightened. He was angry. I could almost feel his glowering look.

"Can you see anyone else running in the road?" I shook my head. "No!" He went on to question me, "Why then were you running instead of walking like a normal person? I don't want to see you running again in the town. Walk!"

"Yes uncle" I was mortified, tears welled into my eyes as I turned and continued on my way. For all his sternness I had always felt that my uncle had my best interests at heart. I have since wondered at his anger that day and what might have really caused it. At Hurst, many years later, I still enjoyed running. I had embraced athletics with enthusiasm. My successes were admired, maybe even envied by my peers. I was certainly encouraged by my achievements.

I had done particularly well in the inter-school athletics matches that took place the summer preceding my trip to Turkey. The biggest event was the annual Informal Athletics Meeting of the seven Woodard Schools For Boys of which Hurstpierpoint was the first to have been founded by Canon Nathaniel Woodard. It was the turn of Worksop College in the Midlands to host the occasion.

I have hazy recollections of what in fact was intended to be a social occasion though its pretext was an inter Woodard School athletics gathering. The most vivid of these, though rather confused, was a visit to nearby Welbeck Abbey the home of the Dukes of Portland where there were said to be strange goings on. Things that brought *The Phantom of the Opera* to mind. I recall listening to the story of how the particular Duke, terribly disfigured, was compelled to spend his days driving about in underground tunnels in a horse drawn coach. It was said that he only ever came out into the open once it was dark and no one could see his deformity.

I was recently spending the day on a visit to Clumber Park with my wife. We had driven that way through the Dukeries a great many times on our way to Beryl's family home in York. On an impulse I turned off our habitual route and drove towards the town of Worksop. There was a prominent road sign for the college off the main road. I turned off and headed up the long drive to Worksop College.

It was 60 years ago almost to the day that I had last been there. I wondered how much I would be able to remember of the school where I had stayed and won the junior ½ mile to great acclaim:

> "Hurst gained two firsts and a second – good results from so few competitors. It is interesting to note that Grigsby's time (2min 16.6sec.) in the ½ mile was better than the senior's (2min.17.2sec.) in that event."

I pulled up as near to the main entrance as I could on a vast car park. It was a warm sunny day, we had enjoyed our lunch earlier at a restaurant in what was left of Thoresby Hall in Clumber Park. Turning up unannounced at the school, I was not sure how I would be received, nor did I have any idea as to what surprises might be in store for me should I be permitted to wander about. I had said to Beryl as I got out of the car, "I don't suppose I will be all that long. It depends on my reception and what I come across. See you shortly."

I was shown by two of the boys along a cloister to the main entrance. A pleasant receptionist greeted me and took down some particulars after which she pinned a badge onto my jacket. This identified me as a 'Visitor' – "Feel free to have a wander about but the dormitory areas are out of bounds to visitors. Please return your badge when leaving."

I do not think I was away for more than about half an hour. "You haven't been long! How did it go?" Were Beryl's first words when I opened the car door. I got in before replying. "Strange. Try as I would, I could not recall much. In fact, I was able to add little to what I already could bring to mind of Worksop College. I had a general picture of the school from the outside, especially the chapel. Unlike Hurst, it was an all red brick construction. As I was leaving, the receptionist accompanied me to the main entrance. I had asked her if I was correct in believing that the athletics track was beyond the chapel. She pointed it out to me and it was as I had imagined. Not very enlightening I am afraid to say. But I am glad I made the effort to come this one time!" With that I started up the engine and we drove away.

The visit had the effect of prompting me later on to delve further into the tale I had heard all those years ago about the strange Duke and his underground tunnels at Welbeck Abbey. It transpires that the fifth Duke of Portland as a young man had fallen in love with a well-known opera singer of the time, Adelaide Kemble who lived in London. He was certainly not disfigured. He used the tunnel for trips to London. His journeys would begin at the stables where four fine horses would draw his coach along a tunnel for a mile and a quarter then a further two miles by road to Worksop railway station. The Duke's coach would then be rolled onto a flat railway wagon and be fastened down for the trip to London. The Duke remained inside his coach, with blinds drawn, for the entire journey.

Inter-schools athletics match against Charterhouse at Hurst. I am seen winning the ½ mile team race for the second year running. Mr R.E.Bury can be spotted to the right with his stopwatch

A tale no less extraordinary than the one I had originally heard but which still leaves me pondering. A further more laudable twist emerges. The subterranean excavations are said to have provided a living wage for 15,000 workmen for 18 years! If true, a remarkable accomplishment which would have alleviated the widespread unemployment and poverty of the time. It is little wonder then, why the fifth Duke of Portland it is said had come to be known as "The workmen's friend"!

There were other athletic events that I can bring to mind. An important one for me was the athletics match away at Charterhouse School in Godalming on the 1st of July. I had been selected with two other boys to represent Hurst in the ½ mile. I won the race in a time of 2 mins 12.8 secs. This was considered a very credible performance on a grass track. There were few cinder tracks in those days.

That year, in 1947 the Athletics were moved from the Easter term to the summer. This change was very much for the good. The warm weather led to better track performances. I won the three middle distance junior events – 440 yards – 660 yards and 1000 yards, setting new records in all three. My time of 56.2 secs for the 440 yards was judged 'Best Junior Individual Performance' for which I was awarded the victor ludorum. A record that stood for several years.

My performances on the track in the summer of 1947 were to be the zenith of my athletics career at Hurst. Though I continued to win track events in what were to be my remaining two years at Hurst, my earlier achievements were not sustained as I would have wished. I had lost heart, I felt demoralised. Even so, I was to have the distinction of winning the school open cross country race for two successive years in 1948 and 1949. I believe this was never again to be repeated.

It was a single incident that brought about my loss of heart. I can remember the incident clearly, still. It took place during the summer term of 1948, just prior to my trip to Turkey. There had been other things going on which compounded my sense of decline. Looking back, it is impossible for me to know how these events might have been related and if indeed they were related how one might have played on the other.

The confrontation took place on the running track during the final of the intermediate 440 yards race. One of the participants, M.K.Russell barged into me on the second bend out of sight of the masters, including Mr G.Lambert the senior sports master. All were standing at the finishing line. In a race lasting less than 60 seconds, obstruction of this sort can make the difference between winning and loosing. Though I had recovered some lost ground, he breasting the tape with me just on his shoulder. He had won. At that instant in full view of those present, I gave Russell a fierce push, sending him sprawling. He had cheated me, and was no longer a sporting rival, but an enemy.

My retaliation had been deliberate and overt. I had acted in the expectation that those masters present as adjudicators would question what had caused me to behave in that unusual manner. Questioning that would expose the cause of my grievance. I was mistaken! At that very instant, Mr Lambert dashed across to me, grabbed me and rebuked me for un-sporting behaviour.

Nothing was said, nor as far as I am aware done to investigate the incident.

I was seen as being unquestionably in the wrong. Worse still, I was branded an undesirable, a bad sport, and un-gentlemanly. Now many years on, the outcome still rankles with me. There have been other occasions since when I have heard about or even seen acts of retaliation condemned out of hand. I put this down to laziness – *'taking the easy way out'*. My sympathy has sometimes been with the *'guilty party'* driven to retaliate by gross provocation. How can this be reconciled with the British sense of fair play? I suppose my upbringing has something to do with this. Where I grew up people did at least acknowledge that a normal person would not behave badly without good reason.

As in the adage, *'you are judged by the company you keep'* I was to discover that it is difficult to shake off a reputation. I recall Mr Bury telling me, "Pat, Hazzan is a bad influence. You would be better off not associating with him." As far as I can recall, there was no explanation given for this. I do remember though that at about the same time, I had been reprimanded for associating with one of the kitchen staff. Joe Plush, an ex stoker who had served in the Royal Navy during the war. A Mancunian like Geoffrey Hazzan, he was a lonely chap with whom we had struck up a passing *'matey'* sort of relationship. In my case, Joe was the only person outside the school that I had any sort of contact with in England. It was either his regional accent or some injury to his mouth that made it almost impossible for me to understand what he said. Joe had an abnormally thick bottom lip. Geoffrey did most of the chatting with Joe as the three of us played with a soccer ball that he produced. The fact that we used the main rugby pitch for our kick about had probably not gone down well with the school hierarchy. I never knew what became of Joe Plush as he vanished just as he had appeared – out of the blue.

I had grown to set great store on friendships throughout my boarding school days. These friendships more than anything else, made up for the absence of parents and family. When I returned to the English High School in Istanbul, I knew that I would only be away from Mersin and my family for just a term at a time. Even then, I sought and found a close friend in Neil Baker an English boy from Ankara. We had much in common. We were both deferential, modest and retiring.

The other English and European boys were much more self assertive and gave off an aura of familial superiority. The source of this pride usually coming from wealth or position and fanciful imagination as in the case of my friend Alain Giraud who boasted to me that his forebears were '*buccaneers*'! Neil and I were in a permanent state of paucity when it came to money. It was to be my first experience of how a problem shared could bond two individuals together.

Neil was my age, very English with fair hair and blue eyes yet like me he spoke good Turkish with no accent. We managed to keep in touch though we parted at the end of the war when I came to school in England. We met again in the mid 1950s in London, I was serving my apprenticeship in Lincoln and Neil was working for one of the Anglo-Middle East oil companies. I remember visiting Neil in his basement flat in Knightsbridge just before he took a posting with the same oil company in the Middle East. That was the last time we saw each other.

"Yallah ya binah!"

Those three words of encouragement that were repeated from the track side as I ran, drove me on as nothing had ever done before. They were yelled out repeatedly, each successive time, the voice of my well wisher got shriller, almost frenzied! I felt such a surge of emotion that this call brought to me. I gritted my teeth in a supreme effort to make it to the tape well ahead of my rivals. Those yells of encouragement in Arabic could only have come from one person, my friend from Alex!

Geoffrey Hazzan and I had become close friends ever since we were introduced to each other by George Hill early in our first term at Hurst. His expectant mother had returned all the way back to her home town of Eccles from Alexandria so that his birth would be in the UK. Otherwise, he had been brought up in Egypt. We both recognised what a lot we had in common – languages, taste in food and above all attitudes. It was the shared background that drew us together and made us life long friends. Through him it was that I came to be invited on occasions to the Balen's home in Hove. Leon Balen was in the same House at school as Geoffrey.

The three of us were picked up by his parents for the day, invariably a Sunday. We were sometimes dropped off on the seafront promenade to have a wander about – the Laines, the Pier, and Gizzy's ice cream parlour were our favourite haunts. Mrs Balen was a dark attractive woman and a generous soul. In every way, she reminded me of many of my family's lady friends in Mersin. Her husband was a quiet man. I was lastingly impressed with the way he dressed – always in a beautifully tailored lounge suit and expensive looking shoes. He wore shirts that were a subdued pastel shade to match his suit. His shirts were silk with concealed buttons. He never wore a tie. His wife always referred to him as '*Nat*' and he called her *'my darling'*. Sunday lunch was a lavish meal and greatly appreciated after the *'not so lovely grub'* served up at Hurst. She always gave us each some '*tuck*' to take back to school. This always included a glass jar of *'dripping'* – beef dripping of course!

I left Hurst in the summer of 1949, Geoffrey stayed on for another year then went to Manchester University. Returning to England to serve my apprenticeship in Lincoln I used to meet Geoffrey from time to time. On one of the earliest occasions after we got reunited he asked me, "Did you do your National Service?" I replied briefly that I had not. Surprised, he then went on to quiz me, "How did you get out of it?" Where others might have resented such probing, we knew each other well enough for me not to mind in the very least. I replied, "I returned to Turkey straight after leaving Hurst. Besides, I never got any call up papers and I wasn't going to go out of my way to ask for them!" I jocularly explained. I well remember what he then said, "Pat, as a Jew I could not take that chance. I did my National Service!" At other times, he made it clear to me that not only did he have to do what was right and expected of him, but he had to be seen to be doing so. In short, Geoffrey was predisposed to see himself the victim of anti-Semitism.

In the three years away from my home, family and friends, it was inevitable I suppose that I would seek a close relationship of the sort I had previously, and with some one within easy reach. There was nowhere else for me to have found this other than at Hurst, for school was my home from home. The chance of finding a female to be a soul mate at the school was non-existent. Given these constraints, it was inevitable that this attachment would be with one of the boys, a Michael John Fisher who was in my house.

I find it difficult now to understand what it was that drew me to Fisher, other than the total absence of female company. It was of course the very thing that lead to the reputation that most public schools, Hurstpierpoint College no exception had acquired. Prior to becoming co-educational, they were reputed to be hot beds of homosexuality. This though was claimed often by those who had not been to public school and could not therefore possibly know.

I remember hearing of so called '*crushes*' that a junior had for some senior prefect or a rising star in sport. But it was I recall more usual to hear about the new boy who had appeared on the scene much to the delight of seniors who had fallen for his cherubic locks and coy smile. Some of them were reputed to have a passion or a '*pash*' for him. In those enclosed single sex communities I have been talking about, there was another dimension – young, unmarried masters. They would themselves have been not long out of boarding school or the armed forces living cheek by jowl with members of the same sex. Stories surfaced and spread, in some instances also including the young unmarried masters. It was difficult to judge fact from fiction, reality from fantasy. As I recall, there certainly was latent homosexuality, however I am also of the opinion that it was less often practised.

Michael Fisher, though a couple of months younger than me, on the strength of having been at Hurst a term or two earlier was my senior. Academically he was ahead of me by one class. He was an accomplished golfer and at school played the less physically demanding games like squash and tennis. He was asthmatic and in winter suffered badly with chilblains. These conditions, his slight stammer and a rather girlish preoccupation with his dress and habits gave him an effeminate aura. In appearance, I could not say whether Michael was good looking or not. He was neither muscular nor hairy thus lacking in the two defining features of manliness. He was an average build, with what might be described as an unblemished fair complexion and thinning flaxen hair. From this detailed description that I can now piece together, after these many years, Michael must certainly have been unmistakably effeminate, at least in my eyes.

I am now unable to bring to mind how this relationship came about nor when the attachment that I felt for him started. It is likely that it was something that developed gradually. Of one thing I am certain, I was the prime mover. I grew to be possessive of Michael. I wanted to monopolise him entirely for myself during the all too little free time we had out of school hours. For his part, he appeared to be happy and accepted my attention though I must emphasise it was in no way whatsoever sexual. With hindsight, the inescapable truth is that I was a victim of *'real and inescapable unrequited love',* with nobody to turn to. Had Michael been a girl, things would have been very different.

Michael had a friend, H R Edwards though unrelated they were like peas out of the same pod. They were close friends having been through the junior school at Hurst together. They had come to the senior school at the same time and into Red Cross House. From my very earliest recollections they must have been really close friends. Edwards, I never knew his first name, was for some reason called 'Rag' on occasions. He was an unassertive, quiet boy who appeared to live in Michael's shadow. I came to be jealous of their friendship and set out to destroy it. The one thing in the entire unhappy situation that I have come to regret and feel ashamed of.

I had never felt jealous of anyone in my life before. I could not have had any idea what torment it could cause nor for that matter how badly it could make a person behave. Without realising it, and for no better reason than his friendship with Fisher, I began to dislike Edwards. Where previously our paths never crossed, I started to take an interest in him. I set out to demean him. Rather than use his proper name, I called him 'Rag' – I can now think of few other words in the English language that sound more degrading than 'Rag'! I have never forgotten his look of utter wretchedness when on one occasion my taunting had brought him close to tears.

In spite of all that I have said about Michael, outwardly our relationship could have appeared no different than that of 'school chums' for he was another of the boys who invited me to spend part of a school holiday at his home. I can recall his mother and younger sister but I never met his father who had some prestigious position in International Banking. Michael had told me that his father spent a great deal of his time abroad. The family home was in a salubrious part of Bognor Regis one of the seaside towns in Sussex. The one thing that stuck in my mind was the lighting on the first floor landing. It was by wall mounted gas lamps with filaments that glowed – they engaged my attention as they reminded me of the 'Lux' paraffin lamps used in the Gozne hotel. My stay with Michael's family was immeasurably more agreeable than the holidays in Devon. Strange thing was that I never talked about girls with Michael, nor anything to do with any aspect of sex.

At the English High School in Istanbul and later at Hurstpierpoint College the subject of sex, between men and women was a frequent preoccupation. The boys gawped at photographs or illustrations showing all manner of sexual acts performed between men and women – 'dirty pictures'. Erotic literature was smuggled in by some of the boys and passed around to be read and discussed – 'smutty talk'.

I had left all that behind me in England. However strong the attachment that I had come to have for Michael, our separation from each other had not troubled me in the least. As far as I can recall, I neither thought about him nor did I miss him once I was back with my family and familiar surroundings in Turkey. This shows conclusively that my relationship with Michael had come about in order to fill the emotional vacuum I had been subjected to during the three long years away from my family. Further more, it also becomes evident that it was only of a temporary nature. An innocent relationship, however ill conceived…

My two months summer holiday passed very quickly. There were some memorable times. I have already touched on what made the region of Mersin into such a singularly special enclave. I found myself once more in that unique '*millieu*' but with the benefit of being so much older and dare I say, wiser in years. I was thus better able to comprehend the people, their behaviour and customs, the likes of which I would have otherwise never come across. For the first time, I really grasped how very different life in Mersin was from what I had experienced during the past three years in England.

In days before air conditioning, those who had the means continued, as their parents and grandparents before them, to spend the summer months in Gozne. This enabled them to sleep in the cool mountain air but in their waking hours, they had to put up with the lack of sanitation, the absence of piped water and electricity for lighting. The village of Gozne was divided by a river. Upper Gozne was the larger of the two halves, with several shops, cafes, the village school and Mosque. Lower Gozne had always been preferred by the Christians who rented houses there for the season. As a consequence of demand, there were some well appointed dwellings. They were the ones with an adjoining '*privy*'.

Lower Gozne was blessed with an '*Otel*'. It was the only one and privately owned by *'Otelci Teyfik Bey'* one of the village elders, an '*aga*'. It stood on a prime site – with the best fountain, bakery, general store and butcher near by. The *'Otel'* scored better on rustic appeal than comfort or utility. The entire accommodation was constructed in bare wood going up three floors under the lee of the sheer rock face of the local mountain. Each floor comprised a long balcony accessing bedrooms built along its entire length on the mountain side. The other side of the balcony was open and gave an un rivalled view of Mersin and the sea beyond. Open flights of wooden stairs went up to each of the floors. They were steep and rather rickety. Standards of construction in Gozne in those days were not unreasonably high.

Due to the reliability of having consistently dry summers, it was usual in that part of Turkey for cafes and restaurants to be in the open, though under the shade of trees. For the same reason, the well compacted, hard and level ground was devoid of any artificial surface. This large expanse of the *'Otel'* was shaded by three enormous weeping willows. They provided perfect shade for people having meals in the restaurant. The *'Otel'* was only open for the summer season, when it was at its busiest from Friday evening for the week-end when people came up from Mersin to escape the heat. It was the one and only meeting place in Lower Gozne for grown ups and young alike. Nowhere else have I come across such a basic, austere hotel yet one that was so well patronised.

Like a magnet it appeared to draw people to itself. But maybe more interestingly, it seemed to encourage them to let their hair down much to the delight of all those present. One such regular at the '*Otel*' was a Mersin business man Murad *Bey*. He was popular and seemed to be known by all. Having dined in the restaurant and had a few glasses of raki, Murad *Bey*, rather rotund and a fun loving extrovert wanted to show off his *'a la Turka'* dancing. He called the *'Otel'* waiter over, "Garçon!... come my son... I want you to do something for me."

"Whatever you desire, *effendim*." The waiter replied. He could probably guess, knowing Murad *Bey's* habits, what was coming. He also knew from past experience that Murad *Bey* was generous. He always tipped lavishly. He waited patiently to hear what he was to do.

"I want you to go and fetch the '*davulcu*'. Bring him back here along with his '*zurnaci*' partner." It just took these two self taught musicians to produce the countries traditional music. The rhythmic beat of Turkish folk dance music relies on the big bass drum or '*davul*' accompanied by the wailing and sometimes shrill accompaniment of the '*zurna*'. *A* double-reed instrument, not all that dissimilar in the sounds it emits from the bagpipes but I like to think more versatile and melodious.

It was not long before the waiter reappeared. With him were two elderly villagers; one of them out of sight behind his drum, the other unimpeded, carrying his flute-like instrument. Both looked somewhat dishevelled having been awakened from their slumber. The *'koylu'* of Gozne were no different from villagers everywhere in Anatolia, they slept and awoke each day with the sun. They had played for Murad *Bey* many times before, they went up to where he was sitting at his table and greeted him in the customary manner, '*salam aleykum*' to which he gave the customary response, '*aleykum el selam*'.

They seated themselves on chairs that had been made ready for them and without further ado struck up to the delight of Murad *Bey* who rose from his seat and started to dance. Many Turkish folk dances are derived from the '*koylu*' way of life, often imitating movements they make when working like the famous '*harman dali*' conjures up the gathering and harvesting of the corn. It was not long before one or two others joined in to the delight of all present who clapped enthusiastically in time to the drum beat. Some years later in the 1960s film of *Zorba the Greek* that wonderful dance scene with Anthony Quinn reawakened in me memories of the very similar carefree spontaneity and zest for life I had witnessed that evening in Gozne.

The '*Otel*' was at its busiest on Sundays. On occasions there would be tombola. Families in their droves would flock to the café for these events. Drinks were never offered as prizes, in deference to Islam. In any case whether Muslim or Christian, few people were interested in alcohol. Usually prizes were local produce such as baskets of fruit, chickens, even livestock. There was a festive atmosphere, which in those days took little to create. The waiters were kept busy serving glasses of strong tea and small cups of Turkish coffee, for the grown-ups and soft drinks for the children. '*Vishne*', the sweet syrup of the morello cherry diluted with water was a regional favourite.

Billy, my cousin, I recall coming home late for lunch once. The rest of the family were already all seated at table in the hall having their lunch. As usual, the big double doors to the outside were open and there he suddenly appeared. He had in tow, on the end of a rope a young ass. Hearing that he had won the animal as first prize in the tombola, his mother was in fits of laughter. Though quickly recovering, she declared that she did not consider it much of a *'trophy'* for where was it to be kept and fed – what was to become of it when the family went back down to Mersin!! In spite of Billy's protests and howls of anguish, the donkey went. I never knew where to or how it was disposed off.

I have already made some reference to Edouard Butrous. At the time, in his late 40s, he belonged to one of the notable Christian émigré families from Syria who had settled in Mersin. It had been generally accepted by the town's *'beau monde'* that Edouard, a confirmed bachelor, was destined to remain as they say, '*celibataire*'. Much to the surprise and I daresay pleasure of his many friends, he produced a very glamorous young wife called Nadia. Her family, the Asfours were said to be amongst the notables of Beirut. She was a great deal younger than him. Tall and elegant, even when in primitive Gozne, she some how managed to look well groomed. It was said by many who knew her that she resembled Rita Hayworth, one of Hollywood's greats of the time.

That summer, Edouard Butrous booked a row of the best rooms on the top floor of the '*Otel*' for his entourage. Before getting married, he had lived on his own on the top floor of one of Mersin's old Armenian houses. A prestigious property near the Catholic church. It had an uninterrupted view of the Mediterranean. Since Nadia came on the scene, he had sought out a respectable widow. Madame Janine, a pseudonym as I cannot recall her real name, was a typical Levantine. As Edouard explained, "She will keep house and cook for Nadia and myself. In time, Nadia may want to get more involved. Nadia is still so young, Madame Janine could serve as a mother figure, after all she has lived in France and appears to be of a certain standing. I was lucky to find her." So it was that Madame Janine accompanied the newly weds to Gozne that summer.

Edouard, no longer the *'celibataire',* set out to pamper Nadia, young enough to be his daughter. He lavished all manner of gifts on her.

One day when the *'beau monde'* of Lower Gozne were arousing themselves from their siestas, she was spotted coming down from the '*Otel*' dressed in a smart pair of jodhpurs and boots, the likes of which had never before been seen by anyone around. Nadia carried a riding crop in one hand and in the other safety head gear. On the dusty road below was a tan coloured filly saddled up, its reins held by the '*seyis*' who would be in attendance. Evidently Nadia had done some riding in Beirut and Edouard had bought her the young horse as a birthday present.

Probably blinded by his desire to indulge his bride, Edouard had completely overlooked the all too obvious. The village of Gozne in the lower reaches of the Taurus mountain range was by no stretch of the imagination horse riding country. Even where the terrain was reasonably level, it was littered with rocks and stones. Lush undulating meadows, green and soft under foot ideal for a gallop did not exist up there. Nadia's horse riding was restricted to the short stretch of dusty road in the vicinity of the hotel. As a consequence of this, the daily excursion became a spectacle that could be conveniently watched from the '*Otel*' café. I can recall the scene. Nadia resplendent in her *'a la franga'*, or as we would say European style riding habit. Atop her filly also with its *'a la franga'* leather saddle and accompanied by the groom doing his best to keep up whilst listening to Edouard calling out instructions from the top floor of the 'Otel'. For a time, this hitherto unknown display in Gozne, much to the delight of '*Otelci Teyfik Bey*', became a veritable crowd puller.

It had always been my family's custom to call it a day and return down to Mersin shortly after the first rains in Gozne. Not surprising as when they did come they were torrential. There were two or three wooden bridges soon after leaving the village. I recall times when one or two of them had been washed away by the rapid rise in the level of water in the river brought about by the accumulation of debris during the long dry summer. End of season Mersin was not at its best. A lot of people being still away either in Istanbul or the more adventurous in Europe. It was an opportune time to get together things, mainly edibles to take back with me to England. When I could find some I always tried to get some *'batareh'* – hard fish roes encapsulated in bees wax.

So much tastier than the caviar everyone in Europe went mad about.

Whilst on my shopping mission down town, I decided to have my shoes polished by one of the several *'boyaci'* on the back road near the market. Out there, great pains are taken to get as near a perfect shine as possible – not something to embark on if you are in a hurry! I certainly was not in a hurry. The *'boyaci'* next to the one polishing my shoes returned looking disappointed, he told his friend, "Fatma is a damned nuisance. I've just been to try and see her for the second time without success. She was again busy. I'm not going to bother again today, maybe tomorrow. I'll see how I feel."

The said Fatma, turned out to be what my friends called a *'fille de joie'* or what we less romantically refer to as a *'working girl'* in the town's one and only government controlled brothel, just round the corner. Fatma and all her colleagues were not permitted to walk out of the brothel into the town. Even if they wanted to do some shopping, they could only go out in a horse drawn carriage of which there were any number in circulation. As much as anything, this protected the girls from any abuse they might otherwise have been subjected to. Better-off men did not go to the brothel, they arranged for the *'fille de joie'*, maybe Fatma herself, to call on them. The outcome of this was surely, "Same dish, better presentation, more expensive!"

I still have my first British Passport. That seemingly indestructible instrument of identity with its rigid dark blue outside cover the front embossed with the National crest and the words – British Passport –

United Kingdom of Great Britain and Northern Ireland. At the very bottom of the page in a cut out panel I am identified as Master Patrick Grigsby. On one of the inside pages a stamp impression in ink by the Yesilkoy Airport, chief of police is dated 19/09/1948 and certifies my departure to London by aircraft.

I had enjoyed my holiday but I am unable to say with any conviction whether as my house master, Mr Bury had written in my end of year report, I was returning "fired with a new zeal to succeed." Nor can I now recall whether I had the least idea that it was to be my last year at Hurst and that in less than 10 months, I would be returning to Mersin for good.

Chapter 11

It is said by some that hindsight – being wise after the event – is a wonderful thing. I am not so sure! However wonderful hindsight might be, it cannot serve to change anything that has already come to pass. I am also mindful that I must not let hindsight influence how I actually felt and what actually took place on my return to Hurst on the 19th September in 1948. I will continue to tell it as it really was. I had just returned from a visit to my family and the place I still called home for the first time after an absence of three years.

At the time approaching my 17th birthday, I felt that my family and I had grown apart. We had lost contact with each other. When I had been with them, there had been efforts on both sides to make up for this hiatus. Time was approaching for consideration to be given to my career. Parents in that part of the world vied with each other on the subject of their children's career, especially in the case of their sons. With their English origins and their schooling in the UK, my family's attitude was rather different. Less demanding, more liberal, I believe they were as much concerned for my happiness as for my career.

It was my uncle who once more took an interest in my future as he had done when I was about to travel to England for my schooling. He spoke of Ruskin College which was in Oxford but not part of the University and The London School of Economics. Though without much thought as to the long term and sort of career that they would fit me for. My mother on the other hand was more pragmatic, though her notion of a career was limited to just three professions – medicine, engineering and the law. Beyond these she might also have been influenced by her friends, those of whom had been involved with local members of the British Diplomatic Service. To them, what could be more prestigious! The British Empire was still held in awe, especially in a place like Mersin with its growing maritime trade.

My uncle was a staunch Socialist, in spite of his family background for after all he was the grandson of General Henry Selby Rickards. His education had been curtailed when he volunteered to join the British Expeditionary Force in France at the start of the First World War. Having survived, when he was demobilised in 1918, he spent some time at University in Cyprus. He was a self taught Socialist and therefore a great admirer of the movement's founding fathers, especially Kier Hardy. He was a member of the Fabian Society. There was nothing that he would have liked more, even as a mature student, than to have gone to Ruskin College. In his mind, there could be no better reason than this for him to sponsor me at Ruskin College once I left Hurst.

As for my mother's perspective, it was very different from my uncle's. Much of my mother's views had been shaped by trauma in her life. My father's tragic death left my mother almost destitute in Alexandria with me to bring up. She had been obliged to return to her family home in Mersin.

Had she been on her own things would have been different for her, but she had me, a four year old to try and integrate with my grandparents. My grandfather had little time for me, at the time I was the only grandchild yet one too many. With no training after leaving school in England, my mother had taken up teaching English, mainly by giving private lessons. It was not surprising that she had often told me, "First thing is to get your School Certificate. Work hard and try to get good marks in the subjects you are studying. Then, when you leave Hurst, we will have to see what can be done." Her ambitions for me did not go beyond finding somebody to employ me. In return, I would have to work hard and serve them well. She spoke about *'starting at the bottom of the ladder and working your way up!"*

I was thus destined to grow up in my grandfathers' home in Mersin. He had come out to Turkey in 1890, only four years after his own father, General Rickards had died in Beirut. He brought his substantial inheritance, in gold sovereigns I had been told, to Mersin with him. This was shrewdly invested in *'bricks and mortar'* as his physical disability deprived him of an active working life. A wealthy property owner, yet he was ever mindful of the fact that rents were a fixed income. Growing up, I was to hear members of my family on many occasions declare that, "*we have to budget carefully as we only have a fixed income to live off."* It is not for me now to debate the logic nor for that matter the justification of such reasoning. Another thing, all my family, with the exception of my aunt Olga who had for some years, savoured the life style of the leisured class in England, were moderate in their way of life. I was to grow up repeatedly hearing the Victorian adage *"waste not want not"*.

During the summer, back with my family I was once more imbued with their way of life and attitudes. Though only three years older since last in their midst, I was more mature than might have been expected and better able to grasp and digest the concerns shown by my uncle and mother for my future. They summoned up for me life after school, career choices, even prospects of university. My mother's pragmatism had got home to me in her words *'First thing is to get your School Certificate."* So simple, and so obvious, I had made it my immediate priority on returning to Hurst.

That September 1948 Christmas term at Hurst was different from earlier ones. Two things made it so, one personal to me, the second common to the entire establishment. After two years in the Removes, I had moved up into the V Form and would be sitting for my School Certificate. The extensive preparations for the school's centenary celebrations were being spoken of already though I have to say, my own preparations took precedence – each time the exams came to mind, I heard my mother's exhortation, *"get your School Certificate!"*

Mr Bury's words *"fired with fresh zeal to succeed"* intrigued me though I was not sure what the word *'zeal'* really meant. Responding to Mr Bury's wish in the affirmative would have made me a '*zealot*' but I was not a fanatic, nor a bigot and certainly not a fiend. No, I was not '*fired with zeal'* but rather I had come to my senses just in time. Until then I had not been motivated to study, let alone subjects that I felt would be of no practical use to me. That some Greek wise man in Samos had worked out "that the square on the longest side (which came to be known as '*hypotenuse*') of a right-angled triangle is equal to the sum of the squares on the other two sides" was interesting but it meant little to me. I know, I have exaggerated to make my point.

Whatever I might have previously thought, I came to realise that the School Certificate was an objective that I needed to attain if I were to stand any chance of making good in my life that lay ahead. Thus motivated, I became determined to succeed and this was the very first milestone on that steep road which is life's struggle.

What I was not then aware of was the handicap that I had created for myself by my ill-fated emotional involvement with Michael. As for Edwards, he had left Hurst and I am now unable to say when or under what circumstances. Looking back, I remember I had felt bad about this and wondered why he had departed so suddenly. I felt great remorse at the way I had behaved towards him. The fact that once he had gone there was little I could do to put matters right only added to my feelings of guilt. As time went by Michael was promoted, moving up in the House. After all he was the archetypal product of the system – he worked to the book – compliant and unquestioning of accepted practices – not the sort to rock the proverbial boat – a veritable asset. He was also an accomplished golfer and used to be invited to play some of the masters, including Mr Bury. By contrast, after the incident on the running track with M.K.Russell, my standing had plummeted, especially with the senior sports master, Mr G. Lambert. I had become a bad egg, a liability! I felt isolated and even more of an '*outsider*'.

I became increasingly embittered without knowing against whom or what to direct my feelings of resentment. I had never had anyone I could turn to, nothing had changed in that respect. However much I might have longed for Michael to be my best friend, even a soul mate, it was he who was at the very root of the problem that was consuming me. I was to realise once we were parted, that however innocent and passive, the relationship from the very start was ridden with sexual undertones that were never to be fulfilled. This pent up frustration and hostility within me led me into trouble.

The passage of time has blurred my memory as to the events that led Mr Bury to subject me to the drastic steps that he did. I can now only assume that he must have viewed them as grave. I have no other reason to come to this conclusion other than the fact that the punishment he meted out was so very draconian. I was to be subjected to what I can only describe as public ridicule for the entire school to witness. The profound effect it had on me caused me to dwell on what might have caused Mr Bury to treat me in this way. With my family so far away in Turkey and out of reach, I expect the poor man, was at his wit's end to know how best to deal with the situation. Even had he been able to discuss things with my mother, I doubt if that would have brought forth any solutions. At some point he must have decided that the usual forms of disciplining, including caning which was much favoured at the time, would not work on me. In his desperation he decided that there was but one way to discipline me. I recall being summoned to his study, the last of several earlier occasions. All these years on, his judgement, word for word, or at least the sense of it amounted to this:

"I have decided to demote you. You will be moved into the junior dormitory. During the day, you will spend your time not in the senior but in the junior dayroom. At meal times in the hall, you will sit at the most junior table. Have you anything to say?"

I hardly had the chance to digest the implications of what was to be my disgrace. I was overwhelmed with despair. Lost for words, all I wanted was to get away. What could I possibly have found to say that might have changed his mind, made him relent? In my despair and humiliation the only other time I had felt so injured came back to me standing before my uncle in Mersin. I had been a mere child then. This time, as then in what must have sounded a choking voice I replied, "No Sir."

Without further ado Mr Bury, as my uncle had done, dismissed me abruptly, "Off you go!"

It is difficult for me now to describe how I felt, still harder to give an account of the manner in which I bore my ordeal. I am not even sure for how long I was subjected to this '*demotion*' as he chose to call it, probably a week, maybe longer. Being '*reduced in rank*' at an English public school where the culture of seniority counts for so much, and where moving up the pecking order is almost as important as academic achievement, will illustrate the stigma attached to such demotion. Its harshness can be measured by the fact that I can bring to mind no other instance of this treatment being meted out during the whole time I had been at Hurst.

Now I believe it had the effect of demeaning me in front of the entire school. I must have felt overcome with shame for as long as it lasted. I have come to believe that the troubled state I was in could only have been exacerbated by such a process leading to ridicule and mental torment. Though the demeaning process of my '*demotion*' was his very own brainchild, I never had nor now have any bad feelings towards Mr Bury for reasons that I have already explained. His report for the term which I quote in full below says it all. It is also interesting to note what he says about my '*obtaining a high position in the House*'. This implies that I was considered to still have a future at Hurst and that my departure at the end of that year had not as yet been decided.

> "P.C.N. Grigsby:
> I have found him very difficult to handle this term owing to the problem of his friendship which has obsessed his mind to the exclusion of all else. He is now in a more amenable frame of mind and will, I hope, settle down to the many tasks in hand for the advancement of his own career. I fear that another outburst will prove fatal to his chances of School Certificate and of obtaining a high position in the House.
>
> R.E. Bury"

* * *

At the time, disciplining was administered by the cane. Painful but quick and above all, private. To some it was even a source of bravado. It did not usually carry the humiliating stigma of an audience. By contrast, the treatment meted out to me was intended to be both public and prolonged. It involved being seen by the entire school, including the most junior boys, the masters and other staff, over and over again, as an object of ridicule. This had a profound and lasting effect on me. Even now a strong sense of injustice grips me if I hear of a human being subjected to any form of humiliation. No one should be deprived of their '*izzeti nefis*' an often heard phrase in both Arabic and Turkish, '*self-respect*', in the mistaken belief that it is a legitimate form of punishment. It is claimed that the greater purpose of punishment is to bring about improved behaviour. How can this be justified by treatment that sets out to demean? Humiliation causes bitter resentment, even hatred and rage. Worse still, sometimes the victim's resolve to get even.

For all my turmoil and despair, neither could I blame Michael. To the contrary, I have since marvelled at the way in which he tolerated my involvement in his life which at times must have taxed his patience. Neither have I ever known whether he realised that beneath my professed wish to have his friendship there was a deeper infatuation – what I have heard sometimes described as '*unhealthy*'. It has since been suggested to me that he must have been flattered by my attention – I can't say how true this might or might not have been.

As with so many of my contemporaries, Michael did return to Hurst after I had left. We must have kept in touch as we did meet just the one time. It was in 1956, one year after I had got married. Michael came to visit us when we were living in the 'Spinney' bungalow in Drayton Manor, once part of the Robert Peel Estate on the outskirts of Tamworth in Staffordshire. At the time he was with one of the major oil companies Shell or BP, I am not certain which. He had his golf clubs in his car and told Beryl and I that he would take time off to have a round of golf with some old friend or a new customer, "Wonderful thing golf! It has always stood me in good stead. It now serves me as part of my stock-in-trade. My boss encourages this. Mind you, I have never needed any encouragement to play a round. It keeps me supple and fit. Have you ever thought of taking it up Pat?"

"Not really, I have just joined the Tamworth Rugby Club."

I cannot say that we found much to talk about since we had last been together at Hurst. Perhaps we might never have had much in common. When our paths crossed again in Drayton Manor, what little we might have once had in common had gone, vanished into thin air. By then, I had served my engineering apprenticeship in Lincoln, moved to David Brown Tractors in Meltham and left them. Most importantly of all, I had got married to Beryl and moved to a new job and life in the Midlands. Michael had evidently chosen to remain a bachelor, he never mentioned whether he had a girlfriend or not. He still looked much the same, maybe a bit stouter. His flaxen hair was thinner on top. It was to be the last time I saw him. Sadly I got to hear by chance that he died suddenly. A fatal heart attack.

My last term, the summer of 1949, preparations for Hurstpierpoint's centenary overshadowed all else. That term was to be memorable for me personally as well. I cannot say when I heard that it was to be my last term at Hurst. Nor how I came to be told. It might have been my mother who broke the news in one of her letters or Mr Bury himself. I am now inclined to think that the news came from my mother. I can recall nothing of what she might have written, still less the reasons given for the decision. It did come like a bolt from the blue – not just a surprise, more of a shock. I suspect that I might have been relieved yet at the same time saddened. It was later in life that I came to realise how much more I could have derived from Hurst but for my problem and my premature departure that stemmed from it.

I have but two recollections of the Centenary celebrations. Hurstpierpoint being a church founded school, the service in the chapel was to feature prominently. The BBC was involved in a recording of the service. We, that is the entire school and myself, had to attend numerous rehearsals to ensure that everything went smoothly on the day. Coming to the end of the last of these rehearsals in the chapel a boy had raised his hand to draw attention as he had something he wished to say. Mr A. Tregonning, the school's director of music beckoned him to speak up. "Please sir, if I am not mistaken, proceedings in the chapel will be going on at eleven o'clock through to 12.00 noon. Unless something is done to stop the tower clock, there will be chimes at both these times. Won't that impair the sound recordings, Sir?"

Mr Tregonning's otherwise stern countenance changed into a broad smile as he acknowledged the boy who had spoken, "You are quite right Laurence. Thanks for bringing the matter to my notice. Well done!"

Perhaps in the light of all that was going on inconsequential yet something about it struck me. The boy, P.B. Laurence was a contemporary of mine in Red Cross. Not particularly popular, he had earned his nickname "the lip". We had little in common and I did not care much about him. Struck by his forethought, I remember going to him later to say "Well done". None of the staff nor any of the other boys had thought about nor realised the consequence of the loud and prolonged chimes of the tower clock. Perhaps it was that it brought back to me memories of my stay in the Mason's flat nearly four years earlier when I had arrived at Hurst.

It was the one and only time in four years at Hurst that I was to receive guests – Mrs Herga accompanied by Cicely her daughter just down from St Andrew's University had both come from London to be with me. I now know that the centenary celebrations took place on Saturday, July the 23rd, 1949 and were attended by more than 1500 guests. The principal guests of honour were Her Royal Highness Princess Alice, Countess of Athlone, her husband Major-General the Earl of Athlone, Dr Geoffrey Fisher the Archbishop of Canterbury, His Majesty's Lord Lieutenant, the Duke of Norfolk.

Strange, I have no recollection of any of the proceedings that went on for several hours. Nor can I remember seeing any of the dignitaries who were present. Looking back this might be explained by the sheer numbers involved and constraints imposed by the school's layout. This did not disappoint me as pomp and ceremony hold little fascination for me. By nature and upbringing I am given more to spontaneity which is the product or outcome of impulse.

Mr Bury's last task was to get me shipped off safely back to my family in Turkey. I have since pondered on what he might have felt as he set about tackling this final chore – relief, I suppose! In my efforts to describe my school days at Hurst, I have had to do a good deal of pondering. As a consequence I have brought to mind almost forgotten occasions, which at the time might have left me unmoved, maybe even bored. With the long passage of time, they now hold for me a different perception.

One such experience was part of a school holiday in Brighton which I spent with Mr Bury. The consequence I suppose of his failure to find some where that he could have sent me to on my own. We stayed in small private hotel on one of the main streets in the centre of the town. Less than five years after the end of WWII, Britain was then still in the throes of post war austerity. I can visualise my bedroom which over looked the noisy street below. It was sparsely furnished with a steel bedstead, lumpy mattress, and flannelette sheets. As far as I can recall, there was also a small wardrobe and dressing table. It was gloomy, in need of redecoration and dimly lit.

No en-suite in those days, I did however have a washbasin with hot and cold running water. There were toilets and a bathroom on the same floor. I found out that if I wanted a bath, I had to pick the right moment to make a dash for it before somebody else got there first. No television either in those days, not even a black and white set. In the little sitting room, conversation was *de rigueur* unless you chose the *early to bed* option. I recall Mr Bury announcing that he had got us tickets at the local theatre to see *The Linden Tree* – I have to confess, I cannot remember anything about it. One day, soon after breakfast we caught the bus to Eastbourne, it was a pleasant ride. What I was not prepared for was the return trip. He broke the news casually telling me, "We will walk along the cliff side over The Seven Sisters and back to Brighton. It will do you the world of good." I had little choice in the matter. Pretending to be delighted and full of enthusiasm. I made the only reply expected of me, the usual "Yes sir!"

I well remember that walk over the seven hills. It was akin to tackling a mammoth switchback except for the fact that as we were not running, we derived no momentum from the previous descents to carry us up to the top of the ascents that followed. It was the strenuous day's trudge that made it so memorable. That, and the fact that it was mercifully not raining nor too windy. We passed close by the lighthouse. It was to become memorable as I seem to remember some years later hearing that it had to be moved or perhaps dealt with in some other dramatic way to prevent it disappearing over the cliff side. A *rendezvous* for lovers the cliffs were also a favourite spot for suicides.

Looking back over these many years, I have felt increasingly that Mr Bury surpassed what might have been normally expected from a housemaster. At boarding school the housemaster's lot, whether in time or effort, is demanding in the extreme. I can now only surmise that he came to be my guardian through the kindness of his heart and succumbing to my mother's entreaties. Widows can be most persuasive, my mother was certainly no exception.

Our short stay together in Brighton testifies to his dedication, if nothing else. Yet, I knew so little about this kindly man. The little I did hear about him was that he had been to Rossall School in Fleetwood just north of Blackpool in Lancashire. He read classics, Latin and Ancient Greek at Emmanuel College, Cambridge. He was demobilised from the army with the rank of captain just after I arrived at Hurst. He spent most of the school holidays with his mother who lived in North Wales, not far from where he had been to school.

I was to meet Mr Bury some 13 years later, in 1962 by which time I had served my engineering apprenticeship and was with Foseco. As the sales manger of one of their subsidiary companies, I was test marketing a new and rather unique product – a portable foundry. I had gone down to Sussex to visit several prospective customers, amongst them my old school. The science master who I had telephoned to fix up my visit had received me and taken me over to the science laboratory where we were joined by a couple of his colleagues. It was towards the end of my demonstration that Mr Bury joined the party. I had presented the aluminium casting, a decorative ash tray that I had produced in the demonstration to the science master. Taking his leave, he had thanked me saying, "I was most impressed at how conveniently you were able to melt the metal and produce a cast shape. Most interesting. I'll be in touch with you. I must go but I know Mr Bury wants to have a chat with you."

Left to ourselves, I recall Mr Bury sitting down and asking me what I had been up to since my departure from Hurst just after the centenary celebrations. As I cleared up and put the equipment away into its large case in readiness for my next demonstration, I brought him up to date. I told him about my rather chequered career and married life – Beryl and I by then had acquired three daughters. I described life in Birmingham and the Black Country, topics that seem to fascinate people in the southern counties. As for Mr Bury, he was still housemaster of Red Cross and seemed to know how all '*his boys*' were making out. I had asked him what he thought of the revolutionary process I had demonstrated. I recall his very words in response to my question, "Pat, I know nothing about all this new technology. I am only a poor classicist."

Those were his very words to me by which I shall now always remember him, for I was never to see Mr Bury again to thank him properly, though belatedly, for all he had done as my guardian. Given his small frame and his mannerisms, even his speech, I earlier likened him to Monty. For all that, he remained a modest, kindly man. Indeed, his description of himself as "only a poor classicist" bears this out. It is little wonder that one of my all time favourite films remains to this day *Goodbye Mr Chips*. Had an actor like Cyril Cussack been cast in the title role instead of Robert Donat, he would have better matched the image I have of my own housemaster. As time has gone by, there has been such a lot I would have liked to have spoken with him about but then that also applies to so many others.

It was to be Mr Bury's final chore. For it was he who had sorted out my sea passage back to my family in Turkey. It must have been no mean task for him to have sought out the Ellerman & Wilson Line in Hull and booked me a one way trip on one of their cargo-passenger ships. I boarded the MV Domino in the Pool of London. I can still recall being dropped off with my cabin trunk alongside her where she was moored in the Royal Albert Docks. Standing on the dockside, looking up, she appeared surprisingly small. Mr Bury had described the MV Domino to me as a cargo-passenger vessel plying between the port of London and Constanta on the Black Sea, her last port of call after Istanbul where I would disembark. Standing on the dockside, I was struck by how very different she was from the SS Franconia that big impressive looking Cunard liner, serving as a troop ship on which I had journeyed to England four years earlier.

Centenary celebrations over and the School Certificate examinations behind me, it was towards the end of July '49. It was my parting with Hurstpierpoint College, the end of my schooling, I was returning to my family for good. I wonder now how I must have felt as I was about to board the MV Domino.

It is hard to be sure; I suspect it would have been the immediacy that I would have been conscious of and reacting to. Later, with time to reflect, if anything, I would have felt relief at the prospect of moving on to pastures new from what had been an unhappy and disappointing summer term. Deep down I did have many regrets.

I recall it was a warm evening, still broad daylight. I went on board and would soon be meeting my fellow passengers. All five of them as indeed Mr Bury had found out and made known to me.

A gong sounded for dinner. All meals were served in what I shall call, for the want of a better word '*the mess*'. At other times of the day and night it also served as a lounge for the passengers. We had our meals with the captain and three of his officers all seated at the one and only table. It was prior to taking our places that the captain carried out an informal introduction. Present were a young English husband and wife, a Greek lady and Mrs Lister. I had already met the fifth passenger as we shared a cabin. A young man, though some years my senior called Telford. I was to find out later on from Mrs Lister that he was the great grandson of the Scottish civil engineer Thomas Telford, best remembered for designing and supervising the building of the Menai Suspension Bridge and the Caledonian Canal.

The MV Domino had a registered tonnage of 3500. It was one of three identical motor vessels in the Ellerman and Wilson fleet, working the Black Sea and Mediterranean ports. Its main cargoes on that trip was structural steel over stowed with Ferguson tractors destined for Turkey.

After the calm of the channel, we ran into heavy seas and gale force winds in the Bay of Biscay. Throughout the storm none of the passengers ventured out of their cabins. Tables and chairs had over turned in the mess room. The rolling motion had apparently been exacerbated by the cargo of steel. As if by some magic, conditions improved once through the Straits of Gibraltar and into the Mediterranean. Throughout the rest of the voyage, we were blessed with calm seas and brilliant sunshine. I spent much of my time on the forecastle to get a better view of the porpoises that seemed to be drawn to the hull of the ship. These outriders were enjoying themselves suddenly leaping out of the water then gracefully gliding back, surging forward at a tangent circling back to dive under the keel and reappear seconds later on the other side of the vessel. One of the deckhands, 'Smiler' to his mates told me "They do that to scratch their backs." I never checked to find out if it's true or just another mariner's story.

It was to be several weeks before we reached our port of call, Istanbul. Fragments of the voyage still live on in my memory. For one thing, my cabin-mate, Telford left me an indelible image of himself. The first evening he came to table in his dinner jacket when the other passengers were informally dressed. This led to some light hearted banter. Several present had said "he won't make such an exhibition of himself again!" – he did! As he told me himself "I always dressed for dinner". It was some time later that a much travelled passenger informed me "Protocol demands informal dress first evening out and thereafter dinner jackets."

The young third officer, cook and I used to meet in the steward's cabin most evenings after dinner. There was nowhere else, besides the steward had the keys to stores and where the wines, spirits and cigarettes were kept. He would from time to time put four bottles of beer on the table saying with mock reverence "These are on Sir John – we'll drink to his health." He was of course referring to Sir John Ellerman. Another reason why we gathered in the steward's cabin was because he was that little bit older than the rest of us and had been around. He always had a tale or two to tell. Like the one about the first time the ship he was on called at Kalamata on the Corinthian peninsula in Greece.

"My mate and I went to this nightclub called the "Paradiso". They describe them as bars out there. Anyway I had a couple of beers and spotted this bird sitting across the way. After the three piece band had played a couple of numbers and she had not been asked by any of the other punters for a dance, I thought I would. She had blonde hair, most likely dyed. She was a Veronica Lake look alike. My mate fancied the *bint* sitting with her so we went for it."

We were listening intently to the steward, wondering what was coming next at the Paradiso nightclub. The cook laughing suggested, "I know, your Veronica Lake turned you down for some tall handsome Swede off one of the Svenska Orient Line ships that put into Kalamata regularly."

The steward grinned, shaking his head, "You guessed wrong… She accepted! The small dance floor was absolutely packed. Dancing with her, we could hardly move. The place was in semi darkness, they were playing slow foxtrots. We had not been dancing long, I felt something unexpected pressing against me! For all her blonde hair and feminine wiles, she was not a she at all, she was a he… a big he! A chill went through me."

I joined in the laughter, wondering to myself "I wonder if this is true or just another mariner's yarn, like the one about the mermaids." Undeterred, the steward went on,

"I was up to my neck in it! Once the music stopped, Veronica Lake would in the normal way come over to our table for drinks – that's how they get paid. I managed to have a quick word with my mate. We both excused ourselves and headed for the gents whilst Veronica and the other *bint* seated themselves at the table we had been at. They must have had a long wait. We managed to find a back way out of the Paradiso nightclub and caught a taxi to the docks and the safety of our ship."

When we got to Pireaus, the port for Athens we had a night out together. Not I hasten to say at a nightclub but at a *'taverna'* where we had a Greek dinner and listened to Greek music. I had enjoyed their company so much. Many years later, driving through Greece, I was reminded of Kalamata when I bought a large tin of olive oil that came from there "*the best olive oil comes from Kalamata*" was emblazoned on the side of the tin according to the shop keeper's translation.

Throughout the voyage, lasting more than a month, a mild curry and rice was on the Domino's breakfast menu. It was an optional addition to the traditional full English breakfast. I had never tasted curry in my life before. I tried it and liked it. Thereafter during the voyage I always had it and as a result acquired an early taste for curry. This was before the emergence of the so called *'curry houses'* in Britain and much longer before *'chicken ticka masala'* was voted our most popular national dish. The ship's cook told me that curry for breakfast on board ship went back the days of the Raj. It was a time when passenger travel by sea was at its peak between the UK and the Far East. It became a tradition that was kept up by some of the shipping lines.

My voyage, a long one at that on the MV Domino across the Mediterranean to Istanbul had been arranged by Mr Bury for reasons of expediency. It turned out to be my very first and my only *'cruise'*. I have put the word in italics as I am using it ahead of its time. Back in those days, there were no such things. Luxury sea travel did exist but in a very different form from what we have today. Those who needed to cross the Atlantic and were fortunate to do so first class, sailed on one or other of the trans-Atlantic passenger liners usually to New York. The voyage lasting less than a week and was spent in style – in a 'state-room' suite. Gastronomic meals in a top class restaurant. Entertainment was formal and sophisticated – light orchestral music. At dinner, dancing to a top dance band with a vocalist. There might have been a swimming pool. For exercise, passengers took brisk walks around the decks. Some took part in games – deck tennis and deck quoits were in favour. On reaching their destination, passengers would talk about their voyage or crossing. The word *'cruise'* at the time was taken to mean *"sailing around without a precise destination"*.

Now, more than half a century on, the word has come into its own. Cruises, especially luxury cruises have become the ultimate holiday indulgence. Some cruise liners are veritable cities of pleasure with the added novelty of being afloat. Fitted with state of the art stabilisers and given their enormous size, these luxury cruise liners can move at speed but appear to remain motionless to those on board. Once inside, you might just as well be in any of the shopping and amusement malls that have sprung up on dry land, in our large cities. I am reminded of Birmingham's "Star City".

Over-development has transformed the pleasures of a voyage on a cargo-passenger ship like the MV Domino into over the top *'luxury cruises'*. In the past, many shipping lines, especially those operating in the Mediterranean offered some limited passenger accommodation on their ships which as I found out for myself in 1949, had a simple charm of its very own.

After calling into Ceuta to bunker with diesel oil, the MV Domino had headed for Greece. Our first port of call was Patras. The Corinthian canal was not navigable due to war damage that had as yet not been cleared. This meant going around the Peloponnisos, an added distance by sea of some 400 kilometres to Athen's port of Piraeus and from there on to Volos. Here I was invited by Mrs Lister to accompany her ashore to visit a family friend who turned out to have a business making local sweetmeats. I was offered '*kataif*' and '*baklava*' favourites of mine from Turkey. As with some dishes, the names in to Greek would have been derived by the simple expedient in this instance of adding '*i*' and '*dis*' respectively. This Helenic conversion, I am glad to say made no difference to the appearance nor taste of the sweetmeats. The offering of them had permitted me to say '*yasou*' and later '*efharisto*' by way of thanks in my limited Greek. Our final stop in Greece was Thessaloniki the largest port in the far north.

From Thessaloniki we headed back south, crossing the Aegean sea to Izmir in Turkey and then north again to the entrance of the Dardanelles or the straits of Canakkale. Crossing Turkey's land-locked sea of Marmara to Istanbul where I stayed the night of the 4th of September, at that old haunt, the Alp Hotel overlooking the Bosphorus, before once more embarking on that so familiar railway journey to Mersin.

I was about to open another door, one that I had not been through before and beyond it who knows what I would find.

Chapter 12

I alighted from the Toros Express at a nondescript settlement in the middle of nowhere. To me it was a familiar though unimposing place, as I had been there many times before, just passing through. The main line continued on to Adana and from there through Syria into Iraq and on to Bagdad, the terminus of the railroad that stretched all the way from Paris. The express I had been on, sometimes also known as the Bagdad Express, did not hang about, once the few other passengers had got off. It made a hasty departure in a cloud of smoke and steam accompanied by several shrill blasts of its whistle to continue its long journey.

Yenice was the name of the place where I had got off the train. It served as a junction for the local train to the sea port of Mersin which lies to the west. In spite of its insignificance, the station of Yenice did have its one moment of fame. It was in a railway carriage there that it was rumoured a top secret meeting of the 'Big Three' – Stalin, Roosevelt and Churchill – had taken place during WWII. An event probably best kept quiet at the time as Turkey was anxious not to compromise her neutrality.

The local train of two or three carriages from Yenice trundled along dropping its speed to not much more than a walking pace so that it barely jerked to a halt as it hit the buffers at the end of the line. It was like meeting up with a dear old friend every time I arrived at Mersin's humble yet so beloved to me railway station. The place never appeared to change in the 10 years or so that I had known it. It had been the scene of so many of my trips to and from Istanbul when I was at the English High School there. Once more it was the end of the line for my home coming in the first week of September 1949. Though I am now unable to visualise my family's welcome, it would have been the same as all the earlier ones – much hugging, kissing, laughter and the inevitable tears. Tears of such joy each time. Such undisguised emotion, but then, that is the way in the Middle East and indeed how I have always been myself.

"Patrick, you were at your best when we met you off the train. Dressed in your school blazer and grey flannels, I couldn't help thinking – here is what the English public school system turns out. I hope you will always live your life by what they taught you over these last four years at Hurst."

Words that my uncle William came out with a few days after my arrival. I expect that in company with everybody else, being overwhelmed with emotion when I had got off the train, he could not bring himself to utter them. I believe that when he said them, they were no less true for not being spontaneous. They were said from the heart. It was a rare tribute and as a consequence has stuck in my memory word for word. Whatever the future might have held in store for me, however dark the cloud under which I had left Hurst, my uncle at least felt well disposed towards me to have said what he did.

My voyage on the MV Domino had been a most enjoyable experience. Few in 1949 would have had such a cruise, visiting so many interesting places in the Mediterranean. Away from the austerity of Britain, on board we had food that those we had left behind could only dream of. Plenty of relaxation and rest, the sea air and day long, and brilliant sun must have all contributed in equal measure to my appearance of well-being. I stood 5"9 tall and weighed just over 11 stone. My hair was thick and still auburn. On the pocket of my school blazer, was the insignia of my athletics colours and eagle of St John. All of which must have brought back to my uncle memories of Llandovery and his all too short stay at the school.

Praise from my family had always been rare. Over the years, I have consoled myself that it was because they always wanted me to do even better! My best efforts were never good enough for them. I still cling to this belief though it might well have been merely wishful thinking on my part. My grandfather Rickards and my grandmother both had the reputation of being distant and undemonstrative. A quality that my grandfather must have brought with him from England. The British '*stiff upper lip*' and the '*sang-froid*'. Characteristics that some might say served the Anglo-Saxons to set themselves not just apart but maybe even above the rest!

However usual my reception, this home coming, boded differently from all the previous ones. For I was no longer a schoolboy. My school days were forever behind me, that part of my life was over. There would be no going back and yet I had no idea whether or not I had got through the examination for my School Certificate. The suspense whilst I waited for the outcome must have seemed interminable. I was in a state of limbo. I had returned home to my family seemingly for good yet I had no idea what lay ahead of me. Before the end of the year I would be 18 years old. Looking back, nearly 60 years I am sure these were the sort of thoughts that must have preoccupied me. I am now less sure as to how I might have confronted the situation I found myself in immediately after my return to Mersin. Others, but not me, may well have felt "I'm home. Each tomorrow is another day. It can take care of itself, why worry?"

Brooding has always been part of my nature. I would have pondered over what might have been. How things may have turned out for me had my departure from Hurst not been so unexpected and sudden. Back in England, it would have been just a few days before the start of another school year. Old memories flooded back of the start of term that brought with it another bewildered looking bunch of new boys. More to the point, I would have dwelt on what might have become of the school chums, my contemporaries that I had left behind. I wondered, were their circumstances so different from my own? I could recall older boys who had departed. Many of them on leaving Hurst had either gone on to university, or joined a family business after first serving their National Service.

Those who opted for the army went before a selection board. Many, like my friend Geoffrey Hazzan from Alexandria passed their "WASB" – War Office Selection Board coming away with the rank of second lieutenant. They used to come down to the school in their smart uniform. A single sparkling '*pip* ' on each shoulder and their '*swagger stick'* tucked under their arm. It would have been their first visit back to Hurst as *'old boys'* or more particularly OJs. I could sense how proud they felt of themselves and with good justification.

I regretted that these options had not been on offer to me, decisions having been taken for my return to Turkey. I was not party to the whys and wherefores of what had transpired between my family and the school. Like it or not, my school days had been brought to an abrupt end. I had left Hurst under a cloud. I have since reflected on the fact that this humiliating matter was never once mentioned by my uncle. It was only my mother who I recall telling me, "You know Patrick, Mr Bury wrote to me that you had become emotionally involved with some boy. You had become a problem. He went on to say that it would be best if we did not send you back to Hurst. You know, they might have expelled you."

Thereafter my exit from Hurst, just short of expulsion, at least according to my mother was never mentioned.

Over the weeks that followed, my future but more particularly my career became a burning issue with my mother and uncle. Discussions often began with them asking me *"What do you want to do Patrick"* in the vain hope that some how a solution would be found the more often the question was raised. These discussions almost invariably ending in bitter deadlock. As time went on, it became a wider, more profound issue of *"What is to become of you, Patrick!?"*. A crisis of problems that increasingly appeared insoluble, had to run its course. The solution when it did eventually emerge, did so out of the blue and in the most commonplace manner. It not only resolved the burning issues that my family and I had been unsuccessfully grappling with, it shaped my life in a way no one could have foreseen.

My family, along with many of the Christian families who regularly spent their summers up in Gozne, were still there. The heat in Mersin was intense and in the age before air conditioning, it was a respite for me to be up in the cool mountains until the first rains. Many of my early childhood contemporaries were no longer around, particularly the boys. Their families would have sent them to finish their studies in the United States or Europe. Many of them after university would have chosen to stay on where job and career opportunities were so vastly better than in Mersin. My remaining friends in Mersin had dwindled. There were only two in particular left. My cousin Jorj and Fonda Tahinci whom I had known since 1934. My family had been neighbours of the Tahincis long before that, they were Greeks. Though they were a big family, they had only the one boy, Fonda.

Whilst I was still up in Gozne the long awaited letter arrived from England. My uncle who had been down in Mersin brought it. He handed it to my mother then stood with me to hear the news it was about to break. My mother opened the envelope, taking the single page letter out she read it in silence and passed it to my uncle. Overcome by the news it contained she sobbed evidently with joy and hugged me,

"Oh! Patrick, my prayers have been answered. I prayed so much that you would pass these exams. Thank God, you made it, you got your School Certificate. What a relief."

Having read the letter my uncle also put his arm around my shoulder. He had tears in his eyes as he embraced me briefly, his voice quivering with emotion he spoke as he often had in the past, abruptly, "Patrick, well done. Bravo! You now have something to show for four years at Hurst! I am now off for my walk. I will see you later."

I was never shown the letter nor were its contents revealed. It has remained a mystery to this very day. As for my very last school report which had accompanied the letter from Mr Bury, it came into my hands many years later. I came upon it amongst a mass of memorabilia that my mother had carefully put aside and kept. Not surprisingly, I had no distinctions. Of the seven subjects that I took, I failed in but one – mathematics, not surprising either! To my relief and the relief of my entire family, I had credits in the remaining six subjects.

So it was in my eleventh hour at Hurst that my "*frantic last minute swotting*" had paid off. I have since in my own mind questioned whether my Oxford & Cambridge Joint Board School Certificate would have really been of any great worth to me out there. Nor for that matter, whether anything that I had acquired in the four years at Hurstpierpoint College could have served me in that remote corner of Turkey. After all, Mersin was not an outpost of the British Empire which my English public school education had fitted me for.

There were no celebrations, no '*toasting*' with French Champagne nor any local alcohol for that matter, a popular and frequent custom I had come to know in England. My family were not given to making merry nor carousing over such an event. Come to think about it nor were any of their friends in Mersin. It was not the done thing. None the less, my mother did have something to tell me, "We will have to see what opportunities might come up when we return to Mersin. Your uncle seemed to think that it would be best if we could get you into the Levantes' Shipping Agency. Your knowledge of English could be invaluable to them. We will have to see."

It did not take me long to find out that as anywhere else, job opportunities depended on '*who you know*'. In a place like Mersin, even more to the point, your prospects also depended on '*who you are related to.*' I was lucky on both counts, being *'related by marriage to'* Riri Levante. Luckier still for me, the Levante Shipping business was one of the two most flourishing ones in the town. My mother and Uncle William had lost no time in making the appropriate family overtures on my behalf.

Once down in Mersin, towards the end of September, I started working for Emilio Levante Succ., Shipping Agents and Maritime Insurance Brokers. The founder of the business Emilio Levante had come to Turkey from Italy and was succeeded by his four sons, the youngest of whom, Riri, was the motivating force in the Mersin branch. They also had branches in Iskenderun and Istanbul. Like my mother's cousin, Selim many years earlier, I was fortunate to have been taken into the Levante business.

I soon learned the jargon of the trade that brought all types of ships and their multifarious cargoes together. Words and phrases like: clean on board, bills of lading, cargo manifests, cabotage, demurrage, tally clerk, stevedore, donkey-man and a great many others. I got to know the names of the many vessels that called regularly under the national flags of their owners – British, German, Italian, Swedish, Polish, Belgian and Greek. There might even have been the odd one flying what was known as '*a flag of convenience*' – the infamous tripartite known as '*honpanlib*' – made up of Honduras, Panama and Liberia.

The most frequent callers were ships of the Adriatica Line based in Venice. When one or two of their Italian officers came ashore they would call into the Levante offices where they were given a most cordial reception with much backslapping and Latin *bonhomie.* It would not be long before the doors to their inner office were closed so that the *brouhaha* from within did not interfere with the routine of the outer office. A more restrained formal reception was accorded to the Swedish officers of the prestigious Svenska Orient Line. The most magnificent sight afloat was the "Albatross", so aptly named. I would describe her as a *clipper*, bedecked in white from bow to stern, one of the last sailing ships still used at the time for training Swedish naval cadets.

Culture and customs, life its very self in that part of the world I was rapidly discovering was very different from what I had come to know in England. It should not come as a surprise that office life would also be dissimilar. In the 50 years or more that have followed, circumstances in Turkey have moved on. Some of what I am about to relate could sound strange to the ears of people today. All the more reason to tell it as it then was.

Certainly in Mersin and probably in the largest of the country's coastal towns like Istanbul and Izmir, trade with Europe was very much in the hands of the Christian community. Whether through birth or acquired by education and adoption, they regarded themselves as *European* though many were really Levantines.

As I have mentioned already many of the émigré families in Mersin who were Christian had successful businesses and job vacancies. There were even more families who though sharing the same faith were less well off or even poor. Nonetheless, it was through their religion that they also benefited when it came to employment. The other means of selection, *'family connections'* went to filling job vacancies.

Emilio Levante Succ. turned out to be a good example of what I have been describing. Their accountant, an experienced book keeper, Toni Mavroumati, though Greek, was related to the Levante family through his mother. Two metres tall, slim and in his early 30s, punctilious – both by nature and also to suit his occupation, he liked to give the impression of one who keeps to oneself. Edmundo Damiani was part Italian part Armenian and entrusted to deal with the two Italian principals on all routine matters related to shipping and insurance. A communications task that he was well fitted for, having graduated from an Italian boarding school on the island of Rhodes. It would have been difficult to create such a contrast had one set out intentionally to do so. For Edmundo Damiani was not only diminutive of stature, but he had also acquired a premature stoop. His thick, horn-rimmed spectacles made him appear older than his30 years. His quick-wittedness and humour, inherited from his Armenian mother, more than made up for whatever he might have lacked in appearance. Both were heavy smokers, in fact, most people in Turkey liked to smoke, cigarettes or the *'nargile'* – hubble-bubble. These two characters, between them kept the Levante business ticking over notwithstanding the fact that they found much to bicker about. They were the mainstay of what was known as the outer office.

My cousin Jorj had also entered the employ of the Levante's and worked in the outer office. The cotton exporting season in winter was the busiest time of the year for him. He compiled lists of bales of cotton showing the identification number of each and its weight in kilograms from check lists prepared by tally clerks on the dock side. He dealt with the harbour authority's formalities in Turkish each time a ship arrived or departed. There were several tally clerks employed but they spent most of their time away from the office. As in all businesses in the town, there was an office boy, Mahmut who ran errands – not least of all bringing an endless supply of Turkish coffee, small glasses of tea and soft drinks for visitors and staff from the local coffee house down the street.

It is no exaggeration that at times when there were callers in the outer office, it would be difficult to keep count of the languages spoken – apart from Turkish, often Arabic, Italian, Greek, French and less frequently German, Polish, Swedish and lastly English. It was, I recall, after just such an occasion, when things had quietened down that Edmundo Damiani, obscured behind a cloud of cigarette smoke was trying to gain the attention of his book keeping colleague, chirped out, "Monsieur Toni".

In the office, they always kept up a pretence of great formality with each other. Toni Mavroumati, hearing his name called out paused deliberately. Eventually he did glance towards his colleague. Toni's well practiced way of dealing with Edmundo was to appear dismissive. His exaggerated look of irritation and forced smiles accompanied his response, "Well?"

"I just wanted to enquire how you were. We haven't been able to chat!" said the Italian.

"We have now, Monsieur Damiani." Mocked the Greek with a broad grin and a wink to the rest of us. Well satisfied that he had on that occasion got the better of his Italian sparring partner, he busied himself with one of his many ledgers.

I mentioned the great variety of cargoes exported from Mersin. One of the most unusual that I can bring to mind were consignments of goats on the hoof. They were destined for the port of Pireaus. These shipments of livestock were required by the Greeks to help deal with shortages due to the ravages of the civil war. I had visited Athens when the MV Domino was in Pireaus, only a few months earlier. I recall noticing the pockmarks and damage on the front walls of some of the buildings left there by snipers' bullets and other ordnance. Things in Greece would take a while longer to be put back to normal and not surprisingly, Toni was concerned.

Unlike the more usual cargoes of inert materials packed into sacks or bales, live goats presented a tricky handling problem. Herded to the pier, they had to be delivered into barges which were then towed by tugs to where the ship was anchored out at sea. There was then the slow and tedious process of winching them on deck. They travelled to Pireaus as deck cargo. Each time, it was Edmundo Damiani and my cousin Jorj who had the responsibility of making the arrangements for the loading of the goats onto the Adriatica vessel bound for Pireaus. The accountant, Toni Mavroumati persistently poked his nose into these activities.

On one particular occasion, back in the outer office he could no longer contain himself, shaking his head sadly he said, "The proud Greeks, reduced to this humiliation!"

"What do you mean – humiliation?" enquired Edmundo Damiani, always on the alert for a bit of a run in with his bookkeeper colleague.

"Have you forgotten how gallantly they resisted invasion by Italy and Germany during the war? The brave Greeks deserve a better destiny."

"Rubbish! The Allies had to rescue them." Retorted the Italian.

"The Allies were there sure enough. But, the Greeks were always in the front line, backed by the Allies."

"Exactly, Monsieur Toni. The Allies had to keep behind them otherwise the Greeks given half a chance, would have dropped their rifles and run off at the first sight of the enemy."

Edmundo satisfied with himself, reaching across his desk for a cigarette. Toni lost for words, heading for the toilet.

Edmundo Damiani's mother, as I have already mentioned was Armenian. The town in the centre of Anatolia where her family originated from, Kayseri had a large Armenian population. People from there were renowned for their quick wit and humour. Repartee was a popular adjunct to conversation and provided entertainment for those around them intent on listening to their banter. Rarely was there any enduring ill feeling, however personal or even provocative the remarks being bandied about might be. I put this down to the close bond that grew between the people in the communities where they lived. As people did not then move from place to place, these intimate friendships were sustained to the point where they, at least on the surface, out weighed their differences.

Typically, the émigrés of Mersin were a tight knit group whose aspirations were survival in the first place followed by prosperity. They had come to regard themselves as *'Mersinli'* – the children of Mersin what ever their ethnic origins.

What turned out to be a year long sojourn in Mersin back with my family left me with two sets of experience. Firstly, working at Emilio Levante Succ., I gained a grounding in office procedures. Also, through their maritime insurance an insight into the malpractices certain exporters got up to for fraudulent gain. Secondly, both at work and socially I came to have an intimate understanding of the society my family had lived amongst and mixed with. This widened my horizons and served me later in my life to understand the different cultures I came to know. Society, because of its enormous diversity can be likened to a kaleidoscope of human behaviour and relationships. A vast ever changing subject with myriad facets. Few can be more interesting or even as interesting as sexual relationships and morality.

One of the tally clerks working in the Levante business was Iskender Venus, a Christian and also the younger brother of the town's one and only Christian doctor. Dr Victor Venus must have been in his mid 40s. He was popular in the town not only amongst patients for his 'bedside manner' but also as a star in the local football team. As a struggling medical student the young Victor had fallen in love with a prostitute he used to visit regularly. She had helped him with money to complete his studies. When he qualified as a doctor, he was able to marry her and give her the benefit of his good name. Brothels were and still are legal in Turkey though usually confined to towns. In rural areas, it was customary for couples to marry very young.

I recall the occasion when Edmundo Levante came out of the inner office and spoke with the office boy, Mahmut – "Have you seen Iskender? There is something that I want him to do. Where is he do you know?" Standing politely to attention, Mahmut replied, "I do not know where he has gone Monsieur Edmundo." Probably already having an inkling of Iskender's whereabouts he told the boy, "Mahmut nip over quickly to the '*kerhane*' and get a message to Iskender that he is wanted back here. There is something urgent that needs doing."

Mahmut was not away for long. He returned hot and out of breath from his run. Sure enough he had caught up with Iskender who had been visiting one of the girls at the town's only *'kerhane'*. Mahmut was able to report back favourably to Monsieur Edmundo, "Iskender is on his way, sir." In return, his effort was acknowledged,

"Well done Mahmut".

On another occasion, and under very different circumstances, a family friend Madame Victoria Diab went out onto the balcony of their house on the main road opposite the Catholic church. Carriages went by at frequent intervals. She did not have long to wait. She hailed the first passing horse drawn carriage. Calling out to the driver with a hand signal "*Arabaci*!" The driver reined in his two horses bringing the carriage to a stop just under the balcony. "Yes madam. Where did you want to go?"

The Diab family were prosperous merchants and well known in Mersin. Like other well to do Christians, they were regular customers of the only form of town transport – horse drawn carriages. She did not reply directly to his question but asked him, "Do you know my son, Monsieur Mario?" The driver nodded and she went on "I want you to go to the '*kerhane'* and find out if he is there. If he is, leave word that you will wait for him to finish his business. Bring him back with you. If he is not there, still come back and let me know. I will pay for your trip there and back."

The brief exchange most likely would have taken place in Arabic. In those days, most were *'fellahin'*. The driver called out "*Tikrami ya madam*." in thanks and acknowledgement as he cracked his whip and drove off on his mission.

As far back as my memory stretches, in common with my childhood friends, the Mersin brothel had been a part of our everyday lives, commonplace. The *'kerhane'* was a landmark in the town just as the *'patisserie'*, the prison, or the sports stadium were. I also seem to remember occasionally overhearing snatches of conversation among grownups, friends of my family, about the particular establishment in question. In my mind, they have come to be the counterpart of another convention which we in England are dismissive off, arranged marriages. The general view was that brothels safeguarded the chastity of the daughters of respectable families. Visits to them by young men, perhaps even would-be suitors, being overlooked on the grounds that *'they are not made of wood'*.

All the state schools including Lycees were co-educational, yet in those days conventions created an insurmountable obstacle, preventing boys and girls from mixing. On the rare occasions that there was any social mingling, it could only take place under the beady eye of a mature and usually respectably married *'dame'*. These gatherings were house parties or the occasional excursions, usually on foot to some site of historic or other interest. Such assemblies were favoured by the grownups who saw safety in numbers and little scope for any pairing-off. Chaperoning was a weighty responsibility. My mother did sometimes take this on as she was seen to have the added merit of being a teacher; a much respected status in Turkey.

The perception that I had come across in England on arranged marriages put them almost on a par with enslavement. There is no doubt that some were. Even so, forms of arranged marriages, given the strict family upbringing – '*aile terbiyesi*', as it was called amongst the Muslims, did serve a purpose.

I am reminded of a particular instance. The bride-to-be, one of my mother's star pupils for a long time, was the daughter of a prominent family. Though practicing Muslims, her people were Westernised. For some time, she had been telling my mother about her forthcoming wedding to a young recently qualified doctor. It was in fact an arranged marriage. On hearing this, my mother had been surprised as the girl had appeared emancipated in the sense of being liberated from some of the old traditions. On being questioned, she had come out with the following explanation, "My parents were approached by the young man's family whom they knew in Rize before we moved to Mersin. His circumstances and prospects were delved into and discussed. Once a consensus had been arrived at between the families, a date was fixed for the wedding. My mother and father have been married happily for a long time; they know me and have agreed to this marriage in the belief the young man would be suitable for me."

My mother appeared to have been less than convinced with what she had been told and with her usual concern, solicited some reassurance from Nihal, "But how can you marry Dr. Osman without being in love with him?"

It is Nihal's reply that has stuck in my mind all these years and indeed kept alive the entire anecdote, "We have met each other, never alone but in the presence of our parents as is the custom in our culture. He is nice, we got on well together. Love, will come later, with time.

I will grow to love him. What is more important for me now is the conviction that the choice my parents have made for me is sound."

Many years later, I was reminded of this very notion by a dear friend, originally from Palestine, also a Muslim. Approaching the marriage of his only son, we had been discussing customs. He told me, "You know, Patrick people of our standing in this part of the world go into marriage for many good reasons. But '*falling in love*' is not necessarily one of them."

As both these institutions are alien to us in England, they are not often the subject of our conversation. In Mersin, as I grew up, I was to overhear much spoken about them. What is more, there were many different points of view expressed and many personal experiences spoken off. These collectively served to give an image of peoples' attitudes. For all the apparent strictness in upholding social conventions, people were often seen to turn a blind eye or even forgive those who strayed from the straight and narrow.

Even the '*fille de joie*' was let off if her way of life served to provide for her needy family, as was Father Paul who it was said had his way with some of the fallen women duped by him into believing that their sins would be absolved in the process. Such was the generosity of a lady that she offered herself to her older sister's husband to stop him straying. I recall overhearing my mother's closest friend whose much younger husband had strayed confide, "I don't mind how ever many young women he goes with as long as none of my friends get to know that I know what he is up to!"

I was also to find out something about local people's ethics and their conduct in business. An invaluable way of judging ones own standards, whether real or merely professed, is to get to know something about those of others. Apart from shipping and insurance another part of the Levante business was cargo surveillance – an inspection service for European companies who were buying merchandise from local companies to ensure its conformity prior to shipment. An indispensable service, particularly as payment terms were usually against presentation of shipping documents. In other words, the importer would have settled payment before taking charge of the consignment.

A German company was importing sesame seed packed in hessian sacks. Control of the cargo would be done by sampling. A simple yet clever device was used to obtain the sample without opening the hessian sacks. This was a hollow skewer about the thickness of a finger and some 200 mm long. This would be inserted some 100 mm through the sacks at random to get a small representative sample of the sesame seed.

One of the employees from Emilio Levante Succ., acting for Surveillance of Geneva obtained samples in the manner described. The merchant, knowing how sampling was carried out hit upon the following ruse. He saw to it that the hessian sacks were to start with partially filled with the sesame seed. A thin wall tin pipe of about 400 mm diameter, was then stood upright in the centre of the sack and filled with dried sand. The surrounding space between the tin pipe and sack was topped up with sesame seed. The tin pipe was drawn up and out of the sack leaving ample space to be likewise topped up with sesame seed before the sack was securely stitched. The sampling skewer when pushed into the sack, not being long enough, did not reach the column of dried sand in the centre. Of course, the game was up once the first sack was opened by the German importer. This did not particularly trouble the Mersin merchant whom it is said changed his trading name, lay low for some months before resuming his business.

A similar deception was played out by another merchant exporting cotton. Each bale was shipped to the unsuspecting European importer with two or more limestone building blocks secreted within it. On each such occasion, the perpetrators, prominent members of the town, needed little encouragement to talk, indeed boast about their exploits. An almost childish failing which might be what gives rise to the characterisation of *'the likeable rogue'*. There were a few in Mersin.

Business in Mersin was predominantly to do with import/export and was the preserve of the well to do Christians. However, jobs in this sector were less predictable than in the government service or the professions to which the non-Christians were drawn. It was a matter of fact of which all parties were aware. As a consequence, whether the proprietor of the business or one of its employees, both acted with due consideration. The Levantes were no exception, and as my employ was tenuous and my pay modest, I was permitted to take on some outside work.

I worked a few hours a week for Amado Import-Export, a small trading company run by the two Amado brothers. I acted as their correspondence clerk typing letters in English, mainly quotations for locally grown produce such as lentils, chick peas, dried fruit, carobs and so forth. They turned out to be bad payers.

One day I called into their office determined to get what was my due. As luck would have it, they had visitors. Leaving his older brother with the visitors, Muiz came over to the door. He tried to fob me off with their usual promises. Mindful of the visitors in the office, he had been talking in a low voice. I seized the opportunity to put Amado Import-Export to shame for reneging. That evening at home, I told my uncle what had happened.

"You were stupid. You have played into their hands. You gave them just what they wanted, an excuse not to settle up. In future remember, be pleasant to those who owe you money, at least until they have paid up in full."

There were two events that I was party to whilst still in Mersin. My meeting with a famous local who had come to be known in London as 'Mr Hello' and a very different visitor from far across the seas called 'Mighty Mo'. It was my good fortune to have been in England and to have become fluent in English that made both these occasions possible for me. My family being long established in the town also helped.

Ahmet Kirecci was born in one of the poor quarters of Mersin yet came to be honoured publicly by Mustafa Kemal, Ataturk – '*father of the Turks*' – founder of modern Turkey. It was his successor Ismet Inonu, who on meeting him in 1949 persuaded him to change his name to 'Mersinli Ahmet'. He had become World Heavy Weight Greco-Roman Wrestling Champion in the summer of 1948 at the London Olympics. A most amiable giant with blue eyes and unusually fair skin he was characterised by a smooth pate – a perfectly bald head. In London, he acknowledged all those he met with a broad smile and a booming greeting of 'hello', quickly earning himself the nick name, 'Mr Hello'.

I was invited by Mr Knock who was British Consul in Mersin to accompany him to the Mersin '*Halk Evi*' – government house, where a celebratory function was organised in the honour of the 35 year old hero – 'Mersinli Ahmet'. It is not just because he was born and bred in Mersin that he has come to have a special place in my memory. Coskun Parker, the husband of a distant cousin of mine first spotted Ahmet Kirecci. At the time, still a teenager, he was helping in the Mersin bakery. Flour was supplied from the mill in 70 kilo sacks just about the weight that a grown man could lift. Ahmet was in the habit

The London Olympiad in 1948 produced several world wrestling champions for Turkey. I am seen here with Mr Knock, the British Consul at a reception for the Greco-Roman heavy weight champ, that son of Mersin who came to be known as the 'Mersinli Ahmet'

of carrying a 70 kilo sack under each arm. Seeing this display of raw strength, Coskun Parker got Ahmet interested in weight training and athletics. So commenced his climb on to the world stage.

'Mighty Mo' or to give her full name, the US battleship Missouri was there one morning when I awoke. At the time with no deepwater port, Mersin was still what was known as an open roadstead. She must have arrived under cover of darkness and dropped anchor well out in the bay. Some time during the morning, a local government official called at our house with a message from the *'Vali'*, governor of the province. An invitation for me to be at the Mersin *'Tucar Kulubu'* at six o'clock where there was to be a cocktail party for some of the officers of the Missouri. I was to act as interpreter and help entertain the American visitors. My family had lived long enough in Mersin for me to know that it would be indelicate to decline the request. I asked the messenger to convey my thanks to the *'Vali'* and to let him know that I was honoured and would be delighted to attend the reception.

The Missouri had been on a tour of the Eastern Mediterranean 'showing the flag'. A naval tradition that had once been the prerogative of vessels of the Royal Navy. I am unable to say for how many days the Missouri stayed. I had been aboard many of the merchant ships that came to Mersin. Now I cannot help but feel that had I boarded 'Mighty Mo' I could not have possibly forgotten. I have learned since that it was on her decks in September 1945 that General D. MacArthur oversaw the surrender of Japan. What I can bring to mind now was the friendly invasion of Mersin by the hundreds of ratings who were given shore leave and some of whom I got to know. Many of these sailors were not much older than myself.

The town's authorities had generously placed public venues at the disposal of these visitors. One such location was the new Mersin sports stadium near the light house. Entry, probably for the first time ever, was free to all. An arrangement which permitted access for local youths, albeit under the watchful eyes of the local Mersin police and the SPs – Shore Patrols from the 'Mighty Mo'. The American sailors turned up ready to play baseball much to the delight of the locals. None would have seen baseball played live by real Americans though some might have watched it in a film at the local cinema. Most of the youths who came to the stadium were the poor and less educated, to their credit they became animated, shouting and clapping though like myself they would not have known much about the game. The younger kids, many of them scruffy urchins were treated to Coca Cola and American chewing gum. These were still novelties in a place like Mersin at the time.

Going around with the sailors from 'Mighty Mo', I noticed that it was but two of the town's service industries that benefited from their friendly visit. I will come to them presently. Few of the sailors took any interest in the Turkish goods on sale in the shops, nor even the many gold smiths with their window displays of intricately worked 22 ct gold jewellery. Even fewer were tempted into the restaurants or pastry shops both famed for their delicious local offerings. I remember some years later in Antioch an American tourist I met in a hotel asking me, "Do you know where we can get to eat burgers?" I was ready with my reply,

"Sure! There are any number of Turkish restaurants where you can eat them. But you have to ask for *'kebab'*. I personally believe that *'kebabs'* are even better but I suppose I am biased." I never found out how my tourist got on.

Two of the town's service industries I alluded to had a veritable bonanza, a run of business during the stay of the 'Mighty Mo' the likes of which they had never known. On the one hand it was the *'arabas'*, horse drawn open carriages, surprisingly! But not so surprisingly on the other hand was the government controlled *'kerhane'*, to which the sailors were irresistibly drawn. I saw one of the carriages which two *matelots,* in obviously high spirits, had taken over. One of them was driving it with his shipmate sitting next to him. The driver himself was in the back of his '*araba*' with a couple more *matelots,* all in equally high spirits. He was wearing one of the sailor's hats with 'USS Missouri' emblazoned on it, singing a Turkish folk song at the top of his voice.

People in that part of the world tend to be of a serious disposition not given to any tomfoolery, least of all in public. Even smiling is frowned on as it is considered frivolous, lacking in dignity. In that part of the world people are very conscious of their dignity. These cultural mores can very easily lead to misunderstandings. Something that I had grown up to be aware of and careful about. To the credit of the locals of Mersin, who had never before witnessed such high jinks, they tolerantly over looked what was going on. I recall a local explaining to me, "These Americans, they have strange ways of behaving. It does not matter, they are visitors to our country, we have to treat them with consideration. In any case, they are here today gone tomorrow. Bye bye!!"

One of the sailors that I got into conversation with told me that arrangements had been made for the '*kerhane*' to be reserved at a certain period of the day exclusively for visitors from "Mighty Mo" – "It is better this way as otherwise there could be problems with some of the local 'regulars'. It is sound PR – we get this wherever we call." I noticed as we went by there were two SPs outside the entrance to the place.

Unknown to me, as the summer approached, my mother and uncle must have got together and discussed what needed to be done about the delicate matter of my congenital problem. Life working at the Levantes' and once more back home with my family must have filled me with a sense of security. On the other hand, both my mother and uncle must have had concerns about my long term prospects in Mersin, though I myself was unaware of their anxiety.

So it was that the operation, a phalloplasty, that is to say surgery to repair my penis was arranged. It was my uncle who made the arrangements with another of his surgeon friends, Dr Farouk. It was to take place at our house. With my comfort in mind, the oak table in our dining room was duly covered with several layers of blankets and sheets and a pillow on which I would repose myself. As I had not met Dr Farouk Ilhan, my uncle had told me a bit about him and his wife both of whom were old acquaintances of my family. "Dr Farouk was the senior surgeon at the Kabul General Hospital for several years after finishing his medical studies in Istanbul. He also practised in Germany and Switzerland. His wife Muffide Hanim is the very first female to serve as a Deputy in the Turkish Government. He speaks perfect English. You will like him as like most professional Turkish people he is unpretentious. I understand that he will bring the young Dr Kayhan with him. I think you know him."

Thus suitably briefed, I was ready for the procedure. On the day, with my trousers and underpants removed, I settled myself on the table and watched my penis being prepared for its long needed surgery. After it had been swabbed liberally with what looked like tincture of iodine, Dr Farouk proceeded with the help of his charge to anaesthetise my organ which had been transformed into an orange colour. I can't say how many times the hypodermic needle was sunk into it. Eventually, asked if I could feel anything I replied cautiously, "No!" Dr Farouk looked satisfied and, in an effort to take my mind of things, the two of them cracked a few well intentioned jokes. Like, "You will soon be one of us!" and in a more general theme "It is so well numbed, nobody however alluring would be able to rouse it! We would bet big money on that!"

In a more serious vein Dr Farouk informed me, "Recovery will take a while, maybe two or three weeks. When it is fully healed, it will be in perfect working order, *'Inshallah'*, God willing." I had watched the whole procedure. The removal of the entire foreskin. Many years later in England, I related the experience I had undergone to a close friend of mine, Umit Shukru who was a GP. Very down to earth, he told me that necessary though it was, he looked on it almost as one would a criminal assault. I asked him why. By way of explanation, he gave me one of his mischievous winks and said, "Patrick, what is regrettable is the serious loss of substance you have suffered. Now which of us men would want that?" Umit was very down-to-earth about every thing. He did go on to say, "Mark you, it would have been better had your family seen to it when you were in your infancy."

I must have been in bed propped up on pillows resting for well over an hour. There were a couple of towels wrapped around me and I was in my pyjama top. I became conscious of the towels felling heavy. Raising the bed covers, I discovered the towels were soaked in blood. Alarmed at the sight I showed my mother, she called out to my uncle "William quick, get Dr Farouk. Patrick is loosing a lot of blood." My uncle came in to the bedroom to have a look. He told my mother, "I'll call at the Club first, the doctor might be there. If he isn't he will be at home. I'll be as quick as I can." Though it seemed like ages, my uncle was back in a matter of a few minutes and Dr Farouk also on his bicycle followed close behind him.

Examination revealed that a stitch, instead of securing a blood vessel had gone through it. This was quickly remedied by the doctor with the help of Dilber, the young maid, who had been called on to hold the bedside lamp. For both my mother and uncle were squeamish at the gory sight of my penis from which the blood soaked bandages had been removed.

Dilber was doing her best, holding the lamp at an awkward angle to give Dr Farouk as much light as possible. To do this, she was inevitably focused on the scene, my bloody penis. I recall my mother telling her off, "Now then, Dilber you must not look at his penis. Either shut your eyes or turn your head the other way."

I remember poor Dilber's response, "Just as you say Madam!"

This rather comical incident typifies my mother's perception of all matters sexual which I can recall from my childhood. The operation I underwent as my friend Umit had told me was essential and would have been better performed earlier. Looking back, I would describe it in even more pressing terms as '*imperative* '. Adhesions prevented the foreskin from retracting which would have made penetrative intercourse impossible. With her well intentioned determination to keep me on the straight and narrow, my condition must have seemed a blessing in disguise. I am reminded of her words to my uncle, "Up until now this condition has turned out to be his salvation. Who knows what fixes he might have got himself into with women had he been able to have intercourse."

As events unfolded, it was fortuitous that this operation took place prior to the summer season in Gozne. It was coming towards the end of the summer when my uncle William brought the news that Ruston & Hornsby Ltd., were prepared to take me on and train me in their works in Lincoln. It was almost to the year since he had brought that fateful letter up to Gozne informing my mother of the good results I had achieved in my School Certificate.

My mother was for a second time overcome with emotion, "This is all thanks to Mr Rampton. Do you remember William he had told us that his company were always on the look out for young men who they could train to work for them? Look how well Mr Rampton had done for himself to have been entrusted to come all the way out to Mersin from Lincoln to oversee the installation of Ruston engines in the Mersin electric power house."

Much of what she spoke of and the mysterious Mr Rampton's several visits to Mersin had taken place whilst I was still at Hurst. I felt new doors were opening for me. Over the remaining weeks, I would have a growing sense of a new adventure that would take me back to England.

I felt relieved and happy at the career prospects that had opened up for me.

Chapter 13

An entry in my old passport is once more proof positive of my departure from Istanbul by air for London on the 7th December in 1950. But for the hoarding of the many documents and photographs, relics of my past like the passport, I would have had little tangible evidence to go on. The date of my flight back to England shows that I had spent some 15 months in Mersin. An unplanned period that had come to a close in an equally unexpected way. All my relatives, amongst them I include my mother and uncle who like me had been educated in England and my two aunts in France, all returned and settled back in Mersin, their only '*home*'. I am unable to say now how seriously on my return from Hurst I might have felt about settling down like them in Mersin, which I also, at that time looked on as my '*home sweet home*'. After all my first cousin Billy Levante did so and is still living there but my circumstances were very different from the ones he was blessed with.

However unplanned, even slapdash events might have been during those 15 months they had transformed me into an adult. The happy-go-lucky school days were well and truly put to one side. I was anxiously casting about as best I could for a lifeline. I had undergone much soul searching with my mother and uncle prompted by that incessant question, "What do you want to do with your life Patrick?" A dilemma that had at times driven me in my despair to shed a tear or two even though I was 18. I had never acquired that stiff upper lip the hallmark of the English public school system.

As the months slipped by, through a process of what must have been persistent probing, the predicament I was in must have finally got home to me. Seeing the reality of the situation galvanised my determination to come to terms with it but continue to hope for a way out. I was lucky to have been taken in by Emilio Levante Succ., where I gained good experience and earned a crust. My luck was to continue. For as I have already mentioned, salvation came with what at the time must have seemed an unbelievably good offer of employment from Ruston & Hornsby Ltd., to take me on as an overseas trainee. In addition to my apprenticeship, they would sponsor me on a 'day release' mechanical engineering course at Lincoln Technical College. After my training, I would be employed on a permanent basis.

I know that I was over the moon by the truly generous prospects that had opened up for me. My sense of adventure was still further heightened for the simple reason that I knew nothing about the company or Lincoln. Even more challenging was the prospect of being part of the work-a-day life in England. The four years at Hurst had not prepared me for what I was about to experience.

My uncle who had been able to prepare me for life at Hurstpierpoint College I soon discovered knew nothing about apprenticeships. Nor had his schooling in England given him any insight into the country's working life, let alone its heavy industrial life. There was no one in Mersin who I could turn to either. All my friends who went to Europe or the United States for their higher education were at university.

As for Lincoln, I had no idea where it was. My family as far as I know, did not possess an atlas. At school in England I had not taken geography, earlier at the Gazi Pasha primary school in Mersin we had been shown maps of Turkey and I was familiar with its main towns, rivers and mountains. I knew all the places that the Toros Express went through between Adana and Istanbul.

When I was at the English High School in Istanbul, I had been in Sherwood House. The House colour was 'Lincoln Green'. My mother had taken me in 1938 to see *The Adventures of Robin Hood* starring a young swashbuckling actor called Errol Flynn. He and his merry men who lived and roamed about Sherwood Forest were dressed in 'Lincoln Green'. Not much to go on, yet as I was to find out soon after starting at Ruston & Hornsby, all their engines were painted in a dark green, a shade designated by them – 'Lincoln Green'.

Poorly informed though I was, I managed to make it to Lincoln that day early in December. Though I have no way of verifying it, I must have travelled from London by train. I do remember well arriving by taxi that same day, in the darkness of an autumn night, at my destination, Lindum House. To this day, I have no idea what guardian angel arranged this. It was to be one of my very greatest strokes of luck as I was to discover early in the coming year.

Left standing with my suitcase in its dimly lit porch, the taxi moved off. It drove out across the large gravel forecourt and through the open gateway in the high stone wall, back on to Sewell Road. My eyes getting accustomed to the dark, I could begin to make out something of my surroundings. I deduced that Lindum House, was a large two storey, double fronted rather beautiful Georgian house standing in substantial grounds. I pressed a large push button marked 'Bell' in the stone wall.

It was not long before the big mahogany front door was opened by a young female. Wearing a black dress trimmed with white collar and cuffs, a white headband identifying her as a maid. "Good evening" she said and paused for me to introduce myself before she ushered me in, "Please come in Mr Grigsby. You can leave your suitcase here. I will take you through to Miss Larter's office. Miss Larter is the warden."

Officially known as "The Lindum House Club", it was owned by R&H where directors could entertain their VIP guests in the very best of British styles. A wing had been added to the Georgian building for some 20 single bedrooms for post graduate and overseas trainees. I was so lucky to have been accommodated

The said Miss Larter, who in the days ahead I was to hear called "Betty" by the older residents, but never by myself and the other young trainees, was a large impressive looking female. She had no doubt added to her authoritative manner by serving as an officer in the WAAF during the war. Her fine facial features, open and friendly expression qualified her to be described as a 'handsome woman'. Her father I was to find out much later had been in the diplomatic service and she had lived in Russia and later in France. A background that must have fitted her for the post she held at Lindum House officially known as "The Lindum House Club".

On meeting Miss Larter that first evening, shaking my hand she immediately put me at ease by enquiring kindly about my long trip from Istanbul. She then went on to inform me, "Mr Codling wants to see you in his office at Sheaf Iron Works tomorrow morning. He is expecting you at nine o'clock. He is the trainee supervisor. His office is in the main block as you go through the entrance. There will be commissionaires at the entrance who will direct you. I have put you in the "Blue Room" for tonight. I will arrange for you to be moved into the residents' wing tomorrow. I will get Sheila to show you where it is. You must be tired and it is getting late. Sleep well; I look forward to seeing you tomorrow."

Sheila it turned out was the maid who had met me. Once out of Miss Larter's office I could take better stock of what the inside of Lindum House was like. There were several doors opening onto the hall, all polished mahogany with gleaming brass handles and hinges. The parquet floor was also a dark colour giving off the usual pleasant small of polish. Sheila headed up a curved stairway with a dark coloured stair carpet secured in place with shining brass stair rails. Tired as I was I had managed to get some idea as to the sort of place I had come to. Without doubt, it was indeed a fine private home at some time in its past. On the landing, Sheila opened one of the doors and ushered me in, "This is the Blue Room. I wish you a good night."

It had been an exceptionally long, tedious day since I had taken off from Adana very early that morning to Istanbul, the first stage of my journey to London. Turkey being two hours ahead of the UK, everyone in Mersin would have been in their beds for hours. I took stock of the sumptuous bedroom I was in with its adjoining bathroom. The carpet I was standing on went from wall to wall – it was not often that one came across *'fitted'* carpets in England in those days. Linoleum was still the usual floor covering. The carpet was powder blue and I could feel the thick pile underfoot. The curtains had been drawn, their pattern matched the bedspreads on the twin beds. The walls in the bedroom and bathroom were decorated in subtle matching tones of blue.

The "Blue Room" was centrally heated. My thoughts went back to the two most prestigious hotels in Istanbul, the Park and Pera Palas. I had seen glimpses of their bedroom suites when I was invited out from the English High School during the war years by friends and relatives staying at them. They could not be compared with the splendour I saw around me. I decided to run the bath and have a good long soak. Water, hot and cold gushed out of the two enormous faucets, I had seen nothing like it before. As I went on with my day dreaming, my thoughts appeared to be interrupted by a quiet voice – "This isn't going to last. If I were you, I would make the most of it."

Once in the bath, I was dwarfed by its sheer size. Lying fully stretched out, my feet barely reached the far end. Sitting, my shoulders were about level with its brim. I lay back enjoying the sheer luxury of the mass of hot water that I was totally submerged in, thinking "This really is the life!!" I could not help but wonder what my mother and Uncle William would have said had they seen me just then.

Looking up idly at the ceiling through the water vapour a thought suddenly struck me – "I wonder what all this is going to cost?" My family had brought me up to always ask that question. Pondering over the matter, I began to worry, "Will I be presented with the bill for all this?" As if to cut my losses, I got out of the bath, dried myself, put on my pyjamas and got into one of the beds. Such comfort, the likes of which few in Mersin would have experienced. Tired, I soon dropped off to sleep.

After breakfast next morning, I set off on foot down Lindum Hill for Ruston & Hornsby Limited. Though I could not have ever guessed it, that first morning was to be followed by some 1500 similar mornings of '*clocking-in*' at R&H as the place was known to all who worked there. I can still remember the mixture of anticipation and excitement that was churning about inside me. Having not even the slightest inkling of what awaited me I chose to remain optimistic, I felt quite 'high', euphoric. Typically, I was early. This gave me the opportunity to settle myself down by chatting to one of the uniformed commissionaires whilst I waited. At exactly nine o'clock I was shown by one of the female receptionists into Mr Codling's office. He turned out to be a slim man with sandy coloured hair, a small neatly trimmed moustache. Wearing a smart light coloured tweed jacket he had a military bearing. He greeted me, asking me to take a seat whilst he attended to some forms that had to be filled in.

There were inevitably formalities that had to be gone through not only with Mr Codling but in other departments. When these procedures were completed, I returned to Mr Codlings office. Smiling, he shook hands with me once more saying, "That's it Patrick, you are now a part of R&H. I am sure you will do well and enjoy the training you are about to embark on. There will be somebody along presently to show you through to the Apprentice Shop."

My guide, turned out to be a young apprentice in a navy blue boiler suit. Once out of the offices, out in the yard he said, "Come on mate, we can go through the main machine shop".

Heading across the open yard, he went through a doorway. The other side of the door, I was to experience for the first time in my life the embodiment of the industrial world. Noises, odours, sights even vibrations that were all pervasive. I felt I had suddenly entered an excitingly strange new world. It was the curtain raiser to a new life. I felt overcome with anticipation and great optimism. We had arrived. My guide, who had told me his name was Tom and I were outside a glass partitioned annexe. Above the entrance were the words in bold black letters – "Apprentice Shop". Some 20 or so young apprentices were working at steel benches. The sole occupant of a small office was on the telephone. Tom took his leave saying to me before he went off, "That is Mr Osgarby. I have to go mate. Wait here until he calls you in. Good luck… see you about mate." With that Tom went off.

Mr Osgarby was a rotund figure dressed in a dark three piece suit. He never removed his shiny and well-worn bowler. Though not much good at judging people's ages, I guessed that he must have been close to retirement. Having finished on the telephone, he stood up, removing his reading glasses he beckoned me to go in.

"Right young man. I am Bert Osgarby, I run the Apprentice Shop and my commitment is to set you youngsters off on the right path. I understand that you are to be with me for three months. Now then, things you need to keep in mind. First thing, you will clock in on time at 7.30 am. If you are late I will want to know why. If you need to leave the shop you will come and see me first, even if it is just to have a pee. I will not tolerate skiving. Finally, you will know me as and always call me Mr Osgarby. Have you any questions?"

Hurst had prepared me well for this sort of encounter. I was careful to make sure that I conveyed the right impression back to Mr Osgarby. Namely that I understood what he had told me and that I accepted his authority without question. My reply must have satisfied him as he went on to say, "I'm going to put you with Frank for a while. He will show you round. You will also have to go across the road to Knobby Clarke for your tools, a metal tool box and boiler suit. Make sure you get a large one as they all tend to shrink when laundered. Come back here as you will need a requisition from me."

Frank was one of Mr Osgarby's two minions who helped run the Apprentice Shop. He was a small chap with fine features and light blue eyes. He had thick black hair that seemed to stand straight up which is probably why he never wore anything on his head. Instead of a boiler suit he wore a tan coloured gown. He spent his time at the top end of the shop testing the small diesel powered single cylinder compressors. I never saw Frank without his pipe, a straight stemmed thing that he had to relight constantly. He spoke little preferring to keep to himself.

"*Knocking-off time*" as it was known came at 5.30 pm with a hooter sounding. Machines were shut off and all work stopped. Until I became accustomed to it, the silence that descended on the place was palpable. There were large circular stoneware wash stands where as many as five or six of us at a time could wash. Hot water jets were turned on by foot and there was a liquid soap dispenser.

It was either the soap or the Rozalex that had an oily smell. Given the all pervading smell of diesel oil, which permeated ones skin, clothes, even underwear, and shoes, there was little to choose between the three. After '*clocking-off*' and once outside, I merged with the crowd surging out of the main gates on to the main road. Most of the employees had bicycles. Once mounted on them, they took it for granted that they had the right of way over all other forms of traffic. I recall, every evening, traffic was brought to a complete standstill. By the time I got near Lindum Hill walking, most of the crowd had dispersed along one or other of the five roads that intersected there. I remember that first evening heading up the hill past the Usher Art Gallery on my way back to Lindum House.

I barely had time to wash and change when the dinner gong sounded at Lindum House. It always did, at exactly 6.30 pm. I had hesitated outside the dining room. A rather gruff voice addressed me in a friendly, engaging sort of tone which I was later to find out sounded like an Africaans accent, "Come on man! … Don't hang about. Come in. You can sit where ever you want. It is first come first served. By the way, I'm Bob and this is Fitz."

The speaker, Bob Ackermann was a large hail and hearty Rhodesian, 'a wild colonial boy'. As for Fitz, I never recalled his surname though I found out that he came from one of the Latin American countries. There would have been some 18 or 20 of us residents at the long, elegant polished mahogany table. A marvellous three course dinner professionally served by smartly uniformed waitresses. I would have been surprised if either of the town's top hotels of the time, The Saracen's Head and The White Hart, could have surpassed Lindum House. Sometimes the dining room had to be cleared and the table re-set for a second sitting at 8.30 pm. Usually for directors and their guests who would have been received earlier by Miss Larter for pre dinner '*aperitifs*' in the directors' lounge.

After the residents' dinner, coffee was always served in the residents' lounge. This was a sort of day room where there was a black and white TV and radiogram with a collection of 78s. Out of the array of records, that were frequently played, two vocals have stuck in my mind over the years – *Music, music* sung by Teresa Brewer and a nostalgic love song *Have I told you lately that I love you* by a female vocalist of the late 40s whose name alas I cannot bring to mind.

Greatly appreciated as they were at the time, it was not only the excellence of the culinary offerings and creature comforts of the place that have remained with me all these years. Lindum House was also where I made many good and long lasting friends. One in particular, Herbert Stanley Good, a Canadian from Montreal. '*Hank'* as he must have been nicknamed even before we met, had arrived shortly before me. We were the same age and turned up everywhere together. As we were similar in height and build, we even shared items of clothing at times. This was not surprising as we were always short of money. It was not long though before we were referred to by every one who knew us, as "*Hank and Red*". At the time I had auburn hair. Strange how we so quickly became '*bosom buddies'*. Looking back now, like me, he must also have wanted to have a *'soul mate'*. Now I shall never be able to find out for he passed away in 1997. Herb who I often think of is still my *'bosom buddy'*. We did share some memorable times.

As little as a week, maybe at most two weeks after arriving, it had become apparent to me that I could not afford to continue living at Lindum House. My cash crisis had obviously not taken long in coming. My mother and uncle must have interpreted Jerry Rampton's words over optimistically when he said apprentices were paid during their training. Just how much, became clear when I opened my pay packet at the end of my first week at R&H. My salary was £3.0s.0d less a few pence stoppages. Not quite enough to cover the full board of £3.10s.0d at Lindum House but adequate for the £2.10s.0d 'digs' I had located. They were off Monk's Road. One of Lincoln's busy and well known main roads. It was just the other side of the canal from

R&H's Sheaf Iron Works, Clayton Forge, Penny & Porter and other engineering works.

Though we had only known each other for a matter of days, it was Hank that I had confided in about this crisis. He in turn, I recall had tried hard to put me off moving out of Lindum House into 'digs' in the town, "Hell, Pat! Do you want to turn into a '*peasant*' stuck down there on Monk's Road…eeeh!!?"

Herb used the expression '*peasants*' often. According to him, Bob Hope, the comedian had immortalised it in one of his films. It was in a crowd scene that he called out, "*scatter peasants!*". The term stuck. Herb was warning me against living with what we call '*hoi polloi*' the common people, the '*plebeians*' as in ancient Rome. After the cloistered world of the middle classes at public schools, I was very shortly to finding myself in 'the real work-a-day England' amongst the working class. It was to prove a revelation.

I did leave Lindum House, in spite of my awareness of all its comforts and many advantages. I had no option. It was certainly in the most sought after and privileged position, at the top of Lindum Hill. The cathedral stood with the remains of the roman castle and East Gate nearby. Not surprisingly, R&H's managing director, Colonel Harold Riggall, D.L., J.P lived just around the corner. Of more practical interest to Herb and I and some of the other overseas trainees were The Peacock, The Adam and Eve public houses and The Assembly Rooms. It so happened that Lincoln Prison was also just down the road, though of no particular interest!!

According to an entry in my identity card I moved to 10, Arboretum View off Monk's Road on the 19th December 1950. I continued to see Hank every day at the Works and also at the local Technical College.

We were both studying for our ONCs and we hoped in time to gain our HNCs. This could lead to an AMIMechE – Associate Member of the Institute of Mechanical Engineers. At the time I recall being told by many of the older, more senior residents at Lindum House that achieving an HNC or AMIMechE was every bit as good as getting a BSc.

My landlady at No.10 was a Mrs Schofield, a widow. She has survived in my memory for her strange, almost resentful perceptions of industry for which perhaps she should be forgiven. Engineering companies like the ones just across the canal from No.10 she collectively referred to as *"forges"*. They spawned the *"blue collar"* workers, as they do grimy smoke and industrial effluent. Her two sons and daughter worked for the Lindsey County Council. It was casually mentioned to me that it was in no small measure due to their grammar school education. They saw themselves as "*white collar*" monthly paid staff. Superior to the *"blue collar"*, weekly wage earning shop floor workers.

It was the very first day at No.10 that I fell victim to Mrs Schofield's prejudices. That day in the Apprentice Shop, as part of my training, I had been grinding smooth some iron castings. Though I had removed most of the graphite dust from my face and hair before '*clocking-off*', there must have still been traces of black when I turned up at the rear entrance to No.10. Mrs Schofield let me in. Seeing my face mottled with black smuts she became most irate, "I have never had anybody from one of the *'forges'* come into my house before. How on earth do you get yourself so dirty?" she wailed.

Taken aback and not wishing to inflame her further I kept quiet. Several times I had heard men at the Sheaf Iron works dismiss the state of their unwashed hands when handling a bun or a sandwich during a break, explaining, "*It's clean shit. It will do no harm!*" I wondered to myself, what might have been her reaction had I passed on that explanation.

She had not finished. Her anger had turned into indignation as she ended her tirade telling me, "I would have never taken you in had I known this would happen!"

Having vented her disapproval and also made her thoughts known to me on '*those who work in forges*', she disappeared into an adjoining cubby hole. She was back in a trice, dragging a large galvanised steel tub from where it had been kept out of sight. Out of breath and her face crimson she only just managed to get her words out. Pointing to it she spluttered, "There you are! You will have to manage with this. I suppose you will want some hot water."

As I have mentioned before, some things remain stored in one's memory bank and so clearly too. This incident has stuck not simply because of what she said but because of Mrs Schofield's manner, her indignation in particular. Even now I find that in certain circumstances indignation can be ridiculously funny.

There was something else about that incident. An impression of social divides and narrow-mindedness. The perception that because one man's skill is in his hands and he wears a boiler suit, he somehow must be intellectually sterile.

I suppose one might describe it as ironic. Many apprentices on day release went to night classes at technical school and gained qualifications on the par with university degrees. Some instead of going into the armed forces to serve their National Service opted for a life at sea in the Merchant Navy. They served their time in the ship's engine room, sitting exams as they went along. Eventually obtaining a chief engineer's '*ticket*' I was to meet just such a person, Alan Judkins, a New Zealander. Known by his friends as "Crew-Chief" he wore a boiler suit on duty but was an equal of any graduate.

There was no bathroom at No.10 as I can recall the four of them going off with their towels rolled up under their arms to the public baths. Nor for that matter was there a toilet in the house itself. The only one, aptly referred to as '*an outside toilet*' was in the backyard of the house. I managed a nightly hot bath in Mrs Schofield's galvanised tub. It was some time later when I mentioned that they had a dog that I was told the galvanised tub must have been what the dog was bathed in.

Aside from what I learned later about the dog, I did not mind using the tub. After all, that was as good as a bath ever came to be in Gozne, the primitive mountain village in Turkey to which my family fled for three months every summer. It also reminded me of my nightly wash, helped by my mother dispensing the meagre supply of warm water.

I stayed with the Schofields for about two weeks. It was not all gloom and despondency. I did come away from No.10 with some happy memories though strangely, I can bring nothing to mind of Christmas. Nothing that is except Mrs Schofield's eldest son from an earlier marriage who was the manager of a Wines & Spirits shop on the approach to what was called The Steep Hill. He must have turned up on Christmas day and I over heard him telling his mother that he had 'cashed up late' on Christmas Eve, a reminder that shops were open then even on the day before Christmas.

It was the custom at about ten o'clock every evening to have '*supper*' – all types of pastries, cakes and scones with butter and jam washed down with cups of strong tea poured from a giant teapot that was kept well insulated by a tight fitting knitted cosy. What made this late night spread memorable for me was the then popular 'Jack Jackson Show'. The Schofield boys tuned into it on the radio. Jack Jackson, a trumpet player had formed his own band. He was occasionally interrupted by a cat's plaintive '*meow*' when he was introducing the show. Somebody told me “It sounds as if he is strangling that bloody cat” – precisely! It was that distinctive screech every now and again that livened up the ‘JJ Show’.

Once more it must have been my mother who came to the rescue with the ‘remittance’ of some funds that permitted me to return to Lindum House in time for the New Year of 1951. Thus united once more, Hank put it this way – “Gee! I think we are so lucky to have landed in this place. Man, its like we were in a five star hotel. My school chums from Lachine High, back home would not believe it. We even have our meals served by maids – cute ones at that. Don’t you think Sheila is the cutest? Yes siree, I shall stay at Lindum House as long as I can.”

We did just that!

Chapter 14

It had not been long since my initial short stay in Lindum House. I was extremely lucky early in the New Year of 1951 to be accepted back as a resident. I will explain why. Ruston & Hornsby Ltd. had about 600 apprentices. The vast majority came from local homes. The minority who did not have homes nearby were accommodated in digs or in one or another of the company's many hostels around Lincoln. The company employed a billeting officer who looked after these arrangements. Ruston & Hornsby Ltd. also had a variety of trainees sponsored by overseas agents, associate companies and even customers sent for various terms of product training. The Lindum House Club, could only accommodate a mere 18 or 20 of these, priority being given to overseas trainees and no doubt their importance and standing. Of course, without the arrival in time of the much needed financial help from my family in Turkey, I would not have been able to make my return to Lindum House.

What I have come to realise as the years have gone by was how providential my return proved to be. Had I not been favoured with such good luck at the time, the rest of my life might have been so very different. At the time I would have had no possible way of knowing this. I was very happy to be back with my *'bosom buddy'* Hank and the other residents I had got friendly with. I would have embraced all the creature comforts Lindum House had to offer. So it was that 1951 augured well for me.

Lincoln had in such a short space of time proved to be so very different from my earlier experiences of England and Hurst in particular. I was meeting and rubbing shoulders with the vast rank and file of the British public. Now for the first time, I was exposed to the '*real work-a-day world of England'*. Staying with the Schofield family at No.10, I had been given a most revealing insight at first hand of the divide between "*blue collar*" and "*white collar*" workers. Though I say workers, the terms "*blue collar*" and "*white collar*" in practice applied not only to them but to their entire families. On the shop floor at R&H I was to find that there was a great spirit of '*bonhomie*' amongst the "*blue collar*" lot. Aside from the leg pulling and practical jokes, it was also where I was to come across that uniquely British sense of humour and wit. I was to learn later that many much loved comedians did come from what was then known as the *'working class'*. I was happy mixing with all and sundry, to understand and show them respect as I had been brought up to do from childhood in Turkey, but as an '*outsider*', which I was and chose to remain.

Each day in Lincoln brought new experiences. After the four years of public school regimentation, and the year of soul searching in Mersin, I felt liberated. Sure enough, there were still vestiges of an umbilical cord. It had become obvious that I was still dependant on my family for funds to supplement, at least for a time, the modest allowance I received each week from R&H. In the Apprentice Shop, I had found that I had an aptitude for the various skills in the use of tools and equipment that I was being trained to use. This boosted my confidence, making me optimistic and convinced of a good future with R&H. In particular the prospects of working for them in the Middle East. Motivation gripped me as never before.

Such a lot had happened since my arrival in Lincoln. I had settled into three months induction under the watchful eyes of Mr Osgarby in the Apprentice Shop. At the lunch hour, I made a beeline for the canteen at Sheaf Iron Works. The quality of the food there came as no great surprise. It was not all that much worse than what I had got used to at Hurst. There were some strange daily offerings at the canteen.

Things I had never heard of before, like spam fritters and banana fritters – the second, was a dessert. There was also something called brown Windsor soup about which I remember somebody telling me, "Now that really is something! A creation of the House of Windsor if you please! You must try it." On checking the veracity of the claim, I found out that like many other things I had heard, it was a 'fairy tale'. Some of the *'old timers'* in the works used to have fun sending new apprentices on wild goose chases for things like "a left hand spanner", "a bucket of steam", or "a jar of elbow grease". There were many others, if only I could bring them to mind.

That first day, Mr Codling had told me that after my prescribed stint in the Apprentice Shop I would be moved about in the Sheaf Iron Works. It must have occupied acres, much of it under cover, comprising what I came to know as *'shops'*. Anyone of these in itself, could be taken for a factory. The largest were the machine shops – on either side of gangways were lines of machine tools for grinding, milling, boring. Lathes, enormous things for turning the big crankshafts of R&H's big powerful marine engines. Other *'shops'* were devoted to assembly work. Engines were built up in different erection shops each devoted to a particular model of diesel. Most importantly, there were the *'test beds'*. Every Ruston diesel engine had to be run *'on test'*, put through its paces on dynamometers which verified the horse power it was capable of producing. This often in the presence of outside inspectors from Lloyds, Bureau Veritas or The Crown Agents. In each of these *'shops'* there were many scores of men operating the machines. Some just out of their apprenticeship, some veterans but all dedicated.

Had what I have described been some university, its hall of residence might well have been Lindum House, and what a wonderful one it would have made. I was privileged to be in the midst of such a collection of residents. They had come from so many different countries. Aside from this, I also learned a lot from having the opportunity of meeting

12 cylinder VOX turbo charged diesel developing 2,400 bhp on test in Ruston's Sheaf Iron Works

occasional visitors who came as guests for just a night or two. Many of them veteran engineers or businessmen, from whom I was also to benefit so very much. I doubt whether elsewhere I would have gained so much practical knowledge and experience.

In the end, the way things worked out, I was to spend almost four and a half years at R&H in Lincoln. For four of those years I lived in Lindum House. For Hank and I, outside recreation had been restricted on account of our limited financial resources. Neither of us were pub-minded. On the other hand, we both rather liked the company of girls. Hank having been to a co-educational school in Montreal was at ease with them. I on the other hand, having been at a male only public school, was handicapped. I was happy to be guided by him. During week days, when we were not attending evening classes at the Technical College, we sometimes went to the cinema. On weekends, we had a choice of dances at local venues. If we were really short of funds we went down to the Ruston Sports and Social Club, entry to which was free. Being free, we got what we paid for – not much! Even so, it was a lot better than nothing and we always managed to enjoy ourselves.

Dance halls were meeting places, launching pads to a date. When it came to dating, there were a number of inescapable realities. However altruistic the girls might have been, a young chap without money was handicapped. Even in those far off days when austerity was a way of life and the aspirations of most girls were modest. Hank once unburdening himself at a dance, told me, "Did you see that girl with whom I have been dancing? She's really cute. She travelled over with the band from Nottingham. She is a secretary. I'm sure we would get on well together. In fact she asked me if I would like to look her up, maybe take her out this coming Sunday. Hell! Pat to do that I would need some sort of a *jalopy*, even a beat-up Chevie!"

For all that, the girls usually took to Hank! He was I believe, good looking and often taken for an American. As the general perception at the time was that they were loaded with money, the mistake was something else in his favour. He had told me that the Ruston Agents he was employed by in Canada were paying him half his salary whilst he was in Lincoln and he got the same weekly allowance which was all I received from R&H. On his own admission, he was not too badly off. Hobnobbing with females, dating was new to me. It only added to my lack of confidence. Not surprisingly, I did sometimes think "What on earth am I to do – short on looks, worse still, no one would ever take me for an American like they do Hank. There must be a way out of this for me!"

It was only a day or so after my return to Lindum House, my luck changed for the better. I had caught sight of a new member of staff. Dressed in white overalls, she was young, curvaceous and lively. For all her liveliness she appeared demure. Where I had been brought up, great store was placed on modesty in a female. She was known by everyone as Miss Cussins. I found out that her first name was Beryl. From the first time I had seen her, I had wondered to myself whether she would consider going out with me sometime. With some guidance and encouragement from Hank, I summoned up all the courage I could, I knocked on Miss Larter's door. I had made sure that the said Miss Cussins would be there. My luck held! Our first outing as I seem to recall was to the Odeon cinema.

Beryl Joan Cussins came from York. She had just finished a three year course in domestic science and institutional management at Berridge House a private college in Swiss Cottage, London. She had been referred to Lindum House to do a year's practical work catering. The thesis she had to prepare whilst at Lindum House secured her diploma. We took to seeing each other on the nights that she got off duty early. Our evening strolls took us past Lincoln's famous prison. In those days at that late hour, there was no traffic on that quiet stretch of road. We had the place to ourselves. We walked with one arm round each other's waist, keeping in step so that we did not lose our

Herbert S. Good, my 'bosom buddy', aka Hank the Yank – a veritable car devotee, he complained at the lack of white wall tyres and leopard skin upholstery in the UK

Beryl, my fiancé at Cleethorpes

balance. As the winter wore on into spring, our walks took us into the surrounding countryside.

Coming as we had from such different origins, we found much to talk about. We chatted incessantly and never ceased to marvel at the slimmest of odds that had brought us together in Lincoln, leave alone at a place like Lindum House. The topics of our conversations were boundless but almost always something to do with ourselves. We spoke about our early childhood, so different one from the other. Yet for all that, there was one thing we had in common. We had both lost a parent and experienced the trauma of its consequences. Strangely, both of us, we discovered from one another, had gone short of encouragement and praise in our homes. This shared childhood deprivation did not cause us to mope, to the contrary it strengthened our attachment to each other. Together, we felt able to make light of almost anything that confronted us. Even my continuing cash crisis appeared to be less of a handicap. With my sense of humour which often thrived on irony, we both found much to laugh about. We took life as it came. I had got myself in the habit of brushing caution aside with the words, "God will provide!"

I still spent a lot of time with Hank down in the Works and at the Technical College, he remained my '*bosom buddy*'. In fact, Beryl often joined us to form a threesome on various outings. I recall one long weekend in particular when a childhood neighbour and friend of Beryl's from Newcastle University came to stay at Lindum House. Avril Johnson was a dark, striking female who during her stay got several of the residents in a state as she was rather well endowed. A bunch of us were having a late dinner sitting at the round table in the dining room. The main part of the meal over, we were having some fruit. Avril was eating grapes, trying to avoid swallowing the pips, several of them had dropped down her cleavage. As somebody remarked later, it caused quite a titter! There was a furore when the likeable Aussie, Max Burfoot very gallantly started to help Avril recover them from between her ample breasts, thus causing a further titter. The popular American singer of the time, Guy Mitchell's big hit *She Had a Dark and Roving Eye* might well have been inspired by Avril. It was not long before it appeared amongst the collection of 78s at Lindum House. An apt reminder of Avril Johnson's long weekend.

The more Beryl and I chatted, the more we appeared to share ideas and aspirations. We discovered that we had so much in common. Lindum House had taken on the guise of home for us both. We knew that our good fortune would be coming to an end. For when Beryl completed her year's practical experience she would be moving on. That summer we made the most of whatever happened to be going on. There were tennis teas at weekends, the annual fancy dress party, a grand seaside picnic. All thanks to Lindum House and its residents. We did sometimes get lifts from residents with cars for an evening out in Nottingham invariably ending up at the Palais de Dance. Probably the pinnacle of our highlife was when we made it to The Assembly Rooms in Lincoln for a charity ball, always an evening dress affair.

Beryl and I had become inextricably involved with each other. We could not imagine our future lives any other way. We were in love! As for me, I had found that soul mate that I must have so needed since I was first packed off to the English High School in Istanbul as a boarder. We did get engaged on New Year's Eve 1951, it was a quiet affair, just the two of us! A week later Beryl departed from Lindum House. It was to be her first management job which took her a long way off to St.Albans. We were to be thus parted for almost the next four years spending much of our limited means on travel and hotels. Yet another cash crisis to be over come, and it was.

Quite early on at Lindum House, I discovered a way of augmenting my weekly pittance. Overseas trainees flying back to their countries had no further use for purchases they had made on arrival in Lincoln. They were more than happy to pass these on to me for disposal. Apart from gramophone records most of the stuff was clothing and

Lincoln's Assembly Rooms to which we occasionally treated ourselves.
From the left – Murid Murad, Anne with Ray Warner-Lacy, Betty Larter, Bernard Opperman, Beryl Cussins with me, Keith Taylor-Smith, all from Lindum House

An annual affair, usually in fancy dress, always informal and certainly multi-national. On this occasion from the left we are –Brian Woolfenden, Beth Calms, just visible behind her Mo' Farouk (India) mustachioed Bernard Opperman (S.Africa), Colin Meek (Pakis'), Daphne Kendall with top hat, Sylvia, Jay (India), old Etonian Martin Cordeaux with cloth cap

footwear. I had discovered a second hand shop up Lincoln's famous Steep Hill. On having a word with the owner, I was pleased to find that he would make me a fair offer on clothing. I used to call from time to time with a few items to dispose off. It was raincoats and if I was in luck the occasional overcoat that brought me the best return. Gramophone records, 78s I kept and still play some of them which have come to be part of my collection!

As and when I had some items to dispose off, I used to take them round to my dealer friend on a Saturday morning. The proceeds safe in my pocket, I would walk down Steep Hill and call in at Boots. In those days, their cafeteria was a popular meeting place for coffee. The *'young bloods'*, male and female flocked there in their various groups – from the nurses' home, teachers' training college, young Conservatives, a group of public school boys serving their apprenticeships at R&H and the multi-nationals from Lindum House. There was little if any crossover from one group to another. Nurses excepted.

During my time there, the Lindum House set read like a gathering of the League of Nations – Jean-Piere Togneri (France), Murid Murad (Jordan), Mufid Shishakly (Lebanon), Bahadin Al Mahdi (Sudan), Omer Bese (Turkey), Per Torn (Sweden), Carlos Cabrera (Canary Islands), Graham Bunbury and Bernard Opperman (South Africa), Enrico Cappa (Italy), George Palau and Cesar Manchieno (Equador), Alan Judkins (N.Z), Herbie Good (Canada), Sunai and Tian (Siam), Trigo Barton (Argentina), Emilio Conde (Cuba), Max Burfoot (Australia), Jabar and his brother Faizel Wazir (Iraq), Keith Taylor-Smith (India), Muhammad Farouk (Pakistan), and Bill Dupres (Rhodesia).

Another character who used to join us was Nasif, a wealthy Saudi. Not surprisingly, he chose to live in a rented flat with his kept woman. As I would expect, a full figured sensual looking female. Nasif was a heavy weight chap. His horn-rimmed spectacles had thick lenses. He boasted that his poor eye sight was a result of his sexual excesses. There was a running battle between him and Bahadin Al Mahdi for leadership of the several other Muslims in the town. They were always falling out on account of this rivalry. I recall one Saturday as I was leaving Boots he button holed me saying, "Pat, will you be seeing Baha?" When I said I would, he continued, "Tell him from me to fuck off!" He hesitated, having second thoughts maybe, recovering he added – "But say it to him politely!"

Bahadin Al Mahdi or Baha as everyone used to call him, was very different in appearance from his Saudi rival. Tall and lanky he had a mass of fuzzy hair, he was black. Baha always dressed in three piece tailor made suits. He liked bright ties and wore gold cuff links to round off his sartorial elegance. He cultivated an air of sober dignity to which he then aspired though sadly for him not always successfully. For paradoxically, he was by nature a friendly soul who craved popularity. It was his quest for this popularity which sometimes led to his undoing. Baha lived precariously on the horns of this dilemma.

Returning to his origins, Baha was the great grandson of Muhammad Ahmed Al Mahdi, the famous (or infamous depending on how one perceives history) religious leader. A leader claiming to be Messiah, the word Mahdi in Arabic means 'he who is guided right.' Little wonder then that my friend and fellow resident Baha had no mean a legacy to live up to. A challenging task and one difficult to accomplish as a trainee going through the different work shops at R&H in post War Britain heading for egalitarianism.

One evening, we were having our customary coffees in the residents' lounge. It was a time of relaxation, a pause, before we dispersed our various ways to spend the evening. I recall Brian Woolfenden a Cambridge graduate working at R&H was stretched out in one of the armchairs. He was studying the crossword in one of the daily papers. On seeing Baha, he asked him in his over exaggerated casual way, sounding almost bored, "Baha. What is another word for 'blackmail'?"

All of us present had been taken in by Brian appearing to be studying the crossword, from which he had picked this out. Several suggestions were put forward, all unsuccessfully. Brian unwound his tall frame out of the chair to leave the room, saying as he went out, "A Sudanese Postman!"

I knew that the mere mention of the word *'black'* in whatever context upset Baha, yet he laughed along with every body else. He had heard many other wisecracks aimed at him or his origins, like the one about the camel corps and the Sudanese Navy.

Down in the Works though, things were rather different for him. In the particular incident I can bring to mind, as much as anything it was the peculiarities of Vic Smith a *'ganger'* that Baha fell foul of. 'Big Vic' as he was known was indeed a larger than life character. He enjoyed practical jokes and used to take liberties with the tea trolley girls much to the delight of onlookers. Big Vic was that particular shop's senior trade union official or *'convenor'*. It was said that he was an ardent Communist!

When Baha approached Big Vic to borrow some special tool, he was told to "Fuck off!"

Easily upset, Baha had responded, "Hold on! You can't talk to me like that!" not aware of Big Vic's political leanings he added, "I am a Prince!"

Practical joker that he was, Big Vic must have seen red at what would have appeared to him as a 'Princely put-down', especially when Baha went on to demand an apology from his larger than life Communist adversary. No one had heard of *'political correctness'*, behaviour then was largely a matter of judgement. Not for the first time, the little

Horizontal diesel assembly, Sheaf Iron Works.
From left – Graham Bunbury (S.Africa), Cecil and his brother 'Big Vic' Smith who was shop convener, and myself

A bright Sunday morning on the Lindum House lawn just after breakfast – my mentor, Ivan Stewart from Dungannon, Baha the great grandson of the Sudan Mahdi and to his left myself.

confrontation ended up with a meeting in Mr Donaldson-Palmers office. He was personal director and adept at pouring oil on the troubled waters. The Mahdi family were valued customers in the Sudan!

The most amusing, if not bizarre of Baha's escapades could only have been told by him personally, as it involved a late night encounter with the local constabulary and his trip down to the '*nick*' for '*further questioning*'! It all started innocently enough late one evening in the residents' lounge. Somebody had remarked that it would take an olympian performance to run round the block in 10 minutes. Others present agreed but not Baha, who getting up from his seat said, "I'll have a go."

With that, he proceeded to prepare himself by taking off the jacket and waistcoat belonging to his dark three piece suit. He slipped off his tie. He then removed is shoes and socks, rolling his trouser legs up. Thus stripped down he was left standing in a white shirt which showed off to great effect the bright red braces that held his trousers up. I was reminded of the fishermen I used to see as a child in front of our house in Mersin. They also were thin wiry chaps and had their trousers rolled right up just above the knees to expose their skinny though sinewy legs like Baha. It was the braces that seemed so incongruous. After a bit of running on the spot to impress and loosen up, he set off into the night.

It was a quiet, dark autumn evening; people living in the vicinity of Lindum House were home for the night. The roads were deserted. There were large private houses with spacious grounds, behind the high walls bordering the pavements along which Baha was loping.

"Oi! Where do you think you're going."

According to Baha, this was how he had been pulled up by one of the two policemen in the patrol car who had wound down the nearside window. As the solitary figure flitting in and out of the black shadows cast by the big trees beyond the wall did not stop, the car lurched forward and the same voice called out once more, "Hey! We want to have a word with you."

The policeman got out of the car, and is said to have muttered, "Blimey!"

Little wonder really. Confronted with the sight of Baha standing there, hands on his hips panting. In the light cast on him from a nearby street lamp, beads of sweat could be made out glistening on his ebony face. Out of breath, his lips were parted to reveal his pearly white teeth. The look of surprise revealed the luminous whites of his wide open eyes.

"And who are you?"

"I am Bahadin Al Mahdi."

"Oh yes! …and where are you from?"

"Khartoum."

"Right, Sir. I will have to ask you to accompany us to the station."

The 10 minutes that had been originally estimated for the run had been surpassed by almost half an hour when there was a ring at the Lindum House front door bell. A bit later, in came Baha still barefooted. Most of us were still in the lounge. As time had gone by, there had been some speculation as to what might have become of him and whether someone should ring the police.

"We were just on the point of telephoning the Police station."

Baha laughed, "That is where I have just come from!"

I have since pondered on this curious encounter that dark night. What a surprise it must have been for the two local constables. They might well have described it in their jargon as 'having a reason to be suspicious of the said black man running barefoot with his trousers rolled right up to his knees and wearing fancy braces.' A hitherto unheard of incident probably in the entire county and beyond. It was a first. They must have felt it their duty to detain him for further questioning down at the local nick, just for the record.

I would guess that at the time there wasn't a single black face to be seen in Lincoln. Well, apart from my friend Baha's. I came to the conclusion that the constables who apprehended him could never have been to the Lincoln Races. Yet the one and only time that Hank and I went, whom should we run into but Prince Monolulu, said to be the most famous black man in Britain. Tall and rather eccentric in his colourful garb with a spectacular array of coloured ostrich feather plumes in his headdress. He was a 'tipster' seen at many horse racing venues around the country. He even had a catchphrase which he shouted out repeatedly, "I got a horse…I got a horse!"

Lincoln in the early 1950s was a sedate cathedral city, dull I suppose by today's standards. There rarely were any serious incidents. The only other run-in with the police led to three of us, all residents of Lindum House being summoned on a road traffic offence. John Pierre Togneri had given Hank and I a ride on his motorcycle. We were spotted by the police proceeding rather precariously down the road which lead to each of us receiving a summons. The greater embarrassment was to find that R&H's Managing Director, Colonel H Riggall who was a J.P was on the bench when we attended court.

Since arriving in Lincoln and with the benefit of living at Lindum House, I had found it easy to mix with the foreign trainees. My family's close ties with Syria and Turkey had in particular drawn me to those who came like myself from the Middle East. One such person was Murid Murad a Jordanian but of Palestinian parentage, born in Jerusalem where his family had property and had been living prior to the creation of the State of Israel. He was of course a Muslim but as I have mentioned earlier, this was of no consequence to me. He and his younger brother Munjid, who I used to meet from time to time, had both been educated at Victoria College in Alexandria and as a consequence spoke perfect English.

In appearance Murid was a typical Arab, a burly chap with masses of black hair and eyes to match. He was an admirer of all things English, having been to Victoria College in Alexandria. Want it or not he was also an *'outsider'* even in Jordan to which so many Palestinians who had been displaced were forced to move. Of the many who came from the Middle East, Murid was the only one who knew some Turkish. When we were on our own, he loved to come out with the odd phrase or two such as '*Nasilsin canim*' – how are you my dear? '*Yapma canim*' – come on my dear. A throw back to days of the Ottoman Empire when speaking Turkish was in itself a sign of some standing. Murid professed with great pride Bedouin roots. As I got to know him, I suspected that it was more a statement of how he felt rather than what he really was. The same age as myself, we became close friends right until he returned to work for Naguib Baki the R&H Agents in Amman.

For a time we were both in the Apprentice Shop together. I had discovered that Murid was disposed to taking liberties. He was a practical joker. So I told him how Frank used to catch out unsuspecting apprentices with his clever little ruse, "That is Frank over there, the chap with the pipe, testing the small compressors. He has engaged several unsuspecting apprentices in conversation. He casually points up at the roof beams saying, "Look at those big spiders up there." His victims thus caught unawares, he grabs their privates for a laugh. He has caught several, including myself. I'll tell you, it's painful. Makes the eyes water!"

A short time later, I noticed Murid standing chatting to Frank. When Frank pointed up to the roof, believing he had another victim, it was Murid who grabbed him. If the look of utter shock on Frank's face was anything to go by, it was a wonder that he had not swallowed his pipe! When the apprentices realised that Frank's trick had rebounded on him, they went wild.

Not so long after we had both left Lincoln, I heard that Nevin, the younger daughter of my mother's closest friend Victoria Atalay had married a young Jordanian from Amman. On further investigation it turned out to be none other than Munjid, my old friend Murid's younger brother.

I had several South American friends from Lindum House. One in particular was George Palau with whom both I and Hank were friendly. George was a small, dark chap with native Indian features. His entire face lit up into an infectious smile and he used to often say "Be happy chap! Laugh." Which is what he did. He talked incessantly about his motor bike – a Harley Davidson that he rode about on in Quito, Equador. Cesar Manchieno was also from Quito, a fair skinned blue eyed chap. They never spoke to each other. Cesar must have seen himself as a descendant of some 'conquistadors'. He was rather aloof, I hardly ever had the opportunity to speak with him.

It was an Englishman from Argentina who left the most indelible of marks. Not least of all on account of the strange name, Trigo, by which everyone knew him. An enigma, he described himself as "*V Barton from Bristol*". It was thought that his first name must have been Victor though no one ever used it. Trigo was a large man with a fine head of hair, just a few flecks of grey. He wore a brown fedora when he went out, always perched on his head at a jaunty angle, it was his hallmark. There was something distinguished about him. As for his age, like everything else, it had to be guessed, maybe late 40s. Trigo had just joined R&H. Prior to that he had something to do with the Argentinian state railways.

I had heard him talking with the likes of Brian Woolfenden and one or two others who had been through university and got engineering degrees. He could hold his own with them and had a wealth of anecdotes not only about engine maintenance but design and performance. He was particularly helpful to Hank and I maybe because we were the youngest of the residents and certainly in the greatest need of guidance.

I was not doing at all well at the Technical College. In fact, I had slipped back, failing in subjects that I had earlier passed. Once more, mathematics had been the stumbling block. I unburdened myself to Trigo who had listened patiently. When I finished he asked, "What do you really want to do at Rustons?"

I told him what Jerry Rampton had told my family about opportunities abroad. Since arriving in Lincoln, I had found out a great deal more. In particular about Percy Roberts who was R&H's representative, based in Beyrouth, "I would like to join Percy Roberts, then when he retires, hopefully take over from him." Trigo's reply surprised me. More to the point, it enlightened me and gave me some new found confidence listening to what he said, "You don't need a degree or even an ONC for that. What you require is a good appreciation of Ruston engines and their applications. Listening to you and Hank, I would say you are both going about your training down at the Works in the right way. Don't worry, you have the right temperament and most importantly, the motivation."

What Trigo said was reinforced by a Mr Scott who was the Lloyds inspector based in Nottingham who used to visit Rustons to inspect engines or parts. I remember him also for what he once told me about his work, "I have learned one thing during the many years as a Lloyds inspector. Any fool can reject work on inspection. It takes experience to make concessions, to advise on how a part can be re-worked to be good enough for me to pass. Now that is what makes a good inspector."

I met Trigo once after leaving Lindum House. It was at Birmingham's old Exhibition venue, Bingley Hall, many years ago. He was sales manager of Robert Hyde Steel Foundry in Derby. He had aged but still wore his brown fedora. I never saw him again.

Traditionally at Lindum House on Saturdays and Sundays in place of dinner we had a self service cold buffet. It was a veritable feast. There were cold meats, a choice of three out of ham, beef, tongue, chicken, or smoked salmon with various salads. It was here that I developed a taste for Russian salad. There was always a tureen of soup on a hot plate and a choice of fruit salad or pie for dessert. Nowhere before or since in the UK have I seen the likes of such a copious spread. At these times, especially in the spring and summer we tended to sit at the round table in the large bay window over looking the lawns and garden.

It was on these occasions that we indulged in socio-political discussions for which there was great scope given the diversity of the cultures presented. As I recall, these '*debates*' could get heated but never unpleasant. Even then in the early 1950s, the USA was often the main topic the discussions being fuelled by several South Americans. The two most vocal contributors were an engineer from Cuba, Emilio Conde and a younger trainee, George Palau whom I have already mentioned. Both, for their own particular reasons appeared to resent North American influence in their countries. I heard the term '*gringo*' for the first time, the more usual term was less ambiguous – "the bastard Americans!"

Present at the table one weekend evening was my Turkish friend Omer Bese from Izmir. He was the R&H Agent's senior engineer, a man probably in his 40s who spoke no English whatsoever when he arrived in Lincoln only a few weeks earlier. He had been sitting in on some heated argument about American attitudes. At the end of the discussion, Omer, came out with, "American, dollar gentleman! – No dollar! – No gentleman!"

The cliché was often repeated long after Omer had returned to Turkey. I spent some happy times with Omer a year or two later when I was sent out to represent R&H on the Agent's stand at the Izmir International Fair.

I have already alluded in passing to *One Hundred Years of Good Company* the book published on the occasion of R&H's centenary in 1957. The play on words is so very apt. I came to know some unforgettable personalities in the workshops during my training. They were unstinting in passing on to me their know-how and experiences. After I retired I never missed Fred Dibner's television presentations of aspects of our industrial past. There was so much that reminded me of the years I spent on the shop floor at R&H. Most moving of all was the memory of all the many '*Fred Dibners*' I had the privilege of rubbing shoulders with during my time there.

Mechanisation went no further than a gravity conveyor line for assembly of a small vertical diesel engine. I remember hearing some talk about '*time and motion study*'. Production was largely driven by the men's skill, pride in themselves and in the engines and other machinery that they built. There were whole families working at R&H. I recall being told that dismissal was unheard of. I also remember that when necessary it was the grownup members of the family who would discipline any of their young who went off the rails. The company fostered a sense of loyalty, a good example of this was the Annual Foreman's Garden Party which was staged in the summer on the lawns at Lindum House. All residents were invited to attend.

Prior to the event, any of them who had become Foreman since the last garden party or who had not attended before, were asked to take part in a rehearsal at the Riggalls' house, so that Mrs Riggall could coach them on '*garden party etiquette* '. Imagine the indignant reaction now by the adherents to '*political correctness*', should such a thing be suggested in one of the automobile manufacturers of Birmingham or Coventry.

Following my introductory training in the Apprentice Shop I spent two and a half years on the shop floor. Starting with the VSH range of small high speed diesels and ending my fitting and assembly work on the biggest turbo charged diesels known as the VOX. These giants could produce 2400 bhp running at 428 rpm. They must have been the type of Ruston engine that Jerry Rampton had commissioned at the Mersin electricity generating station. Mr Codling had also arranged for me to spend some weeks in the Diesel Repair Shop, and the department where the fuel pumps and injectors were assembled and tested. These are the most vital organs of a diesel engine.

Finally, I had five months training on what was arguably Ruston's pride, its Gas Turbine. The department was headed by David Fielding who had been with Sir Frank Whittle at British Power Jets. Interestingly, I recall whilst I was there seeing pulverised peat used as fuel for the RGT which had already performed well on various crude oils. It was believed that the RGT would ensure Ruston's survival well into the future.

Nearing the end of my shop floor training which had concentrated on the company's Diesel engines, I was summoned to Mr Codling's office, "It is time you had some experience '*out-working*'. R&H secured an order some time ago from Bradford City Water Works. The two Ruston diesels have just been despatched to the site on Ilkley Moor.

As R&H are the main contractors, it is our responsibility to carry out the entire installation which includes two Sulzer water pumps."

I jumped at his proposal enthusiastically. It was yet another step forward for me. I said that I had heard a song about Ilkley Moor but was not sure exactly where it was. Mr Codling, somewhat unusually for him, smiled. In the past he had been rather abrupt, with a distinct army officer air about him.

"Right that settles it, I will have a word about you with Mr Quixley. As you may know, he is responsible for installations in the UK. It is a relatively small job which is why I thought it would be ideal. You will be able to see it through from start to finish. It will be very good experience!"

Through the good endeavours of Miss Reah, the company's '*billeting-officer*', I arrived at the door of the YMCA on Manningham Lane from Bradford railway station by taxi. It was a Sunday evening. The intention had been for me to be at the Ilkley Moor pumping station site early the following morning. Things did not go quite to plan. From the very start on the Monday morning I had problems. I had left Lincoln with a note from Miss Reah. Included in the two or three lines was a directive to catch the Keighley bus on Manningham Lane. No one had imagined I would have a problem with that! More to the point, nor had anyone dreamt that pronouncing '*Keighley*' would be the cause of the problem.

First time in Yorkshire, I knew nothing about the local accent. There were few passers by on the pavement of busy Manningham Lane that morning. I had asked those who came by where the bus stop was for 'Keeley'. No one had heard of the place, some were even apologetic. Eventually, hearing me say 'Keeley', an understanding expression came over the face of an elderly man I had stopped. He smiled in a kindly manner and proceeded to put me right, "Eee! Lad, you must mean 'Keith-ley'. We don't pronounce it 'Keeley' round here. You are on the right side of the road. The bus stop is a fair way down, a fair walk from here. Good luck. Cheerio." Thankful and much relieved, I hurried to where I would board the Keighley bus.

I have no other recollection of how I managed to get to my destination. I must have been hours late as I seem to recall getting off the Keighley bus and onto another which went up what I came to know as Swine Lane, an isolated, bleak, wind swept minor road on a ridge where the BCWW pumping station had been built. It was not far from Howarth, home of the Brontë sisters and the landscape typical of what had possessed and inspired them. It was my first taste of the Yorkshire moors and I would be there for a few days.

The Bradford City Water Works man in charge at the site on Swine Lane was Alfred Lorley. A portly man, not very tall, dressed in a dark blue durable looking serge suit. He wore black boots and on his head a rather worn looking hat. He was a foreman. I was to learn as the days went by that though he had little education nor training, he possessed immense personal authority and was respected by the two weather beaten chaps who were in his charge and there to assist the Ruston engineer Colin with whom I would be working.

There was little of the day left when Colin told me that he had arranged with Alfred for the BCWW lorry to stop in front of the YMCA and pick me up starting the next day. They dropped me of at the YMCA on Manningham Lane late that afternoon. By the time I had a wash and dressed dinner was about to be served. I was ready for it at the end of what had been for me a long and unusual day. I could remember going down several flights of stairs from my room that morning for my early breakfast. That evening, having got my bearings, it was obvi-

'Out working', one of my stints was helping install Ruston Diesel engines driving water pumps on wind swept Swine Lane near Illkley. I am seen here with Bradford WW foreman Alfred Lorley and to his right the R&H engineer Colin and one of the workmen.

ous that meals were served in what had once been the basement and cellars of a big detached house. There were several similar ones on that stretch of Manningham Lane, at one time the homes of prosperous merchants or mill owners.

At the YMCA once more I was thrown in with young foreign students. There were several who were trainees at Jowett Motors, automobile manufacturers in Bradford famed in particular for their 'Javlin' sports model. I soon got friendly with an Afghan graduate. He was the first and only Afghan I was ever to come across. For some reason, all the years I was at R&H none ever turned up in Lincoln. All I can recall about him was that he was a strict Muslim who neither smoked nor drank alcohol.

Early next morning, I stood on the pavement just outside the YMCA, eyes peeled for the familiar lorry with the letters BCWW emblazoned on the cab above the windscreen. As it slowed down close to the edge of the pavement I could see the figure of Alfred Lorley with Sheila wedged between him and the driver. He had the nearside window down. He signalled me with his thumb and called out above the noise of the traffic, "Pat, get in round the back."

I did! Tipping over the tailboard like a sack of potatoes, ending up in a pile on the floor of the vehicle. It was an undignified entry! I was determined, and did manage, in the days that followed not to repeat the performance. Each day on arrival at the pumping station, a set routine was played out by each and every one of us. Alfred Lorley climbed down from the cab. Not waiting to be helped, Sheila jumped out managing to land on all fours. The two navies removed the canvas covered shelter off the back. This was placed on the grass verge. The brazier was set up by the shelter to provide warmth for the men and was used for the indispensable 'brew-up'. Alfred Lorley and Sheila, a boarder collie, went for a short walk. The BCWW lorry set off back to Bradford. I made my way over to the stone building and joined Colin. He was in the gallery that overlooked the large empty hall which would house the diesel engines and water pumps. All the machinery, right down to yards and yards of pipe work, foundation bolts not to mention boxes of screws and nuts were all waiting there for us.

Colin, one of Mr Quixley's team of '*out-work*' engineers was a slightly built young chap probably in his late 20s. He had served his time at R&H and gone to Lincoln Technical College and passed his ONC. Colin was married and had two youngsters. Even now, I can bring him to mind with his dark blue boiler suit, as yet hardly soiled, leaning over the gallery railings puffing on his pipe as he gazed at the two Ruston diesels sitting on their foundation blocks.

I was impatient to get on with the installation work, building things up, cracking-on. Not Colin. Together we set about checking every section of pipe work against the installation layout drawings prepared in R&H's drawing office in Lincoln. I was reminded of Frank who shaped the steel pipes and cut threads at each end of them so that they could be joined together using a collar or flange. Mr Codling had arranged for me to have part of my training with Frank.

Whilst with him, he had shown me all the '*wrinkles*' that he had acquired over the years getting the pipe work made to suit the many Ruston installations. An error of a few fractions of an inch or the positioning of a bend incorrectly on a section of pipe could lead to the loss of time and money. Avoiding the need to correct mistakes, for whatever reason, once installation work had started on site, was important. That was why Colin was so anxious to check things out before we started.

I had put bends and curves into steel pipes of up to 3" maybe even 4" diameter. This was done by first sealing the end of the pipe by hammering in a wooden bung. Loose, dry sand was poured into the pipe. The part to be bent was heated in a furnace. When it was glowing red, it was placed in a template and bent as required. Once bent, the bung was removed and the hot sand emptied out. Frank had shown me how to cover the cool end with my hand before plunging the end that was still red hot into a tank of water to cool it. At first, seeing the fierce sizzling effect – water boiling and giving off steam, I had been hesitant. Frank had put me at ease, "Don't worry, when you submerge the hot end into the tank of cooling water, provided you keep the palm of your hand over the end of the pipe it will be protected by a cushion of air inside the pipe."

Something of a showman, Frank felt he had to demonstrate as he put it "What not to do!" He succeeded in ejecting over a distance of several yards a spout of near boiling water and steam out of the pipe, by suddenly lifting his hand off its end. An impressive a display as one can imagine. In those days, there was little of the health and safety at work legislation that has been introduced over the past 50 years. Much was left to the foresight and good judgement of the worker. I must point out that where Frank and I had been working, there was no one else in the vicinity who otherwise might have been injured. All of us were then well served by common sense!

I must have got on with Alfred Lorley. For one thing, he took to telling me about his wife's serious problem in pregnancy which had left her in a bad way. Then on another occasion towards the end of the installation work, he came out with these thoughts, "Pat, you know, in life so much depends on how you treat other people. This has nothing to do with education nor class. Take me, my people could not afford to have me continue my schooling. I managed with what little book learning I had. I have been with BCWW more or less all my working life. Now, as foreman I know the job. I would not ask any of my chaps to do something that I could not do myself. The other thing that I am very careful about is to keep my instructions short and simple. This way there is less chance of a misunderstanding which is of service to no one."

The installation had been completed without a hitch. I recall one of Mr Quixley's senior engineers came over from Lincoln. He took Colin and I over to Leeds where we attended a meeting at the Sulzer offices. Once the two diesels had been test run, Colin's work was at an end which also meant the same for me. Mr Codling after that sent me on a number of other '*out work*' jobs including repair and servicing of Ruston diesels.

I was nearing the end of the practical shop floor training that R&H wanted to put me through. As for the engineering theory, I continued to struggle at the Technical College. At one point, another option had been suggested to me. Some of the apprentices at R&H were taking a City & Guilds course which was deemed to be easier. I found out however that it was more appropriate to those who wanted to continue in the works on production, something that had no appeal for me. I decided that for the time being anyway, I would continue the course that I had started. At least if I could get the Ordinary National Certificate in mechanical engineering that would be something.

It must have been Mr Codling who put the choices to me, "Soon you will have completed your 30 months practical training. You now have a career choice with R&H. We have already from time to time talked about these and I believe I know what you have set your heart on, even so, I have to put these options to you."

I had discovered many months earlier that Mr Codling had worked in Egypt and to my astonishment had known my father. They must have come across each other when my father was attached to The Port Said Engineering Works (SAE). However slight this relationship might have been, I felt it must have benefited me. Mr Codling had taken personal interest in my training and in the direction I would choose for a career with R&H. The options that I had known about were in the service department, drawing office or export sales.

We both knew that it had been a foregone conclusion when I told Mr Codling "Export sales" and he smiled and said, "Right Pat. Leave it with me. There are still a few more days, I will need to see you again."

The first stage of my time at Ruston & Hornsby Limited was fast drawing to a close. I was beginning to get itchy feet. Ready to move on, I felt that what lay ahead would be even more challenging than the past.

Chapter 15

Mindful of my origins, past experiences and aspirations, Mr Codling had once more come up trumps. A berth had been found for me in the Middle East section of Ruston's export sales department. This important division that looked after the company's flourishing overseas business took up the entire first floor of the main office block. Its collective duty was to give both technical and commercial support to R&H Agents and Companies outside the UK. The time had come for me to put the engineering skills and knowledge of Ruston diesels that I had acquired in the works, to practical use. I felt a great sense of personal fulfilment and purpose. It was June 1953.

My first day, I found myself in a large open plan office where there must have been a dozen or more sales engineers. They were seated in two lines of light grey steel desks that stretched back to the end of the office. There was plenty of room between each desk for filing cabinets and other office furniture in the same shade of matching grey. The occupant of each desk sat in an upholstered swivel chair with armrests. Very different from the rudimentary bare wooden furniture I had got accustomed to at the Levante offices in Mersin. In addition to the telephone there was also a dictaphone on the desk provided for my personal use. Though there were no hard and fast regulations that I was aware of, the men were in suits. The few younger ones, like myself wore grey flannel trousers and tweed jackets. Neck ties were *de rigueur*. I decided to wear the two piece suit that I had invested in originally for social occasions.

My immediate boss, George Anselm, I was to find out later was half Russian. He told me about his widowed mother who was still living in the USSR. His boss, the joint export sales manager, John Albertini was of Italian extraction. Along with the other departmental sales managers, he had one of the four or five offices that stretched down one side of the open plan office. With my move into export sales, I had joined Ivan Stewart whom I had known for some time at Lindum House. In time we became very close friends. It was one of the senior sales-engineers I was with in the Middle East section, a Michael Martin from Egypt with whom I was to become particularly friendly.

Moving into export sales as I had brought me other benefits, material ones at that. This move had transformed me into a member of '*staff*' with a salary of £5.0s.0d per week. A most generous increase of more than 50% on what I had been given as an *'allowance'* whilst in the Works. Furthermore, the two benefits I had during my shop floor training were not withdrawn. Firstly, I was not thrown out of Lindum House. Secondly, the company continued to allow me a '*day release*' each week to attend the local Technical College.

For all my euphoria, I still harboured a dread. The fear of failing the (S3) examination for my Ordinary National Certificate in mechanical engineering. Paradoxically this was also what added to my keenness to move into sales, the option that least required an ONC.

Ivan Stewart it was who had pointed something out to me, "Pat, you're staff now. It is quite a step up for you. You are now on the R&H promotions ladder. Well done!"

This revelation got me wondering and created a new awareness. Many friends and acquaintances in the works on hearing that I would be moving into export sales had joked about *'the brains department'* as they liked to call those who worked in the main office block. I still had to clock on each morning and clock off at the end of the day just like they had to. On the other hand, they earned wages but I would be paid a salary even though it would still come in the same beige pay packet. The *'them and us'* divide or the *'blue collar'* versus *'white collar'* feud ran deep. I was learning as time went by that the one thing that neutralised it was the sense of humour of the very people who were drawn into this class consciousness.

As I started to find my bearings and settled into the routine of the export sales department, I gained in confidence. For the first time, I became aware that I might indeed have something to offer R&H. Even if I failed to gain technical qualifications, I had many inbred assets. I began to take stock of these. The experience working in the Levante offices. Mersin's cosmopolitan mix of people, typical of the Middle East where I had grown up. My languages – Turkish, French and Arabic that gave me at the very least a basis on which to build. I was surrounded by individuals with whom I had much in common. I sensed that being an *'outsider'* might after all turn out to be another asset.

I had been told that 85% of R&H's diesel engines were exported, it was not surprising that the export sales department was larger than any of the other ones *viz,* home, marine and the new gas turbine departments. This might also explain why the whole of the first floor in the main office block came to be called *'the brains department'* by those on the shop floor. Sarcasm brought on I suspect through envy, what better way of showing grudging admiration.

These departments were so busy, that staff from one hardly ever found the time to mix with staff from the others. I was surprised when I had a visit from a member of home sales who came over to where I was working and started to chat. Chris Beresford had started serving his time down in the Works before me. He told me that he had been in home sales for some months. We used to see each other in the Works and at the Technical College but had gone our separate ways, until then. In the course of our conversation, when it emerged that I had been to public school, he looked amazed, "Good heavens! I never thought of you as a public school type."

The way he had come out with this comment took me by surprise. He had certainly not intended it as any sort of a put-down? Chris did not appear to be that sort of a person. Maybe the remark he had made could be a way of empathising with me, a sign of comradeship. Smiling, and with an air of reciprocal friendship I asked him, "What makes you say that Chris?"

"Well, to be honest apart from anything else, you always appeared serious and mature. I mean, look at that crowd. You know, that chap Baldwin and his pal Rickards and the others. They behave like over grown school kids. They are the sort who never really grow up. Full of airs and graces, they live in a world of their own. You did not come across as one of them."

Chris Beresford's chance remark made innocently enough got me thinking later. I had never spoken to any in '*that crowd*' as he called a clique of public school boys who were serving their apprenticeships at R&H. I had never been drawn to the likes of Baldwin and Rickards. The truth is I was relieved to hear Chris say that I had not come across '*as one of them!*' as he put it! My circle of friends were mostly from overseas, some living with me at Lindum House. I did also have friends from among the many other public school boys, one in particular that springs to mind was John Barnes-Hughes and others who were members of the Lindum Rugby Club.

Long afterwards I still pondered how my mother and uncle would have felt had they heard all that Chris had come out with particularly the bit about me *"not being a public school type."* Such deliberations invariably set off a train of thought that spread out to touch many aspects of my family's and my own mixed origins. Both my mother and uncle were spawned from a mixed marriage, they cherished their Englishness handed down from their father.

It was thanks to the efforts of the two of them that I had attended the English High School in Istanbul then Hurtspierpoint College in England at least in part to satisfy their aspiration that had been made known to me many times by them both. In short that I would become the very personification of *'the English public school system'*. After all, hadn't the Empire been shaped on the playing fields of Eton and Harrow and weren't public schools the very essence of Englishness.

It was the counterpart of the mixed marriage that was the problem that would not go away. As I have already described, it was my aunt Olga when she was with the Scotts in England who opened up the can of worms. It was her two maiden aunts, Edith and Frances Rickards, my grandfather's sisters who saw the marriage of their brother to a Syrian girl as a come down. They refused to receive Olga, who after all was their niece, when she tried to visit them.

Was it not the British who coined the word '*wog*' to describe Arabs and '*dago*' a foreigner from one of the Latin countries, collectively seen by them as inferiors. The very last thing that victims of such insults would do is admit to them. They would try to shrug off the stigma and suffer in silence. Often such hang-ups were not brought out into the open leave alone discussed within the family. They remained submerged in the family's collective subconscious. It was these undercurrents that added to my sense of '*outsider*' though like my mother I strived to adapt to this state.

My mother returned immediately to Mersin after her schooling in England. She spent the rest of her life in the Middle East. Growing up in my grandparents' home, I recall my mother spent much of her time with my grandmother in the kitchen. They spoke Arabic together. My mother was also very fond of her aunt Fouteen who lived in a modest house not far from the Rickards' property. She called on her aunt and cousins almost daily where again they spoke in Arabic. This was how I picked up the language.

My mother's schooling in England had not made her different but rather added to her popularity. She mixed well with the locals, mostly the Christians, be they the less well off or the *'beau monde'* of the town. She also had many friends amongst the Muslim community. When she lost my father and was obliged to return with me to Mersin, she took on the mantle of a committed widow. A standing in that part of the world that earned a woman respect and consideration, especially when she was accompanied by a dependant child.

Left with no pension, she started to give private lessons in English. This widened her circle of acquaintances as well as providing her with a degree of financial independence. She was known by everyone simply as '*Madam Dosia*'. One of my mother's pupils was the elder daughter of Hamdi *Bey* a notable and wealthy businessman living in Mersin. His daughter Neriman married the son of Turkey's first Democratic Party Prime Ministers, Celal Bayar. My mother, who had taught Neriman English to the point of fluency was invited to what must have been the wedding of the year in Ankara. All teachers were in those times held in great esteem. A tradition put in place by Ataturk himself when the great man kissed his teacher's hand in public. Her pupils as a sign of respect addressed her as '*my English teacher, Madam Dosia*'. A form of speech that gave her great pleasure.

Apart from hospitality, people in that part of the world empathise with one another. My mother was sympathetic to the hardships of others. I remember an occasion when we were walking towards the town centre. I must have been seven or eight. As many did, we were walking in the middle of the road which in those days was free from traffic. One of the manhole covers had been removed. I could see a head appear. My mother stopped when she recognised the person whose head I had seen emerging. I was puzzled that my mother had known the grim covered man who eventually popped up, accompanied by the smell of sewage. She exchanged some words with him in Arabic. As we moved off, by way of explanation she told me, "That is Farid, poor chap. He has never been the same since he lost his wife Lateefah. They had a small house in what used to be known as the '*gardens quarter*' of the town. He now lives with one of his sons who took him in. I used to see them sometimes. She grew herbs in a small plot of land adjoining their home, which she sold in bundles. It helped because I don't suppose he was very well paid."

During the period I am talking about, many of the short term visitors to Mersin from England were the country's intellectuals. Professors of archaeology, historians, embassy or British council staff many of whom had been to Oxbridge and the better known public schools. Without any doubt, there was great prestige in being British. There were also the disreputable, adventurers or the *'parvenues'*. The upstarts, non-commissioned officers Sergeant Majors who introduced themselves as *'Major'*. Amongst these, some trading on their 'superior', unadulterated Britishness, did at times cause members of my family to reflect on their own 'mixed origins'. It was this that brought them face to face with that inescapable reality. Unlike myself, for I was at the time very fair skinned, freckled and ginger haired. My father after all was Irish. All my mother's side of the family were unmistakably Eastern Mediterranean in appearance.

The part of Turkey where my family had lived for two generations and where I grew up could be described in a sense where Europe merged into Asia. It was part of that amorphous place known as the Levant to which Europeans, many of them merchant adventurers rushed to make their fortunes. These people, were known as Levantines. Once, a friend of mine overcome with pride, chose to describe his Levantine forbears as '*buccaneers'!* They had amassed their fortunes in Smyrna. It is said that the families of these early settlers intermarried amongst themselves.

After the First World War when the British went into Palestine, the term Levantine came to be used pejoratively. It was used to describe those of mixed Arab and European descent. Also, the Europeans notably French, Italian and Greeks who *'had gone native'*. As these families were spread widely, it is impossible to describe exactly where the Levant lies. It did not identify a geographic feature, place nor country, but it could be described as stretching in a wide arc from Greece through the coastal parts of Western Turkey and down into Palestine. The émigrés who made their homes in the Levant were an amalgam of every imaginable origin, whether of nationality, race or religion including Jews and Armenians. With the widening of its definition, it became something of a slight to be referred to as a Levantine. It implied murky origins, lacking in honesty and trustworthiness.

I am reminded of the Thuma family, a young couple with two sons. They came to Mersin from their native Malta. During their stay in the town, my family got to know them well. The Thuma's had British passports though they had all been born and bred on the island of Malta. It must have been Mrs Thuma who confiding in my mother, poured her heart out telling her how they had been treated as second class by some of the English ex-pats. My mother and uncle empathised with them and I believe did what they could to help them. I was at school in England but my mother wrote and told me that they had decided to emigrate to Rhodesia where they felt their two sons would have better prospects. The last thing I heard was that they had landed on their feet and had invested in some sort of a chicken farm.

During the summer holidays that I spent with my family in Turkey whilst I was serving my apprenticeship at Ruston & Hornsby, my uncle who continued to take an interest in how I was getting on, he often spoke with me about my future.

"You know Patrick, you should think about your future. You're out of your teens now and more or less independent. From what I read and hear, England will have changed even more. I fear for its future. It is over populated and with few resources. The breaking up of the Empire is further aggravating the country's situation and it's standing in the world."

I listened respectfully. But at the time, I had other more immediate personal preoccupations back in Lincoln. The prospects of whether or not I would be able to continue living at Lindum House. How I was getting on at R&H, my long term prospects with the company. Beryl had left Lincoln, the uncertainty of how this might affect our future. All matters that no one at home would have been able to influence and about which therefore, I had kept silent. Wishing to help, my uncle went on about the things he considered relevant to my future.

"I have mulled things over for you myself. Of all the countries that were part of the British Empire the two that would be ideal are Australia and South Africa. The trouble is that Australia is so far away, it is at the other end of the globe. Pity because of the two it is the more stable. This brings me to South Africa. Beautiful country, much nicer in my view than Australia, climate not dissimilar to what we have here. It would suit you. You should have no trouble acquiring South African citizenship. You would be seen to be a white Colonial of English descent. It would be a relief to get away from this constant preoccupation with our origins. You see, it isn't a question of what we are but rather how others choose to see us. Some of these ex-pats from England coming out here see themselves as superior."

Not word for word but certainly one of the things I recall my uncle putting to me. A notion that in the early 1950s would have made sense given my own circumstances and the social climate of the times. At the time, I had pinned my hopes not only for a career but for my entire future on Ruston & Hornsby whom I saw as omnipotent given my time on their shop floor and their world wide standing. In them I saw British Engineering as second to none. England, in spite of the war still had a reputation for excellence – the stamp 'Made in England' carried with it immense kudos.

It was a bit later, when my settling in England looked more likely that my uncle came out with another of his suggestions. Looking back on that, I have found it surprising yet perfectly feasible and certainly with some merit. Here again, there was nothing wrong with his concept at the time, though as the years have rolled on it has probably become less significant. Now it might even sound bizarre, "Patrick, in England people, families who come into money aspire to belong to the upper crust. They resort to all manner of schemes that will elevate them. One way is to acquire a grander sounding name. Take two humdrum names like Brown and Smith, how much more elite if changed to 'Haughton-Brown' or say 'Humphery-Smith'. All you need do is merge your last name 'Noel' with your surname. I must say, 'Noel-Grigsby' sounds good. Have it legalised by deed poll. Wouldn't cost much. Think about it."

I must say, since my uncle came up with the idea, I have come across many double barrelled surnames starting with Noel and wondered whether they might not have been given birth in exactly the manner my uncle described. Needless to say I did not go ahead with my uncle's suggestion. Nor did I ever really know if he had been serious about it.

Growing up in Turkey, I had little to do with my mother's younger sisters, Olga and Rosie. They had both moved away from the Rickards home where I spent my childhood. Olga as I have already mentioned spent a great deal of her life in England, including her later years whilst her daughter Peter was at school. Rosie had moved out of the family house when she married Riri Levante. My mother and her brother had their education in the UK where as Olga and Rosie were at school in France. My aunt Rosie due to her happy and lasting marriage was far less concerned about these hang-ups.

My aunt Olga was dark and very Eastern Mediterranean in manner. She distanced herself from her Syrian origins by the simple expedient of turning against her Syrian relatives. Her marriage to John Catton, at the time acting British Consul in Mersin, was short lived. She, had been rebuffed by her two Rickards aunts who refused to have anything to do with her when she approached them whilst in England. She had enjoyed the lifestyle of the Scotts, an interlude that added to her self confidence and gave her a taste for the good life. She aped the upper crust English, maybe even felt she had become one of them.

She had a way with the rich and powerful, claiming to have had a proposal of marriage from the Duke of Bedford. She said that she declined his offer! Her self confidence and immense charm made her a veritable '*femme fatale*.'

Inevitably, she had those who perhaps through envy, condemned her. She was charged with lacking in loyalty and pursuing those from whom she might derive benefit. She dedicated a large portion of her life to her daughter Peter, spending many years cut off from the lifestyle that she had once made her own. My aunt was generous to a fault. She was also extremely ambivalent never knowing quite who or what she was.

To those born and bred in the United Kingdom and living there as adults, prior to our transformation into a multi-cultural society, the account I have given of the Rickards family's crisis of identity might sound strange. I have no doubt, it probably does now. The little I have said is factual and intended to convey the climate of the times. I hope it will also have shown that much depends on how individuals cope with their *'lot in life'*!

Chapter 16

"Nothing succeeds like success" is an oft quoted axiom, but how can one be sure that it is unfailingly true and therefore reliable? Ruston & Hornsby Limited whom I joined in the early 1950s was unquestionably a global success, surely therefore they would continue to succeed. That was how it seemed to me as I settled into my job in the company's export sales department that summer of 1953.

R&H had vast engineering facilities not only in Lincoln and Grantham but also in Colchester where they had acquired another well known manufacturer of diesel engines which were complementary to their range of industrial diesels.

I will confine myself to R&H in Lincoln where I served my time. Here the company manufactured shunting locomotives and the flameproof diesel mine locomotives that were safe for operation down coalmines. Painted white, as far as I am aware, they were the only machines that left sheaf iron works not painted in '*Lincoln green*'. The boiler works was a completely self contained establishment for the manufacture of boilers and allied products. A variety of pumps were also manufactured for which there was a big market for irrigation in the Middle East. By all accounts, R&H from their earliest days had been forward looking. They still were, given the post war development of an industrial gas turbine. The Ruston GT prototype was on show and actually working in the engineering & marine exhibition at Olympia in1953, about the time that I was moved into their export sales department.

For me personally the name 'Ruston' will always remain synonymous with industrial diesel engines. The range of their diesels was extensive, from the 2 horse power single cylinder vertical VSH to the VOX range. The 12 cylinder VOX, the biggest engine manufactured at the time, was rated at 2,400 horse power. It was the type of Ruston engine installed by Mr Rampton in the Mersin electricity power house.

I soon discovered that Ruston diesels were in great demand in the Middle East – the territory that I was involved with. It was obvious from the volume of communications flowing in daily from the company's many agents which Michael Martin and I had been assigned to deal with, in particular, requests for the number of engines on their orders to be increased or for their delivery to be brought forward. That really said it all. When any of the agents got more and more desperate, we used to go over to the corner of the office where George Anselm, the assistant export manager resided. The availability problems would be put to him. On occasions, he could not find a solution to these pressing matters. As we returned to our own places in the large office, Michael vented his exasperation, in his usual way, "For fuck's sake! – if customers are not satisfied, they will go elsewhere!"

In time, his words would turn out to have been so prophetic.

Michael had a whole array of yarns that he trotted out to suit the occasion as he saw it. The thing about Michael was that he took any set backs personally, something that I was also inclined to do. One of these tales was intended to illustrate the untroubled, laid back attitude sometimes unfairly attributed to the English. A certain John Smith was sent by his company on a sales mission to the Middle East. Arriving at his hotel on the Sunday evening, he pinned a notice in English on the outside of his bedroom door. It read:

"Mr John Smith will be available to take orders from 9.00 am to 12 noon and from 2.00pm to 5.00pm daily Form orderly queue. Wait until invited to enter."

On returning to the UK, his boss asked him how things had gone.

"Not very well". He replied. Concerned, his boss retorted.

"How come?"

"Well, not only are they lazy out there, they are stupid as well!" he explained. By then his boss really flummoxed demanded. "Tell me more." John Smith went on to do so.

"They never knocked on my door! They must have got fed up waiting in a queue, so they just buggered off!"

Rather pleased with his story Michael laughed. I did as well. We always seemed to see things in the same way. Strange how something tragic can also be funny. Still laughing he turned serious, telling me, "I can just picture that plonker. You know, his sort do exist! I had one or two idiots like him to deal with when I was Sergeant in the RASC. The bad news is they'll now be in 'Civvy Street'. God help us."

At the time, it was R&H's high standing as one of Europe's leading manufacturers of industrial diesel engines that led to the availability and delivery problems with which Michael and I were confronted. The classic situation of supply failing to keep up with demand. The front line of R&H's sales force in each overseas country were the local agents. They were getting more orders than the Works in Lincoln and Grantham could cope with whether in manufacture or delivery. Ironically, the problem was spawned by the company's success!

Egypt, our shared birthplace was what drew Michael Martin and I together. He was a good deal older than me. Quite a mixture. His mother was part Greek part Egyptian but a Christian. His father was an Englishman who had been working in Egypt when they met and got married. He spoke a great deal about Alexandria. Apart from that I knew little else about Michael nor the circumstances that had brought him to R&H in Lincoln.

He had a sharp insight into human nature and life. He also possessed that rarest of gifts, the ability to express himself humorously. He was slight of build, and his hair was thinning on top. He wore horn-rimmed spectacles. It was years later when the fast talking 'Sergeant Bilko' emerged on our TV screens that I experienced the reincarnation of my friend. He was the spitting image of Phil Silvers, the American actor who immortalised 'Bilko'. I lost touch with and could never find out what became of Michael Martin. Sadly, he had vanished like so many others that I had come to know at R&H.

There was somebody else memorable in the export sales department at the time. A striking contrast to my ex 'Sergeant Bilko' lookalike from Alex. His defining feature was his gleaming pate, for he was as bald as a coot. One of the secretaries, Anne, claimed it gave him an allure, "it suits him!" Once again, it was a popular TV serial *Kojac* that brought him to mind. In it the NY detective of the same name and partial to lollipops, played by the actor Tele Savalas turned baldness into a cult. Our man in export sales was known solely by his double-barrelled name, MacAllister-Smith. He was a big chap, always smartly turned out in a well fitting double breasted suit garnished with a button hole. Middle aged and predictably, ex British Army. He looked the sort who might have been in intelligence, maybe a captain or major.

MacAllister-Smith rarely moved far from his desk. I can still visualise his big frame propped up on one elbow as he spoke interminably into his dictaphone. He was a very private individual even indifferent. He rarely, if ever found time to speak with anyone in the department. I never so much as exchanged a nod with him. Come to think of it, he never so much as looked at me. It is just that his presence seemed incongruous in the export sales department.

Ruston & Hornsby Limited was a vast organisation. Its many premises were spread around Lincoln and Grantham. Because of its worldwide activities and interests, there were constantly new arrivals, the length of their stays indeterminate. Many here today gone tomorrow! Those who remained, did so sometimes for weeks or even months then one day they also would no longer be there. So many acquaintances of whose departure I would not have been aware until one day I would realise they were no longer about.

In spite of these extensive connections, Ruston & Hornsby Limited appeared to have had little, if any business with the USA. During the years that I was at Lindum House there was never a visitor from the States, that is apart from one single solitary instance. It was during the summer of 1953 that Frank turned up at Lindum House. He needed no introduction as his accent and his crew cut identified him for what he was. More precisely a Texan. He was enormous for his age, just out of university it was said. An Australian, who had been a long term resident whilst working in the new Beevor Foundry, Max Burfoot on seeing Frank for the very first time had typically remarked, "Blow me mate! Now here is proof that everything from Texas is bloody well enormous! Big. Big, with a capital B. Have any of you seen the likes of the chap?"

I never had anything to do with Frank. In fact, I only really got to hear about him following his visit to the town's open air swimming pool with three or four other residents from Lindum House including Max Burfoot. They had all gone down into the town on bicycles. They returned some time later that afternoon, without Frank. Turned out he was at Lincoln Hospital. It was Max who gave an account of the incident, "Well, he appeared to be coping on the bicycle. That is until we got to the bottom of Lindum Hill and the lights changed. The rest of us stopped, he didn't or couldn't. Wallop, slap, bang! The bike, him still on it, straight into the wall. Bingo! Front fork bent double and of course Frank crocked. Nothing really serious, more a case of hurt pride."

Amongst those residents listening to Max's graphic account, Bob Ackermann chipped in, "Tell you what, the Yank never braked. Probably had no idea how to! I'm surprised he managed to ride the damned bike in the first place. These Yanks, when they get to their teens, they are given a motorcar, to go with their spoon and pusher!"

By this time, my bosom buddy Hank had left Lincoln. He was at Broome & Wade Limited in High Wycombe, undergoing a period of training on the compressors they manufactured before returning to Montreal. From when he first came to R&H he was known as "Hank the Yank" being the nearest thing to an American. A term he hated, often responding heatedly., "I am not a bloody Yank. I am Canadian for God's sake."

I have wondered what he might have made of Frank, the first ever *'all American boy'* to have come to Lindum House. Best remembered for his bicycle escapade.

My move out of the Works at R&H had followed on the heels of Hank's departure off the scene at Lindum House in particular and Lincoln in general. This left me in a void which was fortuitously filled by Ivan Stewart whom I have already mentioned briefly. Some years older than me, he was engaged by R&H as a post graduate. I first became aware of him going along the corridor past my room at Lindum

House. He walked fast, whistling always the same ditty – *Westering Ho!* The monotony of it. "Surely," I used to think to myself, "he could whistle something else." It became my pet aversion! What is more, on account of it, I was convinced that the squat fair chap with the pale blue eyes and freckles was a Scot.

I am unable to say what it was that drew us together. Especially now as I look back on the past and the disparity that existed between us. Ivan had a BSc in mechanical engineering from Queen's University in Belfast and a year's experience at the famous ship builders Harland & Wolf before joining R&H. He kept company with several similarly qualified engineers at Lindum House. He and three others owned Riley sports cars. A fourth, Brian Woolfenden ran a Bugatti. They were all employed by R&H. A couple of them were married and the others had steady girlfriends and a few 'bob in their pockets'!

However tenuous it might sound now, we did I was to realise, have a common bond. Ivan Stewart was an Ulsterman. I could recall one of the few things about my father that my mother was able to tell me. Namely, that my father was an Ulsterman. Though he was born in London, his people came from Larne in the North of Ireland. That was about all I knew of my father's origins. I was aware of the religious divide – the people in the south, in the Republic of Ireland were predominantly Catholic. The north, part of the United Kingdom was inhabited by Protestants who originated in Scotland and treated the small Catholic minority as second class citizens.

As time went by and the better I got to know Ivan, my mentor, I was to discover that he had a darker side. Strange how some things stick in the mind and come to be uniquely associated with the person from whose lips they first sprang. "A broth of a boy" that expression of his, has always stayed with me, but also have many other things.

Ivan's chance encounter with the young articled accountant at Lindum House readily springs to my mind. At the time, Price Waterhouse were evidently engaged by R&H to carry out their six monthly audit of accounts.

The two senior accountants were accompanied by a junior. Ivan had got friendly with this young man who he told me originated from Northern Ireland, like himself and his family. He had accordingly joined them at the far end of the long dinner table. The next evening, Ivan came in and sat next to me even though the accountants were as before, seated on their own at the far end of the table. Puzzled, I asked him, "How come you are not with your accountant friend this evening?"

Without looking towards the three visitors, Ivan muttered something I did not catch, "Sorry, I missed what you said."

"He's a '*Pape*'! That's what he is." Ivan replied. I had never heard the word *'Pape'* in my life before.

"What is that?" I enquired. Ivan looked straight at me and spat out vehemently,

"He's a bloody Catholic. A '*Pape*' – he's a follower of the Pope in Rome."

In a matter of a few seconds, that likeable Ivan Stewart whom I had thought was easy going, a great spinner of yarns and full of charm made me aware for the first time of that terrible divide in Northern Ireland. He did change in time. At that moment though he was the personification of the bigoted Ulsterman, a supporter of William of Orange. The '*Orangeman'* who celebrate the Battle of the Boyne each year with their infamous marches.

My unspoken thoughts as I sat next to my friend that evening were, "Here is an educated man, yet so bigoted as to express his hatred of Catholics in this manner. Is it any wonder that the likes of Pat and Mick, digging holes in our roads, react violently in return?"

It was this incident that first brought home to me an awareness of *'the troubles'*. It was the start of my growing conviction that religion was the scapegoat in the bitter struggle between '*the have and the have not*'. The marginalized, the poor and less powerful were the Catholic minority, the '*have not*' in Northern Ireland. It made me wonder about my own father, an Ulsterman. I would in time find enough evidence to satisfy myself that he was not a bigot. Though his first name was William, he had made himself known by his second name, Henry. He was always called '*Harry*'. More significantly I was also to find out that his first wife must have been Catholic. My mother had kept a photograph album that had belonged to my father. It had obviously belonged to his first wife who had been a nurse during the First World War She is featured in many of the sepia coloured photographs in her nurse's uniform. There are hand written captions by the photographs, several showing Catholic churches that she had visited in her travels abroad.

One facet of bigotry is an intolerant belief, usually in a religion. The other facet is obstinacy. What I recall of the sudden break up of Ivan's love affair with Ute could only be put down to his obstinacy; an obstinacy of mulish proportions that saddens me as he was such a caring friend of mine.

Ute was German. She had come to England to perfect her already good English. She was a radiographer at Lincoln General Hospital. Well groomed and smartly dressed, her figure was shown off to good advantage. She was a good looking honey blonde. She and Ivan became inseparable, turning up together at various social functions. Many of us looked forward to their engagement. It wasn't to be. Ute had made a remark about WWII, which Ivan thought was pro-Germany. This led to an argument. He later told me, "She would not apologise. I know I was justified in insisting on an apology. It is a matter of principle. She wouldn't and that is it – I've ditched her."

They never met up again and in due course Ute returned to Germany. Matter of principle or just plain obstinacy. Either way, Ivan gave up something irreplaceable in his life on account of his strongly held convictions. In his mind, choices are stark – either for good or bad. Compromising a sign of weakness.

Ivan who had become a veritable mentor even took an interest in the characters I hung around with. I recall one instance in particular, "That chap Logan is a bad influence. You appear to see him as a bit of a fun character to hang about with. He is a bad egg. I would give him a wide birth."

"Oh! Come on Ivan. You take life too seriously. Besides, bad character or not, I don't have to be influenced by him, do I?" He made no reply, giving me his usual droll smile and a shrug, before he walked off.

When I wrote to my mother telling her that Beryl and I were serious about each other and intending to get engaged I had a long letter back. It was not a congratulatory one that I must have hoped for. Far from it! I may have succeeded already in illustrating how my mother and uncle had always sought to guide me in the way they saw fit. I can hear them now, "Patrick we have always done our best for you as we both love you very much. You know, sometimes you can get carried away, you let your emotions take over. Your uncle and I can see the pitfalls ahead. We can steer you away from these perils!"

My mother, like many of her generation was an accomplished letter writer. She had continued corresponding with some of her childhood friends who had emigrated to the far ends of the world. Writing to me she did not spare herself time nor effort. She set out in graphic detail '*the many pitfalls*' that would await me. The other main theme I could almost have predicted from things I had heard her say in the past –

'your loss of freedom at such a tender age'. Needless to say, the thorny matter of money – or to be precise the lack of it, also featured large. She wound up with the *cri de coeur* straight from the Middle East – *'make a position for your self before getting married and having a family'.* Of course the one counter weight to all these well intended supplications had been overlooked, and that is *love!* Beryl and I were in love and wanted to be together *'for better or for worse'*, isn't that what they say? That was what mattered most to us!

I also remember almost verbatim what Ivan my friend and guide had to say on the matter, "Good heavens man, you're not serious! You are far too young to get hitched to that Beryl. Apart from anything else, she is far too fond of drink. I've seen the way she knocks back the hard stuff. Drink will be her ruination. She will drag you down also. Snap out of it, give her up for your own good. Shouldn't be difficult now that she is away."

There were things going on at R&H at the time which served to distract me from my family and Ivan's cautions on the subject of marriage. Previously, whilst still in the Works, I had already met the two brothers, Ahmet and Mehmet Buldanlioglu who were the R&H Agents in Turkey. They were always accompanied by Monsieur Consolo a Levantine. He assisted them during their discussions with the high-ups in export. I used to be called into these meetings by John Albertini and George Anselm to interpret for them. A lucky consequence of my involvement in this way came about shortly after I joined the Export department, when George Anselm called me over, "Pat, sit down. I want to have a word with you".

He was a squat, thick set figure. Almost as wide as he was tall. He spoke with a thick, guttural voice and had a pronounced accent, which I took to be his mother tongue, Russian! I liked George, as indeed did most others in the Export department. He was thumbing through some papers and talking at the same time, "Buldanlioglu have been in touch. As usual, they have a stand at the Izmir International Fair in August and have asked us for some support. All the company directors, as a matter of policy, are always willing for us to participate. It gives R&H the opportunity to 'fly the flag' especially as you speak the language. How do you feel about it?"

"Wonderful!" I said thinking to myself – "he need hardly have asked".

I was over the moon. Going to the Izmir Fair would be a milestone in and would help my career in export sales. I would be out from England representing Ruston & Hornsby Limited. The prospect gave me a sense of great pride. Also a touch of nerves.

"Good. I expected you to grasp the opportunity. Your mother lives in Southern Turkey, so when the Fair ends you could take your two weeks summer holiday and spend it with your family." I imagine I would have once more made the same grateful response as I had earlier.

At that moment, my prospects with Rustons had never looked, nor felt brighter. Percy Roberts was the R&H representative in the Middle East, based in Beyrouth. He spent his time supporting the agents in each of the ME countries, periodically returning to the UK. It had always been my ultimate ambition to take over from him when he retired and like him, live in Beyrouth.

After finishing with George Anselm, back at my desk, I sat quietly trying to compose myself. By then I was almost overcome with the unexpected prospects of attending the Izmir International Fair that had just been put to me. Another idea was hatched in my mind. Surely

Beryl could get some time off to join me in Istanbul, maybe even come to Mersin with me.

That very evening, I telephoned Beryl at Grimsby General Hospital.

Chapter 17

I was on my way to the Izmir International Fair soon after my meeting with George Anselm, it was mid August 1954. I have since realised the folly of not booking a hotel room for the duration of the show. Nor as it turned out had my boss informed Buldanlioglu who were the Ruston Agents as to the time and day of my arrival. The evening I arrived at Izmir airport on a THY internal flight from Istanbul, there was no one to meet me. I was also in for a startling bit of local news from the driver of the taxi I got into outside the airport.

Had I not been able to speak in Turkish heaven knows where my oversight might have landed me for in those days it was rare to come across any of the general public who could speak in English. The driver tipping his cap back so that he could see me better in the dimly lit street outside the airport building explained the situation, "All the hotels in Izmir and even in Karsi Yaka are full. The town is swarming with *'ecnebi'*, foreigners. I have never known such crowds. It is because of the International Exhibition. I don't know for how long it will go on. It is a great pity that you do not have a reservation."

He appeared genuinely concerned. Much to my growing distress he came out with that well used expression '*Eyvahlar olsun!*' the sense of which is '*Alas, what a calamity!*'

The taxi driver, an elderly chap, took pity realising the plight I was in. As most Turks would have done, he perceived me as a visitor to his home town of Izmir, a friend. By then we had struck up a kind of informal relationship. He spoke, as if confiding in me, "I know a *'pansiyon'*, lodging house where there are always vacancies. It is not the sort of place where a young *'effendi'* like you would normally stay, but we have no choice. Would you like me to take you there? It is not far."

Familiar with their ways and manner of speech in Turkey, I responded as if he were a long lost uncle that I was pleased to have just discovered. I replied with a degree of informality and gratitude, "I am a stranger to Izmir. I have no other plans. I can but put my trust in you. Take me to where you have mentioned."

The place he took me to was in a poorly lit street. It was not one of Izmir's main thoroughfares by any stretch of the imagination. Parting, I thanked him adding the customary Turkish wish for a long life – '*Sag ol*'.

In the room where I was to spend the night, there were several beds. It was more of a dormitory. Tired as I was I had gone straight off into a deep slumber being woken up early by the bright sun light. I was still on my own, none of the other beds having been slept in. I shaved and then showered. The latter proved to be a bizarre experience. The water gushed straight out of a pipe immediately above an oriental toilet that I had to straddle. As luck would have it, the place was clean due to the absence of any other lodgers that night. I smiled to my self recalling how my taxi driver friend of the night before had described it as "where there are always vacancies."

Next day, arriving early on the Buldanlioglu stand at the Exhibition with my suitcase, I was welcomed by Omer Bese, the agent's engineering manager who had spent several weeks at Lindum House with me. We had become good friends in that time. Seeing my suitcase, he enquired jokingly, "You have only just come. Are you leaving us already?"

He listened intently to my tale of the previous night. That day when we went for lunch, Omer got me fixed up at a private hotel run by a charming Greek lady, a friend of his. On our way back to the Exhibition, suddenly struck by the thought, Omer who spoke next to no English asked, "*Pezevenk Henk* – how is he?'

He was referring to my Canadian buddy Hank using his very own rhythmic slang which I have to say is best left untranslated. It brought back memories though. Probably because he could not understand nor speak English, Omer had been very edgy when he first came to Lincoln. I recall the three of us, Omer, Hank and myself going past a public house not far from Lindum House called The Turk's Head even though the sign outside depicted a severed head with a turban, it might well have gone unnoticed. Hank, a joker and a bit of a stirrer, had rather injudiciously drawn Omer's attention to it urging me at the same time to "Tell him, they have several of these heads mummified, displayed on a shelf above the main bar inside."

His sensibilities roused, Omer was well and truly upset and wanted to know what Hank had been telling me. Anxious to avert a punch up, I made some comment to mollify my friend who had not been long in Lincoln. During his stay with us at Lindum House his attitudes must have changed, he actually developed a pretty good sense of humour but continued to call my buddy *'Pezevenk Henk'*.

It was the first time that I had set foot in Izmir on the Aegean coast of Turkey, once known as Symrna by the Greeks who settled there some thousand years before the time of Christ. At the High School in Istanbul, there were a large number of boarders from Izmir, the Anglo-French element spoke incessantly about '*Bornabat*'. I was to discover that it was a district of Izmir known by the local Turks as Bornova. It came to be dominated in the early 19th century and possibly before by the predominantly British settlers who built their prestigious family homes there. It was they who coined the name '*Bornabat*'. I could never find out why.

Nothing much out of the ordinary happened at the Izmir International Fair. As it was the first such occasion for me, I had nothing to compare it with. Turkey's then Minister of Industry, Refik Korultan and his entourage came around on the opening day. As luck would have it, I was on hand to show him and his party around the Buldanlioglu stand. I dutifully expounded in Turkish on the several Ruston & Hornsby diesel engines on the stand operating electric generators and water pumps. Press photographers accompanied this group of VIPs and I was later presented with a photograph of Refik Korultan in which I am seen in conversation with him. The only other recollections I have of the fair were the lunches with Omer Bese at a nearby highly commended '*lokanta*', the famed Shukran.

On my day off from the fair, I was entertained by Alain Giraud, a friend from the English High School in Istanbul. Of all the sights he took me around in Izmir, it was the visit to the Giraud Textile Factory, owned by his father that proved to be the most interesting and indeed enlightening. I remember snatches of Alain's commentary as he showed me around the place.

"This is the old production mill. The machinery must be all of 20 or more years old. All from Mather & Platt in Lancashire. The best in the world! Even the oldest ones are still going strong. My father claims they would go on for another 30 years!"

We were standing in a vast building where there were rows and rows of Mather & Platt textile machines. They emitted a smooth muted sound as they operated. Almost harmonious, akin to the subdued sucking and blowing sound of the steam engines I had seen on test at

Izmir International Fair, summer of 1954

Robey's in Lincoln. Alain motioned to me, "Come. I want to show you our new production lines."

As he finished speaking, he opened the sliding doors into another bay. No sooner were they open and we went in than I was struck by an almost deafening clatter. A metallic cacophony produced by rows of gleaming new textile machines. It was impossible to carry on a conversation. After a while, Alain signalled that we should move back out. Once outside, as we strolled towards the factory entrance, he asked, "Well, what do you think of our new Swiss production lines?"

I was intrigued. A few minutes earlier he had told me how his father extolled the Mather & Platt machines that had been running for some 20 years and might run for a further 30. He had elaborated on the excellent service they had given free from any serious breakdowns. How his father had received good after sales service from the makers in Lancashire. Spares supplied on time. My response was brief, "Swiss? But you told me your father had been so satisfied with the Mather & Platt machines!" Alain's reply was immediate, "Sure, he was" – I noticed how he had emphasised the word 'was'. I must have looked puzzled, Alain went on to explain his father's change of heart.

"Times have changed. My father is a businessman, to survive he has to move with the times! Could you not tell, the Swiss machines run much faster than the Mather & Platts ones. They give a higher rate of production and what is more, they were cheaper."

I felt compelled to get to the bottom of this reasoning. My training and experience at Ruston & Hornsby had given me a different outlook. Quality, long trouble free service and reliability mattered above all else. That was the Ruston ethos. Surely weren't they the attributes that made everything manufactured in Britain the best in the world? At the time, I kept these notions to myself choosing to listen to the rest of the Giraud explanation.

“My father says that textile production technology is moving faster and faster. In say the next five years, there will be new designs of machines. It would then pay us to scrap all the Swiss machines whether worn out or not and replace them with the latest technology. In the meantime, they produce more and cost less than the Platt machines. Our accountant advising my father on investment kept emphasising *‘pay back’*, saying that is what it’s all about!”

What I had seen and heard that afternoon never deserted me.

Some 40 years later, at a luncheon party given by my friend, Marshall Hazzan in Didsbury, I got into conversation with a guest sitting next to me. Bruno Adler, I discovered had been with Mather & Platt, ending up as their sales director. We had been lamenting the demise of so much of the country’s engineering. I told him about my visit to the Giraud textile factory in Izmir during the summer of 1954. In particular the remarks made by Alain Giraud’s father about how ‘times have changed.’ He gave a sigh and went on to tell me of his own experience, “I tried hard to make the board of directors at Mather & Platt aware of how things were changing in the world and therefore the need for the company to adapt in order to survive. No one would listen to me. I was a voice in the wilderness. The consequences that followed were inevitable. All very sad!”

At the end of the exhibition, Omer saw me off. As we parted, he grinned and said, “My salaams to ‘*Pezevenk Henk’*. Remind him *‘American dollar gentleman, no dollar, no gentleman’*! – Bye bye.”

I relayed Omer Bese’s greetings to Hank. Much as he hated being taken for an American, he must have realised it was Omer’s way of reminiscing about the past they had shared in Lincoln. Pleased to be remembered by the Turk, he laughed. Sadly, though I did not know it at the time, that was to be the very last time I ever saw Omer.

On the THY flight to Istanbul, my mind was soon full of other thoughts for I would be reunited with Beryl who was coming out from England and would be in Istanbul that night. My mother's best friend, Victoria and her husband Teyfik Atalay met me when I got out of the plane at Istanbul airport and drove me to their flat. All three of us drove back to Yesillkoy that evening to meet Beryl off the BEA flight. Victoria, meeting her for the very first time, sprang forward to greet her with a flurry of kisses and hugs. Victoria was a very warm, emotional woman, her words of greeting just poured out, "Welcome, welcome, welcome darling, to Istanbul, to Turkey."

Later, the heat of the moment over, she put her arm around Beryl and laughed, explaining in her faltering English, "Forgive me, darling. I tried to appear reserved the first time I am meeting you. I know that the English like to be formal and do not allow their emotions to take over. I thought it would be more correct to say just, 'welcome'. I hope you understand."

Teyfik drove the three of us sight seeing the following evening, late into the night. The European side of Istanbul had changed little. It was barely 10 years since I had been at school in Istanbul. We drove along the Bosphorus past the famous Dolma Bahce Palace where Ataturk had died. It was a pleasantly warm and balmy night. There were many casinos, cafés and restaurants along the edge of the Bosphorus, their bright lights reflected back, shimmering in the surrounding water. We stopped off at a number of these tempting places, as was the custom. People in Turkey had always had a curious habit in those times of adopting fashions from Europe and turning them into local *'crazes'*. The refreshing *'crème de menthe frappe'* was *de rigueur* just then. We lost count of how many we knocked back that night.

We could have flown from Istanbul to Adana airport near Mersin, our final destination. We had chosen to be adventurous, as I wanted to give Beryl a taste of the real Turkey. Our plan was to make the journey by road via Ankara. Stopping the night there would break the long journey of over 1000 kilometres across the Anatolia plains. Few, if any, of my family's acquaintances would have even contemplated such a venture. As for visitors from abroad, the few who in 1954 came to Istanbul might have travelled on the Orient Express and stayed at the Pera Palas hotel. There were no cruises or package holidays in those days nor were there the global chains of hotels. These early visitors to Istanbul would have contented themselves exploring the vast number of it's historic, artistic and religious sights not to mentions places of natural beauty that surround Istanbul.

Next morning still under the soporific effect of the '*crème de menthe*', Beryl and l went down to the side of the Bosphorus where we boarded the Ankara bus. It was barely six o'clock. The sun had risen well before that. It was already pleasantly warm. I knew that it would get really hot as we travelled south east through the vast expanse of Anatolia. The bus was an Austin, fitted out with wooden benches. It was as usual full to capacity. The roof was loaded up high with an assortment of baggage and livestock, mainly chickens. Teyfik had arranged for Beryl and I to share the bench seat in the front with the driver. Teyfik's plan had been for us to have a good view of the country as we went along, in relative comfort.

The driver seated next to me, had an uncanny resemblance to Ali Fuat Firat the headmaster of my primary school. Swarthy with black gimlet eyes. Not surprisingly he turned out like my headmaster to be a Kurd. As soon as we set off, I knew by the way he drove, that he was a man of great faith. The legend *"Allaha emanet"* printed on the plaque above us was intended to ensure his safe passage on the roads he travelled. Even those with no knowledge of Turkish might have guessed its meaning – *"Trust in Allah"*.

Once we got past the city limits, the macadamized road turned into a baked earth track. This might have had the desirable effect of curbing our driver's enthusiasm for speed and reckless overtaking. It did not in the least. By the time we reached Ankara, it was dusk. We had been on the road for 13 hours. The fine Anatolian dust had turned Beryl's summer frock beige. It also had the same effect on me and everybody else. After showering at the hotel, we set out to see what we could of Ankara and have a well deserved dinner at the famous "Karpic" restaurant where during the war it was said high ranking diplomats of both sides were often obliged to dine in close proximity to each other.

It had been a long day with little to relieve the barren featureless expanse we had come through other than the occasional cluster of flat roofed dwellings in some far flung oasis shaded by poplars and eucalyptus trees. Before turning in, I booked the two front seats in a *'dolmus'* taxi that we would share with two or three other travellers heading for Adana.

Ankara was surprisingly cool that night. Situated on a high desert-like plateau the dry heat of the day changes rapidly causing the mercury to fall at night. We both slept well in our separate single bedrooms – that is how things were in 1954! Early next morning we set off in some style in a pristine black Buick. The driver turned out to be a native of Adana. I guessed as much by his distinctive, some might say comical Adana speech. He was portly. The probable outcome of an over indulgence in Adana's famous kebabs! His slick black hair was set off by a luxurious moustache. It became apparent as we got into the journey that he had a problem. He kept dozing off to sleep! A sign that he had been too long at the wheel.

The first part of our drive the second day from Ankara was once more across the near barren sun scorched Anatolian plateau though far more comfortable a ride in the front seats of the Buick. We passed several small '*Yuruk*', nomad camp sites, unmistakably characterised by their tents woven in multi-colours and an awning with four corners supported to provide daylong shade from the relentless sun. These itinerant '*Yuruks*' were accompanied by their herds of goats and sheep who grazed freely. Central Turkey was well served by several big rivers the two best known amongst them being the Tigris and Euphrates that flow south out of Turkey into Iraq and Syria. There were always several big fierce looking shaggy '*Karabas*' dogs about to guard the livestock. They would chase after passing vehicles. On one occasion when near enough, I recall drawing Beryl's attention to a couple of them, "Look, can you see those big leather collars they have? If you look carefully you will see that they have long spikes sticking out. There are wolves who prowl around at night, foraging. They would kill the sheep and goats if it weren't for the '*Karabas*' who are given these collars to protect them."

It was to be the last two or three hours of the drive that would put our driver to the test. The steep twisting descent through the ravines of the Taurus Mountains to sea level. Not only did he know the road. He also appeared to be familiar with the roadside fountains fed from the melting snow on the high peaks of the Taurus. Coming to one, he would pull his car over to the side. Getting out, he thrust his head under the gushing ice cold water. Thus revived he settled himself by the fountain for a quick smoke. Our fellow passengers, all Turks, had successfully kept him engaged in conversation. At the slightest sign of him nodding off, their efforts became both frenetic and physical – a shake or encouraging pat on the back, sufficed.

Beryl and I thus reassured, had been able to view the majestic scenes of sheer rock out crops towering above us, the lush greenery of the forests and occasional meadow. The Cilesian Gates, a narrow defile made famous by Alexander the Great who had managed to find his way through at the head of his army. Soon we were on the cotton growing plains of the fertile Cukurova. Hot and dusty, parched by the mid summer heat. Daytime temperatures soared into the mid 40s centigrade. We got safely to Adana. I glanced for the last time at the plaque on the Buick's dashboard. It read "*Allaha emanet*". A common sight in all vehicles in Turkey along with a variety of *"nazar"* – eye shaped blue glass ornaments to ward off the "*evil eye*".

On board the BEA Viscount, as Beryl and I made the return trip to Heathrow together, we each reflected in silence on our travels and month long stay in Turkey. It had provided each of us with much to ponder on. Mostly interesting and adventuresome some bizarre but come what may, all stimulating and memorable.

Apart from the encounters I have dwelt on, there were numerous other incidents that as time went by took on even greater significance. Beryl's encounter with cockroaches in the Ankara hotel bathroom. Visit to biblical Tarsus birth place of St Paul, lunch at the waterfalls there, where it is said Mark Anthony and Cleopatra used to meet. Middle East hospitality, typified by sumptuous lunch at the home of Victoria and Sukri Diab. Beryl acquires a taste for Syrian and Turkish cooking and learns some key expressions like *'cok guzel'* very nice – *'merhaba'* hello – *'tessekur ederim'* thank you, and many others.

Our shared memories of Mersin very much as it was in my early childhood. A swim at the Plaj that got *'political'* – owner settles old score getting two youths arrested on a charge to which Beryl had to testify by signing a statement in Turkish that she could not read. A few days spent in Gozne – picturesque village in Taurus Mountains with Roman castle, but '*nil mod coms*'. Getting used to sleeping under mosquito nets. In the mornings checking our shoes for scorpions.

Finally on our way back, lunch in Istanbul at *'Abdullah's Lokanta'* famed for its lamb cutlets and *'pilaf'* at the invitation of Mehmet *Bey* the R&H Agent who hearing about our dust ridden bus journey to Ankara jokingly said in Turkish, "So your fiancé has eaten her fill of our Anatolian dust before returning to England, this makes her one of us". Later that day, asking the way, I got into conversation with a young Turk from whom I had asked the way in Istanbul. He bought a kilo of pomegranates from a nearby shop which he pressed us to accept saying, "To a visitor from England a small gift from our country!"

* * *

Back in the export sales department at R&H a short time after the Izmir International Fair, my boss George Anselm called me over, "Mr Albertini wants us to go to his office. He asked me to brief you in the meantime."

I felt a rush of adrenalin, recalling the last time he had been beckoned me over. I ended up going to Turkey. I wondered what was in store this time. I did not have long to wait, George Anselm went on to explain, "It is to do with the Gezira Irrigation Scheme. How much do you know about it?"

As usual, I played things down and said, "Nothing really. I have heard of the Gezira Sporting Club in Alex. I don't suppose it has anything to do with it." George Anselm gave one of his deep throated chuckles and went on to explain, "It is a joint Egyptian/Sudanese project. A major irrigation scheme. It could be big business for Ruston diesels and pumps built by us here in Lincoln and Grantham. The chief mechanical engineer and another have come over to sort out some preliminary matters in connection with the scheme. Just so that you are not taken by surprise, I suspect they are also looking for an assistant – that is where you could fit in! Don't worry you will have plenty of time to think things over. Albertini and I just wanted to give you some prior warning before you meet these gents. I'll give you a call when I get the green light from him a bit later on."

Following this introductory meeting with the two visitors to R&H, both of them Englishmen, I had a formal interview with the chief engineer a few days later. He told me that he was going to need a PA. Experience with Ruston machines and knowledge of Arabic would be essential. If all went according to plan, I would be based in Upper Egypt working there and in the Sudan. R&H would give me more specific training on the diesels and pumps that would be involved in irrigation.

The whole matter set me thinking like nothing ever had in the past. It would be invaluable experience for me. A big factor in advancing my dream of taking over from Percy Roberts as R&H's man in the Middle East. All fired up with the Gezira prospect I broke the news to Ivan Stewart. My family were too far away and in any case they would not understand the implications. I had to tell someone at R&H. As much as anything, I needed approval – a green light! Ivan's immediate response was anything but inspirational., "Come on Patrick, what do you know about irrigation?"

I was well and truly deflated, but not for long. His reply appeared to me as not so much a question, but more of a statement. Having got to know Ivan well by then, I knew it was not said with bad intent. Recovering, I felt defiant. My reply purposely short, "Absolutely nothing!"

I had hoped it would in turn wind him up. It did. I listened to all the reasons he could think of to deter me. I remained silent for a while.

Memories had flooded back of my other friend and colleague from Alex, Michael that Sergeant Bilko look alike. Regrettably he was no longer in Lincoln. We had spoken together so much about what R&H might offer in the Middle East. I could still sense his presence giving me one of his quizzical looks before coming out with what I knew would be his down to earth reasoning

"You haven't got anything much to lose have you Pat? You're not a plonker, common sense will get you by. It will be a great opportunity for you. Go for it."

It was that sixth sense which inspired my reply to Ivan, "But Ivan, unlike you, I have absolutely nothing to lose! No degree, not even an ONC. Albertini has assured these gents that I will be given product training on the engines and pumps. I will spend time in sales technical with Jack Whitsey. Besides, I may never get an opportunity like this again if I so much as falter."

It was round about that time I had finally decided to give up my struggle to gain an ONC in mechanical engineering at Lincoln Technical College. To those who had kept quoting me Robert The Bruce's encounter with the tenacious spider who never gave up, I would still say, "Spiders cannot have much of a brain nor options other than spinning their webs. If Robert The Bruce chose to be inspired by a spider, fine but it is not for me."

I had made a good start in sales and hoped that it would continue to secure my future at R&H for many years to follow. It had been a pivotal career move. Lindum House continued to provide a wonderful life style – for me it never ceased to be '*la belle époque*' of my bachelor days. Besides, where else would I have ever met Beryl who was to become my wife?

Discounting those four years of monastic seclusion at Hurstpierpoint now behind me, the only other place I had got to know in England was Lincoln and its surroundings. It was a staid cathedral city, yet provider of so many happy memories that linger on – like that Sunday at East Gate Court by the cathedral. Morning coffee being served decorously. I was accompanied by two young Siamese trainees Tian and Sunai. They had the temerity of asking, in their faltering English for "Two 'flied lice', please?"

Much to their dismay, their attempt at humour fell flat. The starchy matron, who was serving was not amused! On other occasions, in the works canteen they smothered the food which was unfamiliar to them with lashings of tomato ketchup, which they laughingly referred to as "Thank God Sauce".

It is not to contradict what I have already said, but throughout that time, I was permanently short of cash. There was nothing like the affluence we see around us today, the dark shadow of austerity still hung over the country. Like my contemporaries in Lincoln, engineering trainees and apprentices, I clocked on to work on Saturday mornings. Throughout industry, there was just one week's summer holiday with pay. How then was it that we managed to enjoy life to the extent we did? I have often thought back to those times and pondered that very question.

In the 1950s young people to a large extent found ways to entertain themselves. They socialised either between those of the same sex or mixed sexes. Mixed sexes socialising was referred to variously as 'dating', 'courting' or 'going steady'. It often developed into a more lasting relationship and frequently led to engagement and eventually marriage. Young people's smoking and drinking habits, then incidental to socialising, were constrained by what they could afford. Usually not much! None of my contemporaries had ever smoked or taken drugs – a *'joint'* was what mothers served up for Sunday lunch. I recall a *'gold digger'* being once described to me as a female who expected her boyfriend to pay her bus fare. An amusing exaggeration but it now serves to illustrate attitudes and our way of life at the time.

Public venues accessible to us were modest – dance halls, cinemas and public houses. In Lincoln there were several dance halls – The Assembly Rooms were at the top of the social ranking. I recall some of the dances, formal '*evening dress*' affairs. Attendance was by invitation only and tickets were both scarce and pricey. Like most of my contemporaries, I justified these occasions as a once in a blue moon extravagance! Cinemas were extremely popular. Seats cost a modest 1s.9p. Entry often was only secured by standing for ages in a vast queue.

Their underlying popularity, I was to discover had nothing necessarily to do with the film that was being shown. In winter it was the warmth and the sense of seclusion created in their darkness that held a great appeal to dating couples. The very back row was particularly popular. One or two cinemas, mindful of this partiality amongst their clientele, provided double seats charging slightly more for this favour. Pubs were popular as they also provided a meeting place which was warm and comfortable. For those who required a modicum of privacy, there were quiet secluded nooks and corners. As I mentioned earlier, drinking was part of socialising and not an end in itself.

In company with young people from R&H, I had free entry to The Ruston Social Club. It was not far and conveniently situated for us at Lindum House, at the bottom of Lindum Hill. When she was working at Lindum House, Beryl and I used to walk down there for some of the hops. On weekends overseas trainees and English apprentices whose homes were away from the East Midlands flocked there. Occasionally there were special events nights when aspiring vocalists and instrumentalists from amongst the members bravely took to the stage. They were always given noisy ovations whether their performances were good or plain indifferent.

Even then I was still influenced by the culture of where my family lived and where I had grown up. There were few cars in Mersin, Tarsus and Adana, the three jewels of South Eastern Turkey. By contrast my bosom buddy Hank from Montreal had been brought up from an early age to be a car freak. Let alone cars, the lack of central heating was another of his bugbears. He had other gripes including personal hygiene and the lack of men's toiletries, aftershave in particular. He often came out with, "Jeez man! I am amazed at how backward you people are over here compared with our life standards in North America."

Martin Cordeaux was another of the residents at Lindum House. I really got to know him after he had taken me out several times in his own car. I had never been behind the wheel of a motorcar before. I couldn't have had a driving license because I recall driving Martin's car on one of the many disused war time airfields around Lincoln. The wide concrete runway was ideal for a beginner.

He managed to teach me how to 'double-declutch', to release and re-engage the clutch twice when changing gear. A knack that becomes instinctive of working the clutch peddle in combination with the accelerator peddle to synchronize the gears. Done correctly this ensures a smooth, yet rapid gear change. At the time it was no mean feat, and a habit that one never loses. It was in this connection that I heard he had driven tanks. After leaving Eton College, he had joined the British Army where he served in the Royal Tank Corps. I was to meet Martin Cordeaux again but many years later in Lincoln.

It is said that bad news travels fast. The fulfilling four years of my life at Ruston & Hornsby and Lindum House that I have described were about to be superseded by adversity. Adversity that crept up almost unnoticed and came in many guises. A misfortune that would eventually overcome its victims. As for me personally, I was merely incidental. An innocent party, a mere minnow, caught up in what was to become a long enduring struggle. A struggle with changing attitudes and the emergence of foreign competition.

It is impossible to know when I first started to feel unsettled. It was a gradual process. In the export sales department, there had always been unquestioning faith in Ruston diesels. Not, let me add, blind faith but confidence fostered by the reputation of Rustons abroad. I was once more reminded of Michael, my friend from Alex. He had taken me under his wing when I first started in export. At the time, our agents in the Middle East were clamouring for every thing that Rustons could manufacture. Inevitably there were delays. In his frustration I remember his reaction, "for fuck's sake! – there must be a way around this." He had gone on to predict, "Customers will go elsewhere." Probably less than 18 months had gone by and already *'competition'* – a word hardly ever heard at R&H was becoming a reality. However much R&H responded both commercially and technically, competition wasn't going to go away.

The now popular term '*market forces*' was not then in common use. The adversity that came in many guises, would now be described as '*market forces*'. I recall one of them – '*embargoes*' an official suspension of trade. Two of Ruston's important markets in the Middle East namely Greece and Egypt placed '*embargoes*' on the import of diesel engines below a certain horse power. A move that effectively cut off supplies of diesel engines from Rustons. Steps that it was said had been taken by the Greek and Egyptian governments to encourage manufacture locally.

I was also to be told that the Gezira Irrigation Scheme which had raised such hopes for my future had been abandoned or at least shelved for the time being. But there was even worse news for me personally. Percy Roberts left Rustons to join Johnston Outboard Motors of Brandon, Vermont in the USA who manufactured a wide range of marine engines. His departure was unexpected and left me wondering the extent to which it was prompted by R&H's changing circumstances in the Middle East. A thought that left me desperately uneasy about my own future with R&H. By then, it must have been the early part of 1955.

I was in a quandary. There I was, a 23 year old, engaged to be married yet unsettled in my job. When Betty Larter left, the Lindum House Club Committee must have seized the opportunity to rein in some of her practices in favour of cost cutting. Several of the long term residents like Ivan Stewart and Ray Warner-Lacey were eased out. My turn wasn't long in coming. I had a succession of digs. Life in Lincoln was never going to be the same. Yet, I did not really want to leave Rustons. I was into my second year in export sales. Besides, with no other means of support I would have to get another job before leaving R&H.

Job hunting was new to me and I suspect a dread. I can still bring to mind my very first two interviews. George Wimpey & Co.Ltd., Hammersmith were about to construct a dam in Turkey and were seeking engineering interpreters. I was not successful. Blackwood Hodge in Northampton were distributors of heavy civil engineering plant, Euclid earth moving equipment and the like. They had advertised for sales representatives. I recall this interview particularly well. I was grilled by two young men smartly dressed in dark pinstriped suits. University graduates, and eager to put the latest interviewing techniques on 'selling' to the test. I failed miserably again. It was at their hands though that I was taught an invaluable lesson on 'how to sell successfully!' – even refrigerators to Eskimos. That interview was to serve me well.

I did also have an interview with David Brown Tractors at Meltham near Huddersfield. I can remember my train journey from Lincoln to Huddersfield on the appointed day. I had to change trains at Stalybridge. A dreary lonely place with a solitary soot-stained stone station building. I chose to sit outside on one of the benches, on my own. There was absolutely no one else around. Struggling against tedium and with little else to attract my attention, I gazed indolently at the open countryside. The few cows in the distance appeared motionless. I wondered idly whether they also, like me, could feel boredom. Relief for me did come with the arrival of the Huddersfield train. I have no recollection of my interview. I must have been successful as a few days later I received a letter offering me a position in their export sales department.

I felt no euphoria. After all, my departure from Lincoln was akin to the survivor from a stricken luxury liner striking out in a lifeboat in the hope of finding a safe haven. I grieved all the more in frustration thinking of the aspirations those four and a half years at Ruston's had come to hold out for me. All had come to nought. Maybe it was that disillusionment that spurred me on.

It was Mr Codling who I had met that first day at Sheaf Iron Works and fittingly, I was to see him "*to have a chat about things*" as he put it to me, nearing the end of my days with R&H. I showed him the letter from David Brown Tractors offering to take me on in their export sales department. As he had known my father in Egypt, he was that little bit more personally involved than he might otherwise have been as Trainee Supervisor. "Are you sure of and satisfied with these terms? You know Patrick, once you get there it will be impossible to redress these matters."

I had the usual letters from my mother and uncle in Turkey, "Rustons have been so good to you. You will have been with them for five whole years this coming Christmas. If you move now, you will lose your seniority. You will never find another company who will treat you so well. Think carefully before you decide." Well I had been doing a great deal of thinking and my mind was made up.

I did accept the position of sales engineer at David Brown Tractors. I handed in my notice at Ruston & Hornsby Limited and left Lincoln at the end of June 1955. All those wonderful memories of my training and shop floor experiences and life at Lindum House stayed with me. I continued to see a handful of those Lindum House residents, now life long friends. The priceless legacy that I came away with from Lincoln would remain with me for evermore.

Chapter 18

Much as I dreaded its arrival, unable as I was to stop the relentless march of time, the day came when I had to take my leave. For all its poignancy, I have no way of bringing to mind the exact date when I finally departed from Lincoln. I guess that it must have been the end of June 1955.

I had arrived at the station on my own but with a heavy heart to catch the train to Huddersfield. There was no one to see me off. The oldest and closest friends I had made during my stay in Lincoln had already gone their separate ways. Just as well, for I would have found it difficult, to hold back the emotions that welled up inside me. How different my going from my arrival four and a half years earlier when I had looked forward to a new and unfamiliar way of life with so much optimism and hope.

Funny how thinking back, I could recall the taxi I had caught from that very same station, to deliver me late that night to my destination, a place called Lindum House. It felt like a lifetime had gone by since then and there I was about to leave so many wonderful memories behind me. My eyes must have misted over as I fumbled for the handle of the railway carriage door. I had looked for an empty compartment and luckily found one. Once inside, I lifted my suitcase onto the rack and sat down in the corner of the bench seat. As I had always done, I sat facing the engine. Settled, I was lost in thought, thinking to myself, "It isn't often that I choose seclusion. This time, I want to be left on my own. What is more, I hope no one joins me throughout the journey."

In the privacy of the comfortless, rather antiquated compartment with the stale smell of cigarettes, I lit one myself. I removed my spectacles and gave the lenses a good polish with my handkerchief, absentmindedly wiping my eyes at the same time.

It was late afternoon when we pulled into Huddersfield station and I got out of the carriage with my suitcase. Mrs Ellen Taylor, a widow, with whom I had made arrangements to board had kindly written telling me where to catch the bus for Meltham. It was a rather bumpy ride after Fartown as the double decker vehicle laboured uphill towards the Pennines. Thanks to her precise directions, I had no trouble locating Mrs Taylor's house in a solitary row of terraced stone built dwellings along a quiet country lane. When I got close enough to it, I spotted a signpost which read 'Meltham Golf Club' and pointed in the direction I was walking. But for the Golf Club, the lane would have gone to nowhere but a dead end.

I rang the doorbell. As I waited, I casually surveyed what were to be my new surroundings. There were some big trees on the other side of the lane and beyond them the golf course itself. Evening drawing in, it was deserted. A peaceful rural English setting, yet it was different from what I had been used to in Lincoln. When eventually the door opened, I was greeted by an elderly lady who welcomed me with a kind smile, "Hello Pat. Come on in. I hope you have had a nice journey, all the way from Lincoln."

Mrs Taylor's greeting I was to find was typical of her spontaneity and warmth. Once we were inside, she led me up the stairs to the room she had prepared for me. Left on my own in the bedroom, I had a wash and then stretched out on the double bed until she called me down for the high tea that I was to share with her.

The last few days at R&H had been stressful and difficult to cope with. Some weeks earlier, I had been given notice to move out of Lindum House. I had always looked on my stay there as something of a privilege. My closest friends, all of whom came from abroad, had returned from whence they came. My mentor, Ivan Stewart had taken up employment with another manufacturer of diesel engines in the UK. Beryl had changed jobs several times in pursuit of her career. As for me, it had been a lonely, sad time during which I had been compelled to make a break from all I had aspired to at R&H in the light of world changing circumstances.

I might easily have chosen to soldier on at R&H in the belief that *'better the devil you know'*. The decision that brought me to Meltham was a very difficult one for me to have made. Lying there that evening, I wanted more than anything to make a go of things at David Brown's. I had embarked on a new venture. Within the month, Beryl and I would be married and she would be joining me right there where I lay. I had taken to Mrs Taylor who seemed to be the right sort. At that moment I was balancing my immediate past against what I hoped to make of my future. *'Time will tell…'*

Next morning I caught the bus at the end of the lane for Meltham Mills. David Brown Tractors had set up manufacturing in the old stone built sprawl that had in its day been a textile mill. I was shown into the offices of the personnel manager whose greeting was brief and to the point, "Ah, there you are Mr Grigsby. Welcome to DB Tractors. I will take you straight over to Mr Morgan, who is expecting you."

I recall being led through a warren of passageways. Then finally through a door into a vast area, which might have once been a used for production but then turned into an office. There must have been no more than half a dozen employees seated at desks set well apart as if to justify the large space they occupied. It was a strange scene. Akin to a class with the master at the far end facing his charges. As we made our way to the far end, the personnel manager who had not spoken a word to me since we left his office broke his silence, "Mr Morgan, is in charge of the shipping department. You will be starting with him."

He made my introduction to Mr Morgan the shortest imaginable, giving me the impression that he wished to avoid being drawn into any sort of conversation. He appeared anxious to get back to his own office. I was left on my own with Mr Morgan who with no further ado proceeded to introduce me to three members of his staff whom he said would show me the ropes.

I can bring them to mind as Derek Barrow, a local chap from Dewsbury and Patrick Tyrrell who, judging by his strong Irish accent, came from further afield. Fair, freckled and with pale blue eyes he reminded me of Ivan Stewart though I was to find out that unlike Ivan, he was from the Republic and a strong Catholic. Both were about my age. From what they told me, their time was spent claiming back money paid in duty to HM Customs & Excise on imported tyres. By the process termed a '*draw back*', the import duty paid, was refunded when David Brown Tractors fitted with these tyres were exported.

All tyres had six, as I recall, digit serial numbers moulded into them during manufacture. The procedure entailed fastidious form filling by Derek and Patrick. My thoughts went back to my unfortunate cousin Jorj in Mersin. He laboured slavishly in the Levante office. His was a tedious job, preparing lists on an old manual typewriter, showing the identification number of bales of cotton and against each bale its weight. Hard to believe that there I was listening to Derek and Patrick condemned to an equally pedantic and fastidious occupation filling in HM Customs & Excise '*Draw Back*' forms. A task which I would shortly be undertaking myself. What a prospect!

The last of the trio that Mr Morgan introduced me to was Hugh Evans. An older person, he was a Londoner and had more to say and talk about in general. In fact, he told me a good deal that very morning. He lost no time in putting me in the picture by dropping something of a bombshell, "You appear to have fallen for the DB scam. Welcome to the club."

I was intrigued by his greeting and said as much. He did not need to be encouraged. It was clear to me from his very first remark that Hugh was cynical about everything around him. He was also sarcastic. Cynicism and sarcasm blended together to vent his resentment. Bitterness created by what he perceived as a trick that he had fallen for in joining DB and his inability to escape. He proceeded to explain things to me in more detail.

"Morgan, who runs the shipping department has great difficulty finding staff and even greater difficulty hanging on to them. Not surprising, you will agree now that you have a pretty good idea what they spend their days doing. The export sales manager is a nasty piece of work. I gather you have been kept well away from him. As for the personnel manager whom I saw scurrying back to his '*pen*', he is a stooge. He is manipulated by both Morgan and his export counterpart. You have been duped like several others before, myself included. Those who can, make an immediate exit. The rest don't stop a moment longer than they have to."

That first day I had lunch in Meltham Hall. It was waitress service. Judging by snippets of conversation I overheard, it was considered something of a privilege. There were two members of the export sales department at the same table as myself. I could sense they considered themselves rather superior. I wondered whether they had gone through the ritual I was expected to go through filling in '*Draw Back*' forms.

The privilege of lunching in Meltham Hall I was to discover came at a price. A price which I decided was beyond what I was prepared to pay. I was starting to sense that there was a distinct whiff of medieval class culture about the place. A form of bigotry that appeared to have endured from the worst excesses in this country's past, from 'privilege' to 'deprivation'. In Lincoln mixing as I had with such a motley crowd, I had lost any sense of being an '*outsider*'. In a very short time at David Brown's, cut off as it appeared to be from the rest of the world, I sensed a difference. With one or two exceptions, most of those I had met were parochial and subservient. In the surroundings I found myself in, I felt myself to be an '*outsider*'. What is more, I did so with some considerable relief as I had no wish, nor the intention to get involved.

I have forgotten the name of the personnel manager, let me call him Mr Gray. After all that I had heard and what I had gleaned, I had made up my mind to at least try and see Mr Gray before leaving that very first day. I did get into see him but our exchange was inconclusive. I can even now bring to mind almost word for word our brief exchange, "Mr Gray, you told me this morning that I would be starting in shipping. Can you tell me after how long I can expect to be moved in to export sales?"

His reply confirmed what I had been told by Hugh Evans, "It is not for me to say. That is up to Mr Morgan and the export sales manager to decide." I did not press Mr Gray any further.

* * *

The date for our wedding had been fixed for the 30th of July. Beryl had handed in her notice and left Grimsby General Hospital about the same time as I had started at David Brown. She had also been successful in securing a post at Huddersfield Technical College. We would both be returning to stay with Mrs Taylor after our honey moon in Torquay. Whatever the state of play at DB Tractors, I had so much to look forward to. Ivan Stewart would be joining me in York as my best man.

I must have been at David Brown's four weeks prior to 'the big day'. The brief confrontation I had the first day with Mr Gray confirmed my worst fears. I was determined therefore to find other employment and leave David Brown's as soon as I possibly could. But, in my own good time. After all, I was being paid enough to live on. I made sure that my work, but also my demeanour did not give Mr Morgan any cause to find me wanting. I had got to know and liked my landlady, Mrs Taylor. In spite of constant pain from her arthritis she put on a brave face and kept cheerful. She had trained to be a nurse but spent most of her working life as a nanny looking after the children of the Hirst family in Norfolk. The Hirst name, even then, quite by chance I recalled noticing on spools of thread that my mother had acquired years ago in Turkey.

When I was still on my own, before we got married and Beryl joined me, I used to sometimes sit with Mrs Taylor in her cosy living room having a cup of tea before retiring for the night. She used to adjust her hearing aid on these occasions. Poor thing, apart from arthritis she had poor hearing. She liked to reminisce about the happier times in her past when she was a young nurse. Invariably she came out with anecdotes about her old employers and their children that as their nanny she had brought up. She still felt great loyalty for the Hirst family. When talking about the social changes she had seen in England, one of her adages was, "You know Pat, one of the things that has changed life so much is *'Jack getting to believe that he is as good as his master'* and so frequently the lack of respect that it has brought about."

She would smile wistfully then as if to bring herself back to the present, she would busy herself with the open fire stirring the few remaining embers back to life. It was getting late and I had to be up for work the next day and of course she had to be about even earlier preparing breakfast. Luckily for me, the weather had been unusually good that late spring. Mrs Taylor had shown me a short cut from the rear of her house over a stile straight down across the meadow to Meltham Mills.

I had become familiar with my surroundings. Along the main road, the quiet was occasionally broken by the crackle of a finely tuned exhaust. It was once more Hugh Evans who put me in the picture. "'That will be Angela Brown in her Aston Martin DB2 burning up the road." I say DB2 though back in 1954 it might well have been the earlier DB1. It was still a few years before the first James Bond 007 film made the '*marque*' so famous. To my surprise, apart from manufacturing tractors, DB also built the Aston Martin cars. If the boss Mr Brown's young daughter was to have a car not surprisingly it would be a 'homemade' one, an Aston Martin.

Hugh Evans and I used to meet up occasionally for a beer and a chat. It turned out that he had been a regular in the British Army. What really surprised me was to find out that he had served in the cavalry. In those days, it was still to do with horses, but has long since been mechanised. His unit had served in the Lebanon so he spoke some Arabic. He liked to talk about the spectacular countryside with its cedars and the famous Jabal Druze. When he came out of the Army he landed a managerial job at Heal's the upmarket furniture store in central London. He never told me what made him leave Heal's and London to join DB, after all Huddersfield for all its industrial fame could hardly have replaced London. Whatever it was that persuaded him, Hugh Evans rancour was real. He felt he had been duped in joining DB.

Hugh, middle aged, fair skinned with flaxen hair, was well spoken, he might even have had a commission in the Army. By contrast, Derek Barrow who sat at the next desk to me was dark and about my age. I doubt if he had ever ventured out of the county. He was a most likeable 'tyke' from Dewsbury. Football was his one passion, to the extent that he called off his wedding when he discovered that he was down for a match on the very day! He laughingly told me, "My in-laws to be, never forgave me. The wedding invitations all had to be reprinted and sent out a second time and that didn't half upset them!"

Derek, was a sportsman and a joker. He lived for the day. Unlike Hugh he was quite happy in his job, as long as it did not interfere with his weekend football match engagements.

With our wedding due to take place on the Saturday morning in York, I had left it to the very last minute on the Friday afternoon to approach the personnel manager for some time off, "Mr Gray, I am getting wed tomorrow. I would like to have next week off."

A look of incredulity appeared then froze on Mr Gray's face. When he had sufficiently recovered, his reply was predictably that of the stooge Hugh had made him out to be, "Good Lord! You have only just started working for us. I can't give you time off just like that. You must ask Mr Morgan whether it will be in order for you to be away. It is up to him."

"Thank you Mr Gray. Have a good weekend."

With that, I backed out of his office closing the door behind me. I was aware that Mr Morgan had already left his office. As for me, I set off on my way to York without a care in the world.

I must have seen Beryl on the weekends. It would have been the only way that she could have kept me informed of her preparations for our wedding. I in turn would have told her all that was going on the other side of the Pennines in Meltham. When I got to York that Friday evening, Ivan Stewart was already at Beryl's home. He was keeping her father and stepmother entertained, with his blarney, not to mention my aunt Olga. As she and her daughter Peter were already in England, they were my only guests. I had received many letters from members of my family and friends in Turkey wishing me well. My mother promised she would come over and stay for a few days with us once we were settled rather than make a short hurried visit for the wedding.

There were about 30 guests who attended the wedding. The service was in the village of Heslington at Saint Paul's church nestling in the shade of some large oaks and surrounded by lush pastureland near the Cussins home. An idyllic setting that balmy summer day with everything bathed in sunshine. Across the road, stood Heslington Hall the current owner, Richard Arthur de Yarburgh-Bateman was the 6th Baron Deramore. The property was a modification of a typical small Elizabethan country house that had been built in about 1568. An interesting historic dimension that stuck in my mind, making a contribution to Beryl's and my own '*big day*'.

Beryl was radiant in a long champagne coloured brocade bridal gown. The diaphanous veil she wore obscured her demureness as she was led up the aisle by her father to where Ivan and I were waiting. Both of us standing there rigidly to attention. I also remember how I had fixed my eyes on some spot immediately facing me. That is until I sensed Ivan fumbling for the ring. Beryl and I, thanks to rehearsals the vicar had put us through, managed our lines on cue. We both endorsed our commitments to each other saying "I will". The service drew to a close with Scot Robinson's romantic piece dating back to 1925 but still an evergreen – *Moonlight and Roses*.

30th July 1955 – my happiest day, yet I had little I could call my own! I had taken a week off rather unofficially. I did have three job interviews planned. 'God will provide!' – he had as yet never failed!

Outside in the warmth, my nervous tension melted away. Beryl and I relaxed for the 'photo opportunity' – just black and whites they were in those days. No colour and certainly no cine photography either, nor any sound recordings. The wedding breakfast served between the service and departure of the honeymoon couple was at Betty's Restaurant in the centre of York. It was Ivan with his well-thumbed manual on wedding etiquette who the previous night set about sorting things out. As I have already mentioned, he was my mentor and also drafted most of my speech. He had been best man at several weddings. His speeches were rehashed versions based on a master copy he kept for these occasions.

Looking back now on our wedding day, Beryl and I were relieved and thankful when we boarded the London train later that afternoon. Most of the happenings that day had flashed past leaving an indistinguishable blur that was impossible to unravel. One incident though has stuck in my mind. We had gone back to her family home to change before setting off to London. Phyllis, Beryl's stepmother, usually calmness personified, confronted me. She was holding a copy of the evening paper, *The York Press*, in one hand and waving it at me. I spotted the word 'Weddings' in bold letters at the top of the page at which she had opened the paper.

"What is all this about Beryl going back to Turkey with you?"

She indignantly demanded to know, justifiably I suppose. I was unprepared for such an outburst. I had been interviewed by a young reporter from *The York Press* sometime that afternoon. A keen terrier-like reporter, rather than disappoint him with my predicament in Meltham I had given him a glowing report on my recent move to Yorkshire. More imaginatively, I had included a tale of my prospective posting to the Middle East. I had exaggerated a trifle. I manage to dispel the worst of Phyllis's fears, "Oh that! Well, hearing that I had come from Turkey, the young chap from the local paper appeared rather hopeful for something a bit out of the ordinary to include in his paper. I probably overstated things. There is nothing to worry about. Honestly! Phyllis, we will not be going much further than Meltham when we get back from Torquay."

Beryl had made all the necessary hotel bookings through an old school friend of hers who worked at Cook's in York. These included hotels in London going to and coming back from the hotel in Torquay where we were to stay a few days. London then with its many sight seeing attractions was still a draw to us both, not that our funds would have stretched very far. Going on a spree of nightclubs, theatres and dinners at the Savoy was not an option. Instead, I had other commitments.

As luck would have it, I had managed to secure three job interviews. That such engagements were unusual, even some might say outrageous during a honeymoon had never entered my head. Nor, I have to confess, had I given any thought as to Beryl's feelings about them. At the root of all this was my resolve, my single minded determination to do whatever was needed to hasten my departure from David Brown.

Two of the interviews were in central London at Ferguson Tractors and Vent Axia. The third was with Langley Alloys, a leading aluminium alloy foundry in Slough. I have to say none of them went well for me. I can bring to mind nothing of the first two. I remember much of how I got on at Langley Alloys especially the highlight of my interview. More about this to follow…

Our engagement, which at times seemed interminable was at long last over. I know we had both embarked on it with the intention of getting married sooner or later. I still do not know to this day what made us wait four and a half years. During that time Beryl often maintained that "*two can live as cheaply as one!*" As for me – *"God will provide"* – she herself now reminds me was my usual adage. Expressions of hope in either case, which I now feel with the benefit of hindsight should have persuaded us to take the plunge earlier. On the other hand, had I listened to what my mother wrote in her letters more than once, "*make something of yourself before you get married*," things would almost certainly have been delayed even longer. Rather than struggle to find appropriate answers, we both relied on *providence*. Our long wait must have been our *'kismet'*.

More interestingly, I now ponder on how we both managed to keep the proverbial flame alive for so long whilst we were committed to a state of limbo. The suspense was made all the more difficult by our separation from each other after the first year. It was Lindum House where we had first met just days after we had arrived in Lincoln. I was just out of my teens. It was whilst we were there that we had got engaged. The time we had spent there together, though brief had provided us with some very happy and memorable times. Lindum House had been a real home to us both, for we had both flown the nest – Beryl from York and I from Mersin in Turkey. She, I suspect would not have returned. I still had some vestiges of hope that maybe something would turn up to reunite me with my family and friends in Mersin. Though my departure from Rustons had deprived me of my best ever prospects.

Many things had drawn us together apart from the smouldering physical attraction that certainly drove me. I can remember exactly where on the approach to Lindum Hill in Lincoln late one night, we had shared the pleasure of our very first intimate embrace. We were very much at ease with each other. Neither of us was given to affectation, *"what you see is what you get"*. Faced with catastrophe or in our case austerity, we shared the knack of spotting the funny side of things. We could also laugh at ourselves and our own misfortunes. We could even shed a tear or two, not necessarily by laughing too much!

I recall our very first summer holiday. The train from York got us to Keswick in the early afternoon. We made our way on foot to The King's Arms. Our reservation was for two single rooms with dinner, bed and breakfast for one week. Each morning, after breakfast we set off on foot to explore that corner of the Lake District. Our first expedition was to the top of Scafell Pike. Having conquered this peak, the loftiest in England, we climbed the other lesser ones. One of my enduring recollections was walking up Skiddaw. Everyone else returned from whence they came. I recall persuading Beryl to go our own way back to Keswick, "It's been a doddle coming, let's see if we can keep going straight on and down the other side. It will be a bit more of an adventure."

She agreed, and we did just that only to discover when we eventually got down and found the main road that it was an extra 12 miles to Keswick.

All we ever wanted was to be together. When we retired for the night Beryl would knock on my door after she had her bath and I would nip in to the bathroom for mine. With her door unlocked, I used to casually walk in. A tactic aimed to deal with nosy guests who might otherwise get the wrong idea! These were the all too rare opportunities we had for intimacy. What my buddy Hank used to describe as '*heavy petting without going the whole way*'. A compromise that permitted Beryl to come to her wedding still intact, a virgin. Whenever we had the chance, we spent hours lying together – kissing, hugging, fondling. What Ivan used to amusingly describe as being *'on the nest'*. We also did a great deal of talking, discussing, laughing. We never tired of our own company. Whatever it was, it kept that flame alive.

Our honeymoon hotel in Torquay was by the most basic of standards, modest. Its shortcomings, I have since concluded, a consequence of its bargain-basement tariff. Only two things about the place have stuck in my mind. The first of these were the meals. There was one particular dinner I could not forget. Boiled or poached fish of some sort, followed by tapioca pudding. Not exactly cordon blue. It was this sort of cooking that persuaded us to walk into the town centre and have a second dinner. The other thing that stuck in my mind was funny, in a peculiar way! The hotel had a rash of small type written notices. These Do and Don't instructions more suited to an institution sprang up in the most unexpected places. I can even now bring some to mind. – "Please close the door", "Turn off the light", "Now wash your hands". Even our bedroom was not spared. It did not have an en suite, just a washbasin. A tag by this read – "For washing in only". I have to say, that did tickle my sense of humour. I wondered at the time which of the staff was responsible for these gems.

Once we were up and had breakfast, there was nothing to keep us in the hotel. We went off on bus excursions out of Torquay choosing a different destination every day. Beryl appeared to know the area, "We could go to Babbacombe tomorrow. It is a sheltered cove not far from the town. We could have a swim there. You would like it."

When we got there, it was just as she had described. There were also pedalos for rent. It was a popular spot judging by the numbers who were already there. There was also a large raft moored some way out that was being used as a diving platform by those who swam out to it.

The pedalo man was doing brisk business. I approached him on my own as Beryl had set off swimming to the raft. The plan was for me to take the pedalo out and she would join me from the raft. The chap asked me, "Do you want a single or double?"

From what I could make out, there was room enough for us both on a single. "Why pay twice over?" I thought to myself and told the chap, "Oh, a single will do."

It did not take long for me to get to the raft, I manoeuvred the pedalo to the far side so that we could not be spotted by the pedalo man, when as planned Beryl joined me on it.

Beryl was already on the raft, dripping wet, waiting for me. "Get on!" I yelled. Had I known what she was about to do, I would have added the caution – "Carefully!" Too late for that, she leapt off the raft landing just behind me on the rear of the pedalo. I was a light weight in those days. Just 11 stone. Landing as she did, I was catapulted up like a rag doll. To make matters worse, I was a non-swimmer. Submerged, my arms and legs flailing, I sensed myself surfacing. I realised that I was under the raft which had tipped to one side as the idiots on it were trying to see where I had got to. I did eventually get reunited with the pedalo, minus my spectacles. They stayed behind on the seabed at Babbacombe. It was quite an unnerving experience. Neither of us managed to raise a laugh at the time though it was not long after that we did.

In London again on our way back to Meltham, I kept my appointment with Langley Alloys in Slough. The position I had applied for was as their Middle East representative. I would however be based in Slough. All had gone smoothly until a third man came in to join the two who had been interviewing me. He must have been one of the company's directors. Abrupt and impatient, he set out to bring the proceedings to a rapid conclusion without taking any notice of the other two, one of whom was the export manager. As I seem to recall the first question he put to me was, "Well now Mr Grigsby, what have you got to offer us?"

A most relevant question to be sure. In fact one that had already been put to me and to which I had responded prior his arrival. I repeated the points that I had already made to his two colleagues. He rephrased his question. I could only suppose with hindsight that he wanted to make it more specific to his company and what they produced, "What benefits would you bring to Langley Alloys in promoting the export sales of their castings?"

I went into greater detail describing my family's roots and my education and upbringing in the Middle East. My familiarity with the people, their culture and ways. The year I had worked in the Emilio Levante offices in Mersin. I dwelled at some length on my engineering training at R&H which gave me a good grasp as to the application for raw castings. Finally, my languages, French, Turkish and Arabic that were the common currency of the Middle East. I had always been led to believe that languages were very relevant to successful customer relations abroad.

He paused before speaking. When eventually he spoke, what he had to say astonished me. So much so, that I have never forgotten the exact words he came out with, "Mr Grigsby, you are mistaken about the importance of languages. We find that our overseas customers understand and speak English!"

Not at the time nor since have I understood how a senior person in a company, setting out to build up an export business, could be so insular and lacking in vision. I would have dearly liked to hear what Michael Martin my friend from Alexandria would have had to say on the matter. I did also wonder how wide-spread this failing might be in British industry. It certainly was not at Ruston & Hornsby Limited.

After an absence of just over a week, I was back in Meltham. Nothing for me was likely to have changed at David Browns. Not Mr Morgan nor anybody else took me to task about my absence. Work in the shipping department went on very much as before. Derek Barrow talked incessantly about football and less so about his deferred wedding. Pat Tyrrell persisted with the habit of spelling out his name at the top of his voice in his broad Irish accent each time he spoke on the telephone. As for Hugh Evans, he remained embittered about his plight.

Of course my entire life had changed in that short time. When I returned to Mrs Taylor, I was accompanied by Beryl, my wife. Married, some might have felt the heavy load of marital responsibility descend on them. Like the donkeys I used to see in Turkey struggling under the heavy loads that were piled on to their backs. Strangely enough, as I think back, I felt nothing like that. To the contrary, I was elated to have found a partner to share my life.

But even that does not adequately describe the way I felt. It would be truer for me to say that for the first time since leaving my family in Mersin when I was despatched to the English High School in Istanbul, I felt I had a soul mate. Someone I could trust and confide in knowing that I would not be let down. To add to my turn of fortune, a letter was awaiting me from the Public School's Appointments Bureau. It was an appointment with their Mr Anderson at the Bell Hotel in Leicester.

I was lucky once more. Mr Anderson whom I met as arranged turned out to be most understanding and helpful. He explained things to me this way "You know Mr Grigsby, the Public Schools Appointments Bureau was set up to find job placements for boys just leaving school. From your CV I see that your circumstances are rather unusual. It is some six years since you left school. Not withstanding this, I will do what I can to help you."

I did see Mr Anderson once more when he gave me the particulars of four companies in Birmingham who were looking for recruits from public schools. Though none were remotely involved in export sales nor with diesel engines.

I had no choice but to go along with what Mr Anderson had to offer if I were to have any chance of breaking away from David Browns. I recall Mr Anderson's parting words to me, "I will leave you to get in touch with these companies. Make sure you mention the Public Schools Appointments Bureau and try and see them as soon as possible, strike whilst the iron is hot. Let me know how you make out. In the meantime, Best of luck."

It was to be a most disheartening quest. The immense satisfaction that I had derived from my shop floor training and experience in the export sales department at R&H on their diesel engines was going to be hard to replace. The products these companies manufactured were uninspiring in the extreme. Umbrellas, brass ferules and metal eyelets used in the manufacture of shoes. Lastly, chemical powders pressed into tablets and briquettes for the foundry industry. With this last choice, I recall telling Beryl, "Just think of it. Rustons had two big foundries in Lincoln – Spike Island where they produced the big cast iron housings for their marine diesels and the state of the art Beevor Foundry. I recall it had just been opened when I came to Lincoln in 1950. It was claimed to be the most modern foundry in Europe. How I now regret never having had some of my training time there. I remember hearing Max Burfoot, the Aussie and Alan Winsor who was in charge of RS&J foundry in Ipswich talking all about their experiences. Fascinating stuff as I seem to recall."

Having drawn a blank with the recent interviews I had during our honeymoon and the poor prospects held out by the Public Schools Appointments Bureau I was coming to realise that my chances of ever finding a job that would take me to the Middle East were remote. I could not help but ponder over my decision to part company with Rustons. It was a matter that frequently played on my mind.

I had come to realise and accept that as I did not have a professional qualification, I could hardly stake a claim to a career reserved for those who had gained a university degree. I had to seek fulfilment by some other means. The best I could hope for was to remain on the look out for work opportunities, come what may. To go for the best I could find and persevere in the hope that there would be something in that choice that would give me fulfilment. That said, I remained determined to get into sales, preferably export sales.

Any feelings of despondency that I might have had were dispelled largely by Beryl's support and our solitary walks on the moors near Meltham. Mrs Taylor had become something of a surrogate mother to us both. I never forgot how she had slipped an envelope into my pocket just as I was setting off to York saying, "I know you are skint. It will come in useful on your honeymoon. Good luck love. I will be expecting you and Beryl in a few days. Come when it suits you. You know I don't go out. Cheerio Pat."

To my great surprise, the envelope contained a five pound note. It brought tears to both our eyes – it put '*the widow's mite*' in the shadows.

One of the companies I was introduced to by Mr Anderson in Birmingham did engage me. I was one of five management trainees introduced by the Public Schools Appointments Bureau taken on by Foundry Services Limited who pressed chemical powders into tablets and briquettes. I even managed to make a connection, however tenuous, between them and Rustons. What is more I convinced myself in the process that all I had picked up during my engineering training would be of service to me at Foundry Services Limited. I was more determined than ever to pursue a career in sales.

Mr Anderson had painted a most glowing picture of Foundry Services Limited, whom he had described as an inventive, dynamic company that was growing fast. Unique in their field, they manufactured a comprehensive range of products for the metal casting industry. The company had been founded originally in Birmingham's well known Bull Ring in the 1930s by Eric Weiss and his partner, a doctor of metallurgy, Kossie Strauss. Both had fled the growing Nazi threat in Germany. A modern factory was being purpose built on a tract of land adjoining what had come to be known as Drayton Manor Park, the home of Sir Robert Peel, near Tamworth. The company already had several overseas manufacturing subsidiaries as well as licensees and agents.

On joining Foundry Services Limited, it did not take long for me to realise that the company encouraged hard work and initiative. They had a cosmopolitan mixture of staff, many amongst them proficient in foreign languages. The influence I have no doubt of the two founding partners. The company at the time was still small enough to permit Eric Weiss to impose his authority. I was once more in my element as an '*outsider*'.

I had been interviewed by R.D.Hulme the Works Director and J.C.Noon the Works Manager whom every one knew as 'Bill' Noon. He was to be my immediate boss. Though my starting salary was £350 per year, I was told that as a management trainee, it would be increased from time to time in line with my changing duties and responsibilities.

I joined Foundry Services Limited on the 1st of October 1955.

Chapter 19

I had hoped and expected my move in June 1955 from Ruston & Hornsby Limited into the export sales department of David Brown Tractors in Meltham to have been a logical transition in my career.

In the event, my engagement had been of the briefest duration. Just three months. I had shown the letter of appointment that I had received from David Brown to Mr Codling, the trainee superintendent at R&H who had guided me through my works training. It was he also who had contrived my move into their export sales department. At the time I recall feeling that I was on the way to fulfilling my dream of eventually taking over as their representative in the Middle East. I remember, studying the tone of the letter, he had expressed reservations about it. I ignored his warnings, being anxious to move on. Due to a number of setbacks that R&H had experienced, I had come to fear that the prospects of eventually working for them in the Middle East which I had set my heart on were fast fading.

'Nothing venture, nothing gained', I had followed this conviction that I held and failed. Reluctant as I was to leave R&H, with the benefit of hindsight I now believe that at the time, I really had no other choice. I have also wondered what it was that made me not only ignore Mr Codling's caution but also turn my back on my family's heartfelt plea not to leave R&H.

I have come to the conclusion that these decisions are largely instinctive. I had made my mind up to leave DB on the very day I got to their

Meltham Mills premises as my meeting with their personnel manager will have indicated. Not surprisingly, I came away from there with nothing the least bit commendable. My only legacy, if one can describe it as such, was a strong and lasting addiction to smoking. '*Senior Service*' cigarettes as it happened.

Yet for all that, I was fortunate. Landing on my feet at Foundry Services Limited who evidently favoured public school educated young men to take on management responsibilities in their expanding business. Proof that my old school, Hurstpierpoint College had indeed endowed me with a privileged form of education. One that '*set me apart*' whether for better or worse was not for me to say but at least on this occasion had benefited me. With the passage of time, and taking stock of my new employer's circumstances, I did sometimes even wonder whether perhaps it was the '*outsider*' in me that might also have gained some approval.

My wife, Beryl could not accompany me on this, my second move in three months. To satisfy her terms of employment, she had to stay on until the end of the Christmas term at the Huddersfield Technical College where she was supervising the catering students. We took it in turns to visit each other. On the occasions I made the trip, it was to join Beryl at Mrs Taylor's home along the lane to the Meltham Golf Club. For a short time our adopted home. My return journey by train in the bleak English winter was miserable. On arrival at New Street Station, my abiding memory was a happy one as I hurried across to Lyons Corner House to have one of their individual steak and kidney pies, before catching a bus to Shard End.

On the face of it, the prospects held out to me by my new employers were as good as I could hope for. I was aware that work prospects in the Middle East, the likes of which I had aspired to with Ruston &

Hornsby Limited were unlikely to ever come my way again. A sad fact of life that I was forced to reconcile myself to. However pragmatic I tried to be, this was a ghost that would continue to haunt me for a long time. Little wonder then that my move to Birmingham that autumn in 1955 had not stirred my imagination nor unduly raised my spirits.

I had only ever visited Birmingham once before. It was when I was at R&H and living in Lindum House. Mufid Shishakli who had been at the university there gave Hank and I a lift over in his Morris Minor. It was in 1952, to visit the BIF – British Industries Fair, in those days staged in the redundant aircraft hangars of what at one time had been the Castle Bromwich airfield. It was no more than a flying visit. I had heard Birmingham referred to as '*the city of a thousand trades*'. Birmingham and neighbouring Coventry were the centre of the British Motor Industry, both were *'boom towns'*. Mr Anderson of the Public Schools Appointments Bureau had spoken at some length of the career opportunities they both offered in industry. I was aware of, but had little knowledge of the vast sprawl of heavy metal industries that lay beyond Birmingham known as, *'the black country'*. A strange name though as I was to find out, most appropriate.

I am told that when I first arrived in Lincoln, I spoke English without an accent. I seem to recall that at the time the term 'Oxford English' was used to describe speech free from regional accents. During my apprenticeship and living at Lindum House, I mixed almost exclusively with visitors from overseas and developed a distinctive accent, often mistaken for a South African one. I must emphasize that no one ever found it difficult to understand what I said. The locals, '*Lincolnshire yellow bellies'* as they sometimes called themselves, had a regional accent but it was not a pronounced one.

On arrival in Birmingham I became instantly aware of an unusually strong dialect. Beryl Reed, the comedienne had immortalised *'Marlene'* with her *'Brummy way of speaking'* in a TV comedy serial. I like many others, had assumed that *'Marlene'* spoke the way she did for comic effect. Exaggeration to cause amusement. Sure enough *'Marlene'* was very amusing but the way she spoke was no exaggeration – I became convinced that everyone I met in Birmingham sounded like *'Marlene'*. I have never forgotten Joe Gould's *'yows'* and *'yums'* typical of his *'black country'* dialect. Joe was the senior foreman at Foundry Services and lived in Walsall. I could never tell the difference between the Birmingham and *'black country'* way of speaking.

It was not just their regional accents though that set people apart. The city of Birmingham coat of arms has emblazoned on it the city's motto, a single word – *'Forward'*. Its citizens certainly lived up to this slogan. On her first visit down from Meltham, after meeting Beryl at New Street Station, we had to catch a bus. It was the evening rush hour. I remember telling her as we stood at the stop waiting for the bus, "It's each one for himself here. Stick close to me. We will have to push and shove to get on. *'Brummagem'* is nothing like Lincoln you know, but one soon gets used to it."

On the other hand, people were approachable and ready to strike up friendly relationships. What I noticed in particular was a remarkable lack of formality by contrast with Lincoln. First name familiarity was the norm. I realised that there were striking regional differences in England, something that until then I had not been aware of. Even then I still felt my home was in Mersin and I was continuing to live 'a life apart'. My mother and the rest of my family, my friends were all in Turkey. My move to the Midlands was to mean new friends and acquaintances.

I had digs somewhere in or near Castle Bromwich, Shard End I seem to recall, that first weekend that Beryl came. We had to change buses at Alum Rock, to continue on past the large gas works and coking plant at Saltley. You would know when you were nearing them even if you were blindfolded. The air got progressively heavier with a strong rather sickly smell. An odour that reminded me of hydrogen sulphide, that favourite of schoolboy pranks in the chemistry laboratory.

As the bus went along, we saw little else but back to back terraced houses with the occasional green bushes or trees to soften the scene. The few nondescript shops were poorly lit so it was difficult to make out their purpose. It was a scene of humanity in an inanimate sprawl of bricks and mortar, a stark legacy of the region's industrialisation. Very different from the Lincoln I had got to know so well, whose origins went back to Roman times and before. By contrast, Birmingham – '*city of a thousand trades*' – was itself a creation of the industries it spawned. It had no place in earlier history, unlike the adjoining Royal Borough of Sutton Coldfield with its enormous park where King Henry the Eighth hunted and in return for this granted the town its Royal Charter.

It was inevitable that I would think back with great nostalgia on all that had passed in Lincoln. It is something that I have done many times since and will continue to, earning the all too frequent comment – '*you live in the past*' – from those who know me best. I ponder most especially the myriad experiences during my practical shop floor training in the many branches of Ruston & Hornsby's works. I now feel no shame in failing to obtain my ONC, let alone a Higher National Certificate which had I been academic enough, I could have achieved during my time at R&H. I had been complemented on my practical skills and I know myself that by the time I was transferred into the export department, I knew enough about diesel engines to be able to acquit myself as a diesel service engineer or more correctly '*mechanic*'. Maybe more to the point, by the time I arrived in the industrial Midlands, with

my practical knowledge of engineering acquired at R&H, I was able to make educated judgements on what was going on around me.
I became aware of the proliferation of the motor industry in Birmingham and Coventry which did most to set them apart from Lincoln. The motor industry gave birth to '*mass production*' which in turn promoted '*automation*'. A system of electronic and mechanical robots that took the place of humans. The word itself was coined in the USA towards the end of WWII.

By contrast, at Ruston & Hornsby in Lincoln, engines were assembled starting with the base plate which was first placed on a special cradle. A team of skilled men fitted and assembled its component parts progressively from the base plate up until the engine was built. A crane lifted it off the cradle to go to the test beds. The cradle thus freed was used for the next engine to be built. Almost all the skilled men would have served their five year apprenticeship at R&H. They took great pride in their jobs, which demanded great skill and hard '*manual*' work.

These differences I would come to realise were not as straight forward as I am now making them sound by over simplification. There were many other factors that came to play in these complex differences. In truth, the motor industry is so far removed from that of Ruston & Hornsby that a direct comparison is not possible. Yet how otherwise can one explain how different the thousands of production line 'operatives' in Birmingham and Coventry came to be from their 'time served' counterparts in Lincoln.

This '*mass production*' in the motor industry could be said to have diminished the self worth of the men whose skills were replaced by '*automation*'. Yet, ironically though these men became subordinate, they did better for themselves financially. Since changing my digs, I used to go past Fisher & Ludlows on a bus and marvel at their vast array of cars. I happened to meet a consultant engineer who was doing some work for them. I recall asking him, "All those cars I see stored outside, are they stock?"

To my surprise, the question must have amused him as he laughed, "Good heavens, No. What you describe is Fisher & Ludlow's works car park. All those cars belong to staff who work there."

I felt rather humiliated. Judging by the reply I got, I realised that the question must have appeared rather naïve. Coming from Lincoln, I can hardly be blamed for this slip. R&H did not have any sort of a car park. The fact of the matter is all the staff, whether office or shop floor travelled to work by public transport. Some came on their bicycles. This brought home to me the striking difference in life style between Lincoln and Birmingham which as I mentioned earlier was described as a *'boom town'*.

Anyone coming to work in Birmingham, one of the 'boom towns' of 1955 would have had a job to find accommodation, whether digs, a place to rent or a house to buy. Full employment and good pay acting like a magnet attracted more people than could be catered for, including myself. I was constantly searching through the local paper. One day I thought I had hit the jackpot. The briefest of adverts read "Chalets to rent"

There was a telephone number, which I rang immediately. A lady with a refined voice answered the telephone and gave me an address. The chalets were on Tyburn Road and yes there was one still available. I arranged to call at 6.00 pm. It was dark when I rang the doorbell of the house, a rather substantial looking one.

It was the day after my trip up Tyburn Road to have a look at the chalets. I was at the company's head office on Long Acre, in the publicity department which was run by John Richards. Also present was Rosemary Bassett a rather haughty female with a plummy voice. She had helped me find my various digs and was anxious to hear what I had been up to. I recall going into some detail recounting my experience to the two of them, "The door, I had been waiting outside was opened by a lady. In response to my greeting of – "Good evening." She welcomed me in. "Oh, yes! You must be the young man who rang, do come in." My earlier optimism and expectations were reinforced by the unexpected cup of tea she offered. She chatted on as I sipped from the cup of tea, without actually telling me a great deal.

When I had finished the tea, I placed the empty cup and its saucer on the table. She rose from her chair. "Come on now, I'll show you the chalets."

She led me through her kitchen and out into the darkness. Even when she switched an outside light on I found it difficult to see anything other than half a dozen motionless shadows. They looked like baby elephants sitting in two rows facing each other. As we approached, I realised that they were some sort of huts made of corrugated iron."

John Richards, a taciturn individual, I was told had been recruited with my boss Bill Noon and others through some Ex Services Appointments Bureau set up to find jobs for officers in civvy street. He had been listening in his usual rather disinterested manner to what I had been saying, suddenly chuckled, "Good gracious me. She must have got hold of some Anderson shelters."

At the time, even though I had no idea what an Anderson shelter was, I was able to tell him more about her enterprise, "Well, what ever you say they were, the lady yesterday said she wished she could get hold of more of them. Because what she liked to call her '*chalets*' were in such great demand."

Hearing all this, Rosemary Bassett spoke for the first time, "It is absolutely outrageous! Pat, you should get in touch with the Council and report this woman to the public health department."

I had other things to think of and worry about. In a few weeks Beryl would be free to leave the Technical College in Huddersfield and join me in Birmingham. That however would depend on my finding suitable accommodation for us both. A rather forlorn prospect given my experiences until then.

Salvation when it came did so in a most unexpected way. A farmer some where in the Yorkshire dales was cheating on his wife, he was having an affair. To make things more convenient for himself he had acquired a large caravan, a 22ft Pemberton Star in which to accommodate his lady friend. With his newly acquired love-nest sited well away from his farm and wife, he must have felt safe and at ease to continue his affair.

It was not long before his wife rumbled what was going on resulting in an advertisement appearing in the For Sale columns of the local paper. The advertisement was quickly brought to the notice of my father in law by a member of his staff who was aware of the acute housing shortage in Birmingham. The *'as good as new caravan, only £200, for quick disposal'* not only did it resolve our board and lodging problem, it was I seem to recall, a bargain.

Alerted that help was on the way, I approached my boss Bill Noon. The greater part of what had been Sir Robert Peel's estate, Drayton Manor Park had passed into the ownership of George Bryan and adjoined the site on which Foundry Services new factory was built. There had been good neighbourly relations and as a consequence Bill Noon facilitated my introduction to George Bryan.

The now famous Drayton Manor Pleasure Park was at the time in its infancy. As I seem to recall, there was a small menagerie, a rudimentary open air roller skating rink and cafeteria. There was also adjoining these a caravan site for weekend users. It did not have a residential license. I recall the helpful concession that George Bryan put to me that day, "Tell you what! When your Pemberton Star arrives, get it parked behind the high hedge, at the very far end of the caravan site. Make sure it is well out of sight. I shall have to charge you two shillings and six pence per week. I feel that would be a reasonable charge."

"Yes, perfectly so, and many thanks." I replied, greatly relieved for a second time. Overjoyed as Beryl and I had been to hear that we had acquired a mobile home, there had still been the problem of finding a suitable site. I knew little of the Midlands then, and had been told that the nearest residential caravan park was miles away some where near Solihull the other side of Birmingham.

It was said that the 22 ft Pemberton Star was one of the biggest caravans of its day. We both felt elated when it arrived at Drayton Manor Park, towed by a powerful Rover V8. After all, it was to be our very first home. An outside step by the entrance door permitted easy access to the residential half of the caravan, fitted with a table and comfortable seating for four. This living space was kept warm by a cast iron solid fuel stove. There were few if any *'health and safety'* regulations in those days. We used to stoke the stove up before going to bed as 1955 turned out to be a particularly cold winter. Small though the stove was, it had a mighty roar once it got going. It brought back memories of the stove my mother had from Usta Nedeem in Mersin and the near disaster we escaped.

Beyond a partition in the other half of the van was a pull-down double bed and a wardrobe. The miniscule kitchenette, no more than a sink which when not in use served as a worktop. With the small 'Calor' gas cooker Beryl was able to create her culinary miracles including for the first time, some of the Middle East dishes I so missed. Finally, all credit to the caravan manufacturers, a corner was created for the toilet, which Ivan Stewart, on one of his visits christened '*the thunder box*'.

Thereafter, Beryl and I got in the habit of taking a stroll whenever it was in use by one of our visitors. Best forgotten was the inescapable ritual of emptying the *'thunder box'* or chemical toilet. A chore that befell me!

Not being a residential caravan site, there were no washing nor shower facilities. The nearest municipal baths were almost in the centre of Birmingham at Woodcock Street. A good half hour bus ride away. I cannot bring to mind what the council charged but what ever it was, there was the bus fare also to be found. Worse still, the reception was niggardly.

"I wouldn't run too much cold water. This is all the hot water you get, so you will not be able to top it up with any more hot water."

The attendant went off taking with him the large brass key that he had used to open the large faucet that delivered the regulation amount of hot water. This ploy also ensured that no one stayed too long.

Nearer our home, more convenient though by no stretch of the imagination luxurious the Foseco Work's showers also served us. These facilities were used by the all male work force so we used to wait until the late evening when everyone had gone home and the place was left exclusively to us.

I had joined the Tamworth Rugby Club early on in October. By the time Beryl joined me in our caravan home, I had got to know several members and their wives. The club, on the third floor of a building in Market Street, provided us with a meeting place on Friday nights and the weekends after the game. It had a homely, unpretentious air about it. A quality that I was growing more and more to like about people in Tamworth. The 30 or so active members, ones who actually played, were largely made up of teachers or miners, not surprisingly several Welshmen amongst them.

The club was run by a trio of old hands – George Parker, Charles Curtler and Tom Pullman. The first mentioned, was one of the founders of the Tamworth Rugby Football Club. Charles was a Cornishman from Saltash who had settled in the Midlands after finishing his schooling at Oakham College. Lastly, but by no manner least was Tom, who had come as a young man from his home in Wales to find work in the prosperous Midlands. Maybe not amongst the top clubs in the area, TRFC boasted a worthy Chairman in Micky Steele-Bodger, the local veterinary surgeon who had played for England as a wing forward.

The expression 'binge drinking' had not been coined. In those days, I recall having one or two half pints at the club on a Friday night. The local '*copper*' a tall dark chap used to call in '*just to make sure all is well*' as he put it. I seem to recall, he let himself in '*after hours*' using the door key hanging on a length of string that could be pulled through the letter box to the outside. It was usually Charlie Curtler who greeted him with what he described as '*a jar of our very best bitter.' A* barrel of which would have been earlier lugged up the three steep flights of wooden steps from the cellar probably by Dai Elias, one of the clubs big forwards.

Even the matches were more fun in those far off days. Almost everyone who belonged to the Club smoked. I remember on one occasion a match on the Castle ground that had just started, when the referee blew his whistle and stopped the game. '*Put that cigarette out*' he called to the wing who, well out of the way had gambled on not being spotted '*getting his last drag*' out of the still smouldering stub. On another occasion the game was stopped as the home side had an extra man on the pitch. There was no ill will, to the contrary some laughing and good humoured shouts of '*shame*' after which the games were allowed to resume.

After the match, both teams were provided with tea and sandwiches that had been prepared at the club by some of the wives and girl-friends of the Tamworth players Beryl amongst them. On some other occasions, Beryl and I with one or two other married couples used to go round to '*The Ritz*'. The rather grand name by which we knew a little fish and chips café where now there are high rise flats. One or two of the married members invited us to their homes for high teas accompanied by the rather unconventional offer of, *"Bring your towels, you can take a bath.*" Which spared us the trek to Woodcock Street or the rough and ready Foseco Work's showers.

Beryl had been able to get a job with W.H.Canning & Co Ltd in Birmingham as catering manageress of their director's dining room. I had acquired a bicycle at Kinson's the Tamworth Auctioneers. The snag was that I had not realised how big it was until I tried to ride it. It must have belonged to some lofty 'Bobby'. Its very high cross bar made a sudden stop painful, even perilous. Undeterred, I used to go down to the main road on it to meet Beryl off the Birmingham bus in the evenings.

I managed to get her to sit sideways on the cross bar. Holding the handle bars, I sprinted a short way and mounted the saddle behind her. I pedalled energetically up the long drive, past the caravan site to where we were living. It was the dismounting that did sometimes go wrong. When it did, we tumbled off the thing on to the soft grass near our mobile home. It was the end of another day and an evening that we would share together. We talked at length, discussing our experiences of the day and what we might be faced with in the days and weeks to come.

Our union was to be a real partenership from the very start, after all, we had managed to survive a long, testing engagement. 'Troubles shared and troubles halved' sure enough, but it was also to bring with it other benefits; one in particular. Since her departure from Lindum House, Beryl's several career moves had rewarded her with a significant salary which got us off to a good start in Birmingham. I had just commenced with Foundry Services Limited as a management trainee, one of several who shared this portentous title. My salary though was modest, maybe intended to spur me on in my climb to greater glory. I recall a well-meaning friend describing it as "a monthly insult". Later, on my own I had brooded on the remark. Insult or not, a salary however paltry is better than no salary at all.

There was for me an even more vital consequence to this union. More than anything that had gone before, I had committed myself to a new life. A new life that almost certainly was destined to keep me in England. I came to realise that this new life could not lend itself to any compromise even though I still missed my people and Turkey, my mother in particular. By embarking on this I had put the stamp of eternity on what had been for me 'a life apart' and which now as a consequence would endure for ever more.

That New Year of 1956, the first in our married life, opened up fresh opportunities for me. I still heard the soft voice of my guardian angle, it sounded reassuring, as if it were telling me, *"The future is what you make it. It is all up to you!"*

* * *

It is now, with the passage of time that I am able to see and also to assess the events of my past. These many years, more than half a century, that have gone by brought with them sweeping changes to the people and the fabric of the country itself. I had grown up in Mersin from the age of four in 1935, returning in 1949 after an absence of four years when I was at school in England. I was employed in the offices of Emilo Levante, shipping agents, for a year. I always looked on Mersin as my *'home'*, it was a paradise, an *'oasis'*. My personal circumstances in 1950 were such that the *'oasis'* though unchanged would have figuratively speaking, trapped me as sure as if I were the victim of '*quicksands*'. I was not cut out for a career in Mersin, that was the simple fact of the matter.

I have described how my family's chance meeting with a Mr Jerry Rampton led to my return to England early in December 1950. I have had the greatest regard for Messrs Ruston & Hornsby Limited, manufacturers of diesel engines who took me on as an overseas engineering trainee in their Lincoln works, transferring me eventually into their export sales department.

It was a lucky break once more through the Public Schools Appointments Bureau in 1955 that led to my engagement at Foundry Services Limited in Birmingham.

I have never felt any compulsion to disguise my origins. Nor has the image of being an '*outsider*' which has become deeply rooted in me, ever caused me any inconvenience. I remain indebted to Ruston and Hornsby Limited in particular and to England for providing the wonderful career opportunities that I have enjoyed. It saddens me that the same apprenticeship opportunities that existed in the 1950s in engineering and more generally in industry are not available for the youngsters of today.

The End